This resource made possible by
generous donors to
Chapter 2000
UCC 25th Anniversary
Library Campaign

THE LAST NAZI

THE LAST NAZI

JOSEF SCHWAMMBERGER AND THE NAZI PAST

AARON

FREIWALD

WITH

MARTIN

MENDELSOHN

W. W. NORTON & COMPANY
NEW YORK / LONDON

Copyright © 1994 by Aaron Freiwald
and Martin Mendelsohn
All rights reserved
Printed in the United States of America
First Edition

The text of this book is composed in Weiss,
with the display set in Bank Gothic Medium.
Composition by Crane Typesetting Service, Inc.
Book design by Chris Welch.

Library of Congress Cataloging-in-Publication Data
Freiwald, Aaron.
    The last Nazi : Josef Schwammberger and the Nazi
past / Aaron Freiwald ; with Martin Mendelsohn.
        p.   cm.
    Includes bibliographical references and index.
    1. Holocaust, Jewish (1939–1945)   2. Schwammberger,
Josef.   3. War criminals—Germany—Biography.
I. Mendelsohn, Martin, 1942–   II. Title.
D804.3.F73   1994
940.53'18—dc20   93–13147

ISBN 0-393-03503-4

W. W. Norton & Company, Inc.
500 Fifth Avenue,
New York, N.Y. 10110
W. W. Norton & Company Ltd.
10 Coptic Street,
London WC1A 1PU

1 2 3 4 5 6 7 8 9 0

FOR HOPE

Contents

CONTENTS

Acknowledgments

I owe deep thanks to Martin Mendelsohn, a friend of many years and the one who shares credit for the idea for this book. Marty's perspective and experience were invaluable assets while I was researching and writing this book. I first met Marty during my first week as a legal affairs and politics reporter in Washington, D.C., in 1986. He was then and remains the U.S. legal counsel to the Simon Wiesenthal Center in Los Angeles and an expert on Nazi hunting and Nazi trials. It should be said, too, that Marty served as an informal legal adviser to several of the witnesses who testified at Josef Schwammberger's extradition hearing in Argentina and later trial in Germany.

Writers often say that producing a book is like having a baby. My wife informs me that the analogy is silly unless the writer is female. The other problem with the comparison is that many more people are involved in the birth of a book. I received a great deal of support from many people in a

variety of forms, including hospitality while I was researching on foreign soil. Among others in Argentina, I wish
to thank Dr. Reuben Beraja, of DAIA; Jorge Camarasa, of
the newspaper *Clarín*; Octavio Carsen; radio commentator
Pepe Eliaschev; Raúl Kraiselburd, of *El Día*; Ulrich Rentsch;
Hillel Rubinson and family; Chango Torres; and especially
Enrique Benitez de Aldama, for his generosity, conversation,
and the company of his warm friends.

In Germany, I thank Willi Dressen (and Elke Bartholoma),
of the Central Office for the Investigation of Nazi Crimes
in Ludwigsburg; Dr. Rainer Erb, of the Center for the Study
of Anti-Semitism in Berlin; Arno Fern, director of the Württemberg Jewish community center in Stuttgart (and his
daughter, Yvonne Fern); David Marwell, executive director
of the Berlin Documentation Center; Laurie Levy-Page; and
Franz Sichart and family, especially Anja Sterff, all of Mies-
bach.

In Washington, there were many who were very generous
with their time and help, including Dr. Brewster Chamber-
lain, Susan Morganstein, and Jacek Novakowski, of the U.S.
Holocaust Museum; Warren Eisenberg, of B'nai B'rith; Henry
Friedlander; Charlotte Hebebrand; Bob Kesting and the re-
search staff at the National Archives annex in Suitland,
Maryland; Peter Kovler, of the Blum-Kovler Foundation; and
Eli Rosenbaum.

In Philadelphia, I thank Marta Tarnawsky, at the University of Pennsylvania Law School's Biddle Law Library; Rabbi
Eliseo Rosenwasser, of Congregation Har Zion; and Susanne
Nimmrichter, for translating assistance. The reference librar-
ians at the Free Library and the Annenberg Research Center
were of great help as well. I also thank my entire Philadelphia
family, especially Ted and Bubbles Seidenberg, who welcomed me and gave me enthusiastic support and sound
counsel.

Also thanks to Herb Funk; Raul Hilberg, at the University

of Vermont; Edward Seaton, of the Inter-American Press Association in Kansas City; Elliot Welles, of the Anti-Defamation League in New York; the staff of the YIVO Institute's archive, also in New York; and Zbigniew Chabasiewicz, for serving as interpreter during my visit to Przemysl, Poland. Thanks as well to the elderly Polish man who was carrying a fistful of freshly picked parsley and led the way in eerie silence to the old Jewish cemetery in Przemysl. I never got his name, but without him I would not have stood on that forsaken plot, amid the toppled gravestones and the overgrown bushes and trees, and I would have missed one of the most poignant experiences of my life.

Special thanks, of course, also go to my agent, Kristine Dahl, at ICM, and to the quality folks at W. W. Norton, especially my editor, Hilary Hinzmann. I thank as well Thea Trachtenberg, who was a consistent voice of encouragement and good humor; Steve Katznelson, who let me run up ridiculous phone bills as I read him passages of the manuscript; Anne Kornhauser, who was a first-rate sounding board and critic as I worked through my arguments and analysis; and Susan Freiwald, who provided valuable comments on the manuscript. My parents, Bernie and Leah, were and are an inspiration to me. Lastly, and most important, I thank my wife, Hope, for her faith, her point of view, her patience, and her love.

THE LAST NAZI

MEMORY, JUSTICE, AND HISTORY

Only when an epoch ceases to be haunted by the shadow of its own consciousness of guilt will it achieve the inner calm and outward strength brutally and ruthlessly to prune off the wild shoots and tear out the weeds.
—Adolf Hitler, *Mein Kampf* [1]

In 1945 Adolf Hitler's guiltless epoch, built to pursue evil designs of unprecedented proportions, lay in rubble and ruin all across Europe. In 1992 a New York City doctor who had survived that ruin focused intently on the panel of judges before him in a charmless and bare courtroom in the criminal courthouse in Stuttgart, Germany. An eighty-year-old man, quite possibly the last important Nazi who would ever stand trial, followed the proceedings with a look of detachment, of inner calm.

Dr. Marcel Tuchman had traveled four thousand miles from his comfortable Manhattan apartment to testify at the murder trial of the man whose presence had terrified him many years earlier and whose specter had haunted him ever since. Tuchman had grown increasingly anxious as the day of his court appearance had drawn nearer. The night before, he had hardly slept, anticipating the moment he would confront the man responsible for wiping out his entire family.

Tuchman had built a successful medical practice since moving to America at the end of World War II. His spacious home was filled with fine furniture and African art. He was in vigorous health, too, with plenty of energy to maintain a full schedule of patients even into his mid-sixties.

In spite of his jitters, Tuchman was pleased that he looked healthy and prosperous on the day of his meeting with the former SS Technical Sergeant Josef Franz Leo Schwammberger.

"I suppose one could say I didn't want that bastard to have the satisfaction that he broke my spirit, which he didn't," Tuchman explained later, his speech still colored by a pronounced Polish accent. "I saw him under those circumstances, when I am not his victim but his accuser, and he didn't frighten me, didn't make me anxious at all."[2]

Perhaps the sight of the enfeebled Schwammberger helped put Tuchman at ease. After all, the former SS man had aged dramatically. Wearing a plain beige cardigan and a hearing aid in each ear, Schwammberger gave the appearance of a doddering old man. He looked as if he should be out strolling slowly through a city park among the pigeons and the prams and the other octogenarians rather than standing trial for murder.

Fifty years before, when Tuchman and Schwammberger had last met, the Nazi commandant had loomed large. As the SS officer in charge of three slave labor camps in southeastern Poland, including the one in Tuchman's hometown of Przemysl (pronounced p'sheh-mi-shu), Schwammberger had lorded his power over his terrified prisoners with viciousness. He had cracked his whip on the back of a starving Jewish man and then left him to bleed to death. Tuchman and other witnesses recalled Schwammberger's unleashing his German shepherd to tear at the flesh of Jewish prisoners and his firing his pistol from atop his horse as he galloped through the cobbled streets of the walled-in Jewish quarter. Schwammberger had waved his fist in the air and proclaimed to the hundreds of trapped Jews that he was their God, their Satan.

Fifty years before, Schwammberger had rounded up Tuchman's mother, along with three dozen other Jews found hiding from the local Nazi police. Armed SS guards prodded Tuchman's mother on the march through town to the Jewish cemetery. There she and the others were forced at gunpoint to dig a wide pit. Then she was stripped of her clothes, shot in the neck, and pushed into the waiting hole.

A friend of the Tuchman family somehow survived the graveyard massacre, escaped back into the ghetto, and reported what had happened. Even though he had not been a witness to the killing, Tuchman remembered the fear and the horror fifty years later as he looked at the elderly man at the defendant's table just a few paces from him. When the chief trial judge asked him to identify the withered man, Tuchman was ready.

"When they asked me whether I could recognize him I looked straight into his eyes and I said, 'Those eyes I could never forget.' There was a glimmer of a smile on his face. It was the first expression I had seen all along. It was kind of morose, almost, and there was a glimmer of a smile, like we know each other. It was very strange, very fleeting."

Schwammberger's eyes had made a deep impression on the New York doctor. "A person's eyes don't age," Tuchman declared just a few weeks after his trial appearance. "You see, his countenance has changed. He used to walk with a spring. He carried a whip. He moved very swiftly, and he was everywhere. When he came, he generated electricity around him. And now he walks like a slightly Parkinsonian hypokinetic individual, which he probably is.* But the eyes, if you isolate the eyes, they are still those eyes of 1943, 1944."

In 1943, if Tuchman had looked directly at Schwamm-

---

*Hypokinesia is a condition involving abnormally diminished muscular function or mobility.

berger, it might have cost him his life. Nearly half a century later, if anyone had reason to fear for his life, it was the elderly former SS man, not the Jewish doctor.

When the trial court resumed its session after the lunch recess, Tuchman was called to the judge's bench to identify the bounds of the ghetto on an old map of Przemysl. The exercise was part of a simple test the court had devised to evaluate the accuracy of each witness's memory. The prosecutor and two defense lawyers followed Tuchman up to the front of the courtroom. Schwammberger, too, wanted to see what was happening and joined the huddle. Tuchman's interpreter, a middle-aged German woman who had assisted many Jews in their testimony during the trial, noticed Schwammberger slowly making his way to the judges' bench and hurried forward to insert herself between Tuchman and Schwammberger.

There they stood, two men who many years before had been mortal enemies. "I had fantasized so many times in the past, if I could get my hands on him and choke him to death I would have done," Tuchman recalled.

Instead the doctor gave his testimony calmly and deliberately, as if he were delivering a diagnosis. He restrained himself from the impulse to strike out physically at Schwammberger. "I could tell the story without breaking down, without breaking my voice, just telling the facts as I remembered them. When I came back, I must say, I had second thoughts about being so brave and detached. You know, my younger son, who's somewhat more emotional, said, 'How could you not go over to him and punch him in the nose or spit him in the face?' Who knows? It is conceivable that would have been a more normal reaction on my part. But I didn't do it."

That moment of confrontation in the Stuttgart courtroom was greater than the two men, the witness and the defendant, the Holocaust survivor and the accused murderer. Tuchman had not traveled all the way to Germany simply to seek personal justice. Schwammberger was no ordinary murder defendant. The German government had not spent three hundred thousand dollars in bounty money to track down the former Nazi in an Argentine mountain hideout and then subjected its people to yet another painful recounting of the horrors of the Third Reich simply as a matter of course.

There was something more at stake. The very fact of Schwammberger's trial, coming so many years after the crimes had been committed, was nothing short of extraordinary. The coincidence with other momentous events in German history also made the trial a phenomenon. Schwammberger arrived in Germany to stand trial just six months after the national jubilation over the fall of the Berlin Wall. A few months later East and West Germany were formally reunified after forty-five years of separation.

But Schwammberger's trial had a significance more profound than the simple matter of the timing of the proceeding. For Tuchman and the other forty survivors who testified, for the judges and the lawyers and the high-profile mayor of Stuttgart, for the international media, for newly democratic Argentina and newly reunified Germany, there was a higher, more complicated purpose. The effort to bring Josef Schwammberger to justice was nothing short of a vital reckoning with history.

Had Josef Schwammberger not escaped from a French prison in 1948, had he been extradited to Poland and tried there instead, he would likely have been executed along with dozens of his SS comrades. This should have been his fate. Had his life story ended that way, no one, except his own family and friends, would have given much thought to it. The history books would have found no place for him. As with thousands of Nazi criminals in those first few years after the war, a certain justice, albeit a gross and imperfect justice, would have been done.

Schwammberger did not die in 1948. Following scores of Nazi fugitives, he fled to South America and there enjoyed forty years of largely undisturbed obscurity. Escaping to Argentina certainly spared his neck the hangman's noose, but in preserving himself, Schwammberger assured, unwittingly, that his life would assume many layers of symbolic meaning.

In fact, Schwammberger's case became more significant the longer it was delayed. When the onetime camp comman- dant did finally surface, after decades of hiding, he wore the sagging face of an old man. At that moment he represented the unreconciled Nazi past.

Schwammberger's advanced age, as well as that of the dozens of survivors whose testimony would either make or break the case, suggested that his could well be the last major Nazi war crimes trial. His trial, then, marked the putative end to an era that began in Nuremberg in 1946. In the years thereafter Nazi trials were a key means to making good on the now widely known slogan "Never forget." Me- morial stones, after all, cannot speak. Museums are often sterile, impersonal. Commemorative speeches degenerate into rhetoric.

For decades the trials of Nazi criminals in Europe provided a continuing challenge to all who survived the Nazi era, including and perhaps especially those born long after Nazi Germany's surrender on May 8, 1945. The challenge was to see the past as more than a couple of lines in a history textbook, to see the past really as something more than history.

The atrocities committed during the Holocaust seem in- credible even today. The individual acts of Nazis like Josef Schwammberger still seem unbelievable. But seeing Schwamm- berger living and breathing in the body of an old man helped certify just how real he is and just how real were his atrocities.

The witnesses recounted their half-century-old night- mares, and when they turned toward the man responsible, they saw a frail man, a brittle grandfather who often looked disoriented or sleepy or stupid. Yet there he was still, a surviving, living testament to the awful truth.

The fact that Schwammberger was, and is, so indisputably real remains especially important today as two groups continue to become more powerful: the neo-Nazi and far-right movement in Europe and the United States and the loose network of hecklers who promote the preposterous notion that the Holocaust never occurred, that the slaughter of six million Jews is a myth fabricated by Jews hoping to exploit public sympathy for political power. Schwammberger casts such movements in their proper, sinister light.

As long as there have been people who lived the Holocaust, then there have been people to remind others—if only by their very existence—that the Nazi reign of terror was a dark chapter in human history and not some plague sent from the cosmos to defy all human reason and deny all human accountability. Now, as we are on the verge of losing the living memories of the Holocaust, the challenge to remember becomes only more relevant yet only more difficult.

When we acknowledge that indeed, we must remember, just what will we be remembering? And by what means will we remember? Or simply, why will we remember? Just as Hitler and Göring and Goebbels all have become historical caricatures, will the true colors, the sharp lines, the instantly identifiable realities of the Holocaust fade and blur until the entire period becomes nothing but an abstraction or a slogan? Will the Holocaust become just another reference on the time line of human history? Or has that day already come?

Josef Schwammberger is a symbol of memory but also of antimemory. His story and the decades-long struggle to bring him to justice reflect the individual and collective struggles not to remember or to alter memory just as much as the more obvious and oft-repeated mandate not to forget.

Josef Schwammberger's life is a lens through which to

explore the ways we have—and have not—confronted the Nazi past. Fifty years after the Holocaust we can still inquire of the living. Tomorrow we will have no choice but to look elsewhere for the memories, for the meaning, and for the truth.

ROOTS

[Schwammberger] was a nice guy except that he
killed Jews.
—Sam Nussbaum, Holocaust survivor

Josef Franz Leo Schwammberger was born in the
picturesque Tyrolean village of Brixen, on St. Val-
entine's Day, February 14, 1912. Although the
baby's name was clearly inspired by one of the most powerful
men in Europe, Austrian Emperor Franz Josef, the new arrival
to the Schwammberger family was hardly momentous. Amid
the thunderous clamor of revolutionary upheaval then beginning to sound once more across Europe, Josef Schwammberger's birth was but a hiccup.

Brixen, at the time of Schwammberger's birth, was a
peaceful Austrian town just north of the Italian border.*
Sheltered by the majestic Alpine range and split by the
gentle Isarco River, Brixen was also on the southwestern
edge of a vast but crumbling empire, far from the concerns
of those at the imperial court in Vienna.

*Even today the town's population is only about fifteen thousand.

In just a few years Europe again was consumed by war. By the boy's fourth birthday Franz Josef, the long-reigning Hapsburg ruler, was dead at the age of eighty-six. Soon thereafter, following the defeat of Austria and Germany, the Allied victors erased the lines of one of Europe's longest-lived empires and in the process redrew nearly every national boundary on the Continent.

Before Josef reached an age when he might comprehend its significance, the northern border of Italy was pushed up into the middle of the dense Alpine range south of Innsbruck. Austria, for six centuries one of Europe's preeminent powers and long in the business of adding to its territories, was forced at the conclusion of the First World War to give up the southern portion of its Tyrol Province.

Through the transfer more than two hundred thousand formerly Austrian Tyroleans—German-speaking Tyroleans—came under the Italian flag. There were just half as many Italians in the territory. But despite the disparity in national identity, Italy believed its political interests justified its absorbing the Austrian province.*

After the transfer the name of Schwammberger's birthplace was changed from Brixen to Bressanone. Just ahead of the advancing Italians, the Schwammberger family, including Josef and his two older sisters and older brother, moved north toward the German border and to the breathtaking Alpine city of Innsbruck.

Although at the time young Josef Schwammberger could not appreciate the loss of the Tyrol to Italy, the border revision exemplified a dramatic change in Europe's political

---

*The Tyrol has been a source of contest between Austria and Italy for many years. Italy had long coveted the territory as a buffer against German encroachment. After Austria became part of the Third Reich in 1938, Hitler decided not to press Mussolini to return the land in deference to their political alliance. Even today many Austrians resent losing that turf.

dynamic. The shifting of borders to accommodate discrete national groups, and in some cases in spite of national identity, as happened in the Tyrol, set the stage for earthquaking developments. The changes soon were to have a profound influence on Schwammberger, Europe, and the course of human history.

During the century leading up to World War I, nationalism had become the driving political force in Europe. An entity like Austria's Hapsburg Empire, ruling over distant and diverse ethnic minorities, simply could not continue to exist in a world where Serbs were willing to take up arms to create an independent Serbia, Ukrainians for Ukraine, Poles for Poland, and so on. The ethnic instability finally was overwhelming.

The postwar peace extinguished, at least temporarily, some nationalist brushfires. Poland, for example, was reborn after having been divided and redivided out of existence over many centuries. In other cases, loosely stitched federations of smaller ethnic groups formed, as in Czechoslovakia and Yugoslavia.

But the Allied victors punished the German-speaking countries Austria and Germany for their aggression. Seeking to avoid future confrontations, the Allies deliberately flouted Germanness in reassigning national boundaries.* France helped itself to the coal-rich Alsace-Lorraine, reclaiming the territory from its vanquished nemesis Germany. Other lands settled predominantly by German-speaking peoples were given to Poland, Czechoslovakia, and, in the case of the formerly Austrian Tyrol, Italy.

Peace in Europe was brief. Nationalist movements only

---

*Germany itself had been created in 1871, when the powerful Prussian state managed finally to consolidate the other Germanic principalities. Austria, although German-speaking, was not included mainly because Franz Josef was stubbornly unwilling to give up his multiethnic empire for the sake of one unified German state.

gained strength from the political and economic disorder that followed the end of the war. Militant nationalist leaders rose up to rally those who felt encouraged to assert their national aspirations, such as the Croats and the Ukrainians, and those who felt spurned or maligned by the unprecedented political restructuring across the Continent, such as the unhappily dispersed German people.

It was a confusing, disillusioning time for a young man such as Josef Schwammberger to come of age. The home in which he had been born was now on Italian soil. The powerful empire that had been his country's pride for centuries was extinct. His country's reputation was stained by its defeat in world war. And the language he spoke bound him to other German countries and territories from which he was politically isolated.

In the northern city of Innsbruck, at least, he was nearer the pulse of German life. A jewel of a city nestled in the thick Alpine range along Germany's southern border, Innsbruck was situated on what was fast becoming the front line of the German nationalist campaign.

In 1922, when Josef Schwammberger was only ten years old, Adolf Hitler sat in a prison in Landsberg, just seventy-five miles up the road and across the German border from Innsbruck, to which the Schwammberger family had so recently moved. In the first paragraph of *Mein Kampf*, Hitler reflected on the fact that his birthplace, Braunau, lay "on the boundary between two German states." Identifying what became one of the early top priorities of the newly formed Nazi party, Hitler wrote that "we of the younger generation at least have made it our life work to reunite [Germany and Austria] by every means at our disposal."

Superficially Schwammberger shared other traits with the man who was agitating to restore pride and prosperity to the German people. Like Hitler, Schwammberger came from the modest home of a lifelong civil servant. Schwammberger's father, Florian, worked as a postal clerk, and his mother, Helene, handled the household duties, including raising Josef's three older siblings and the younger sister who was born in 1917 shortly after the family left Brixen.

Also like Hitler, Schwammberger was of below average height and weight—at maturity he stood just five feet and seven inches and weighed only 145 pounds—and had dark hair. In short, Josef Schwammberger, like Adolf Hitler himself, was hardly the model to represent the tall, blond Aryan male whom the Nazi racial theorists later extolled as the highest physical form of German manhood.

Again, like the Austrian-born Hitler, young Schwammberger was desultory and desperate before finding himself and a sense of purpose on the other side of the German border.

After completing his elementary and intermediate school studies—up through the American equivalent of junior high school—and lacking the qualifications to attend the academic high school, the gymnasium, Schwammberger spent two years in a vocational program. He then spent three years as an apprentice to an Innsbruck druggist.

One month after the stock market crashed on Wall Street, with the world economy teetering on the brink of collapse, young Josef managed to land a job as a salesclerk in a pharmacy. His training had served him well.

Two years later, on the last day of 1931, the worldwide depression caught up with him, and he lost his job. Josef Schwammberger was nineteen years old and a prime candidate for the Nazi party.

When Arnold Susskind and Josef Schwammberger met as young men, one held absolute power over the other. Until that fateful moment, however, the budding Austrian Nazi and the Polish Jew actually shared a number of interests and experiences.

Susskind, too, was born just before the start of the First World War and at the edge of the fading Austrian Empire, although at the complete opposite end from tiny Bressanone (né Brixen) where Schwammberger was born. When Susskind was just a few years old, he, too, witnessed the transfer of title over his birthplace, Przemysl, along with the entire province of Galicia, from Austrian to Polish custody.

Living in Innsbruck, Schwammberger was at the forefront of an impassioned nationalist dispute, the prospect for a unified German nation. Growing up in Przemysl, Susskind, too, was right on an important national fault line. During the First World War, Przemysl was captured by the Russian Army and then was liberated by German troops. After Germany's defeat in 1918 Przemysl was situated at the southeastern extreme of the newly constituted republic of Poland.

Both young men came of age amid intense nationalist fervor and even violence. In Schwammberger's universe the ethnic furor concerned pan-Germanism, while Susskind's world, an ethnically diverse community, was racked by powerful and competing nationalist campaigns. The population of Galicia, although joined to Poland, was in fact only about one-third Polish, with one-third Ukrainian and one-third Jewish. In some Galician towns Jews made up 40, 50, even 60 percent of the population. There were more than three million Jews in Poland overall in the 1930s, about 10 percent of the total population. Jews were the second-largest ethnic minority in the country after the Ukrainians.

Through the political chaos and economic turmoil of the times, Susskind struggled to define himself, to resolve his rival feelings for the Jewish people and the Polish state, just as Schwammberger was coming to terms with the conflict between his Austrian birthright and his German aspirations.

The roots of the hateful violence that ultimately impelled Josef Schwammberger to seek to destroy Arnold Susskind ran deep in the history of their peoples. For centuries the

Austrian Germans enjoyed a privileged status in the world. Even lower-income Germans like the Schwammbergers were still members of an elite class, compared with the other subjects of the Hapsburg Empire, the second-class Moravians and Poles and Slavs. The Jewish experience, by contrast, was historically one of hardship, socially and financially.

Jews and Poles had lived together in Central Europe for nearly one thousand years. In fact, Jews may well have settled in Poland even before Christians.[1] The earliest written records of Jews in Przemysl date back to the mid-1400s, but there are references in medieval court records to Jewish families living in the town several hundred years before that.

Jewish immigration to Poland increased dramatically during the fourteenth century, when Casimir III, one of the most honored of Poland's kings, made a point of encouraging Jewish settlement. He believed Jews would bring commercial skills that would help spur Polish economic development.

In spite of the fact that they had been invited, Poland's Jews were rarely treated as equals in the centuries that followed. They were repeatedly slapped with special taxes that forced many families into bankruptcy and kept large numbers of others at subsistence levels. Other social and economic restrictions limited Jewish rights and tended to force the Jewish communities to become increasingly insular.

Outbreaks of violence directed at Jews, often inspired by fantastical fears of "blood libel" and other anti-Semitic myths, were not infrequent. These actions and measures were inflicted generation after generation, long before the rise of nazism and state-sponsored anti-Semitism. The Roman Catholic Church, perhaps the single most dominant institution in the country, openly encouraged such attacks.

Galicia, the province that included Przemysl, was joined to the far-flung Austrian realm in 1772, when Empress Maria

Theresa, Franz Josef's great-great-grandmother, bargained with the Russian czarina Catherine II and the Prussian king Frederick II to split among themselves the lands of the much weaker Polish kingdom. The negotiated elimination of Poland was a mixed blessing for Galicia's Jews.

On the one hand, the Austrians had a somewhat more enlightened attitude toward the Jewish community than the Poles. Jews began to enjoy many of the benefits of citizenship that Jews in Western Europe had already begun to appreciate: relative freedom in commerce, politics, and, of course, religious life.

The Jewish community was still heavily taxed, however. Even worse, the Austrians imposed a system of regulations designed to restrict the growth of the Jewish population. These laws, which had been in effect elsewhere in the Austrian lands since the early 1700s, assigned a fixed number of families entitled to bear children in each regional district of the province. Jews without official "family numbers" often were forced either to assimilate or to remain cut off from the economic and social life of their community.*

As difficult as life was for Jews in Galicia during the nineteenth century, they were far better off than Jews living in other parts of Poland and east in Ukraine, the Baltic states, and Russia. Czar Alexander III's ascension to the Russian throne in 1881 heralded an era of repression aimed at all ethnic minorities, but especially at Jews. Some five million Jews were segregated in the westernmost of Russia's lands, the area that became known as the Pale of Settlement. Many were forced off the land and into squalid urban ghettos. Alexander's May Laws, a series of measures designed to strip Jews of their property, deny them access to services, and undermine their livelihoods, were grim harbingers of Hitler's Nuremberg Laws fifty-three years later.

*The Austrians finally abolished the so-called Familiants Law in 1859.

Fearful of Czarist oppression, many Galician Jews fled to other parts of the Austrian Empire at the onset of the First World War. Thousands relocated to Hungary. Many joined an already well-established Jewish community in Vienna. Others abandoned Europe altogether and sailed to the United States. Large-scale emigration to Palestine also began during this period.

Still, as Arnold Susskind describes his childhood, Przemysl clearly was not the worst place for a young Jew to be, in spite of all the ethnic tension and hostility. A quiet town on the banks of the San River, Przemysl was surrounded by low hills within striking distance of the Carpathian Mountains to the south. Only a hundred miles or so to the east lay the cultural attractions of Krakow, a onetime capital of Poland.

By 1930 the population of Przemysl was about sixty thousand, one-third of whom were Jews. Jews were active in local business and political affairs. For a time there was even a Jewish deputy mayor. Several other prominent Jewish lawyers and businessmen served in the Sejm, the Polish national parliament.

The eldest of four children, Susskind enjoyed a comfortable, happy childhood. His father owned a shop that sold imported chocolates and candies. The store was a popular stop for many of the thousands of Polish soldiers and army officers stationed at the garrison in Przemysl. "The officers used to fool around in the hotels and nightclubs, drinking, and they spent money," Susskind recalled. "In fact, my father's business, he had a few officers were steady customers, made a nice living."[2]

Folding his hands on the dining-room table of his modest home in Forest Hills, New York, Susskind reminisced that "Jewish life was very active." That there were many "activities" (pronounced "ac-tee-vi-teez" with his still-conspicuous accent) was a sure sign, in Susskind's view, of a prosperous community. As a boy he made his commitment, however, to his studies. "I went to Hebrew gymnasium [an academic high school]. I came home, I had to do my homework. We had an aunt living with us. She watched me, and when I did my homework, then I could go out. Oh, and after I did my homework, I had to read for half an hour."

When he did go out, Susskind went to his "organization." The organization was a Zionist group called Betar, founded on the ideas of Vladimir Jabotinsky, a Russian Zionist and one of the leading and most controversial voices calling for a Jewish national homeland in Palestine. The name of the group was a shortened form of the Hebrew B'rith Trumpeldor, which means "House of Trumpeldor." Joseph Trumpeldor, a charismatic Zionist, had succeeded during the First World War in persuading the British government to commission a small unit of Jewish volunteers to help fight the Turks, who were then still the imperial masters of Palestine. The Jewish legion fought bravely at the Battle of Gallipoli, and Trumpeldor, wounded in the fighting, became an international Jewish hero.[3]

Scores of Zionist groups of varying orientations had sprouted all across Eastern Europe in the several decades following the 1896 publication of Theodor Herzl's treatise Der Judenstaat (The Jewish State). Jabotinsky followers were among the most uncompromising in calling for immediate mass emigration to Palestine. Betar, like many other Zionist groups, sponsored programs to prepare members for eventual settlement in Palestine. Betar groups sponsored courses in Hebrew, physical fitness, and agricultural science. But one of the most attractive features of the group, especially to the scores of Jewish kids who had grown up being teased and harassed by their Polish schoolmates, was that it also offered military training. The uniform Betar members wore became a source of Jewish pride.

"I was fifteen when I joined that group," Susskind recalled. "I heard Jabotinsky speak. He came with a warning. He appealed to the Jews of Poland, 'Pack your bags and run away, comes terrible times.' I heard him in a big auditorium. I came home and told my father I was going to join that organization."

In the 1930s Jabotinsky became concerned that he and his followers, with their brown-shirt uniforms and military-style parades, might be seen not as ardent nationalists, like the American general George Washington or the Italian patriot Giuseppe Garibaldi, but as Jewish Fascists. In some circles Jabotinsky's fears were justified. In 1935 Italian dictator Benito Mussolini told Rome's Chief Rabbi David Prato, "For Zionism to succeed you need to have a Jewish state with a Jewish flag and a Jewish language. The man who really understands this is your Fascist, Jabotinsky."[4]

There was diversity of opinion among those sympathetic to the Zionist cause. These internal battle lines continued to define the most prominent split in Jewish politics through to the current differences between Israel's left-leaning Labor and right-wing Likud parties.*

And there were spirited differences between the Zionists and those Jews—and there were many—who were wary not only of Jabotinsky but of Zionism in any form. Many sincerely believed in assimilating, in their loyalty both to Judaism, with its religious teachings and cultural traditions, and to the Polish nation. Many Jews were poor and worried they would never have the resources to emigrate. Others were well off and worried about losing everything they had worked for if Jews came under increased suspicion and persecution.

The Zionist debate swept the entire Continent. Particularly in the east, in Poland and Russia and the Baltic states,

*David Ben Gurion, Israel's first president and early leader of the Israeli Labor party, once called Jabotinsky "Vladimir Hitler." And Menachem Begin's infamous paramilitary unit, Irgun Z'vai Le'umi (National Military Organization), which led attacks on British soldiers and property during the 1940s, was a direct descendant of Jabotinsky's Betar.

where anti-Semitism had been so fierce for so long, where the future of the Jewish population was most uncertain, there was tremendous tension surrounding the Zionist issue. The way in which the problem would be resolved and the speed with which it would be resolved might mean—and certainly did come to mean—the difference between life and death for millions of people.

Even in little Przemysl Jews felt the severity of these tensions. Left-wing Zionists hurled more than insults when Susskind and his fellow members of Betar dressed up and held a parade. "When came a national holiday like Lag b'Omer, we would march.* And they used to throw rocks on us. But Jabotinsky's idea came true. He said no one will give us Israel on a platter. He said you have to be prepared, to train yourself."

In the middle of his last year at the gymnasium, when he was just seventeen, Susskind got the call from Betar headquarters in Warsaw that it was his time for *hachsharah,* a Hebrew word meaning "preparedness." In a sense, *hachsharah* was like National Guard duty, except that these "troops" were spending weeks at a time in the Polish woods or in the mountains, training in camps for the battles, military and otherwise, that they were likely to face in British-occupied Palestine.†

In the middle of the night, carrying only a pillowcase stuffed with extra clothes and a blanket, Susskind stole away to join his comrades in what he believed was a grand mission to train at a model work camp near the Russian border for the day when he would be able to settle in the Holy Land. Only his sister was let in on the plan. "Later I wrote my

*Lag b'Omer, a minor Jewish holiday, occurs on the thirty-third day following Passover and marks the end of a terrible plague some eighteen hundred years ago that devastated the academy of noted Talmudic scholar Rabbi Akiba.

†The British took control of Palestine after the defeat of the Ottoman Turks in 1918.

parents where I am," he recalls. "They used to send me packages because we were starving over there."

He spent thirteen months at the Zionist training camp, mostly working at a lumber mill. "It had an English name, Forest, only I didn't know what forest was. It was tremendous big. Two thousand people used to work there. They had their own railroads and everything." As part of their training, those participating in *hachsharah* also continued their Hebrew-language studies and military drills.

"A Polish soldier would teach us how to shoot," Susskind recalled. "I remember a Mauser I used to shoot. I had a medal for shooting."

Betar also offered political education. One day during Susskind's preparedness training, Menachem Begin, the future prime minister of Israel, visited the camp to deliver a political speech. "He was traveling to all those places. He was at that time a great speaker. He looked with the glasses, just the way, not good-looking, only energetic, and you could see that mind was different, that he has a great future."

When Susskind returned to Przemysl, he began writing articles for the Betar newspaper, the *Tribune*, which was published in nearby Krakow. Committing himself full-time to the cause, he also worked to organize other Jewish communities and to get them involved in *hachsharah* activities.

In 1935 he received at last a coveted permit to emigrate to Palestine under the auspices of Betar. But he never made the move, never fulfilled his dream, because the British, at that time increasingly sensitive to Arab pressure and fearful of renewed Arab violence in Palestine, had agreed to impose stricter limits on new Jewish settlements there. Although illegal immigration to Palestine continued in considerable numbers throughout the 1930s, tens of thousands of Polish Jews like Arnold Susskind were stranded.

From a young age Sam Nussbaum was taught that his survival would be linked with his ability to work hard and prepare himself for difficult times. That may be a harsh lesson for a young boy to accept, but in Nussbaum's case and under the circumstances of the day, such dire warnings as wisdom provided him with the critical margin between life and death when it came his time to encounter the Austrian commandant named Josef Schwammberger.

Nussbaum was born in Przemysl in 1920, several years after Schwammberger and Susskind. But in those several years Europe and indeed the world changed dramatically. Austria had been reduced from a grand empire to a third-rate state. The Bolsheviks had captured power in Russia. Germany had been laid to waste and was teetering on the edge of revolution. Galicia was no longer a distant province but had become a vital district in a country brimming with national pride and promise. And Europe's Jews, nowhere more so than in Poland, were beginning to sense the imminent struggle.

As a boy Sam Nussbaum could not fully appreciate the meaning of these world changes or the significance of his being a Jew in an increasingly hostile, anti-Jewish world. Rather he concerned himself with youthful pleasures, such as soccer, the demands of his schooling, and his family obligations.

Nussbaum was the son of a grain merchant, and he and his family lived modestly. "We didn't have much then," he recalled as he sipped coffee in the kitchen of his spacious home in Overland Park, a well-appointed suburb of Kansas City. "We had a percentage in a mill, and we had a little store. Over on Słowackiego Street. I remember that."[5]

Nussbaum's mother and five younger siblings helped out in the shop. The father reserved for his eldest son responsibility for making deposits at the bank. "About three o'clock, when they got through [counting the receipts], I would go on my bicycle back to the bank with the cash in my boots," Nussbaum reminisced, still proud that he was the one his father entrusted with such an important chore.

When Nussbaum finished elementary school, his father contracted with a Jewish plumber to teach the trade to young Samech, as his parents called him. His family could not afford to send him to the gymnasium, the academic high school that Arnold Susskind had attended. Just as with Schwammberger, Nussbaum's father decided it best for his son to learn a trade.

Lack of financial resources was not the only motivation for the elder Nussbaum's pushing his son into a trade. The father believed the training would better equip his son for the rugged life of a Jewish settler in Palestine if they somehow managed to find the means and the money to emigrate. "He said to me, 'Samech, pick up a trade and learn a trade, and I will try to see that you go to Eretz Israel.'* That's what he told me. That's the only reason he wanted me to learn a trade."

Nussbaum's father was also interested in having his son learn about the arts, so young Samech studied the violin. "I was pretty good, too," Nussbaum reflected. "My father used to take me to weddings, and I would play the violin. But a plumber's fingers are heavy. And then the war came."

In the end those plumber's fingers did not help Sam Nussbaum get to Israel. Time after time in the trying years ahead, however, they did save his life.

*Eretz is a Hebrew word meaning "land" or "nation."

CHAPTER 3

UPROOTING

If things don't get better, depend on it, they will
get worse.
—Yiddish proverb

Month after month passed, and Josef Schwammberger simply could not find work. He continued to stay with his family in the house they
all had lived in since moving to Innsbruck. Schwammberger
spent his twentieth birthday and all of the following year
on the unemployment rolls.

There could not have been much comfort in knowing that
his personal economic misfortunes were part of a worldwide
depression. In 1931, the year Schwammberger was laid off
from his job in the pharmacy, there were nearly six hundred
thousand Austrians without work out of a total population
of barely seven million. Many others were able to find only
part-time jobs. Both Schwammberger's and Austria's prospects looked bleak.

As French Premier Georges Clemenceau had gloated after
the Hapsburg Empire's defeat and dissolution, Austria was
simply "what [was] left over." And the part that was left was

acutely ill equipped to sustain the severe economic downturn that came a decade later. Giving up its imperial holdings had a devastating economic impact on top of the political consequences. In the days of the empire many of Austria's most important industries and much of its raw materials had been located outside the country itself.

The sufferings of Austria's weakling economy only compounded the national identity crisis that had been festering since the defeat of the Central Powers in World War I. For so long it had seemed the natural order for Austrians to lead, to be prosperous. Vienna had been not only the center of a vast and wealthy empire but a vital hub of European culture and ideas. Now Austria was a feeble power riding the reputation of its past.

Exacerbating this challenge to the national character was the fact that Germany, although also beaten on the battlefield, was at least still united as a German nation. German Austria was not a part of that union—by Allied decree—and German Austrians were not sure whether they should be separate from or together with their brethren to the north. Some feared being overshadowed by their much larger neighbor, but many Austrians still believed they ought to bind their fate to the greater German nation rather than to some rump Austrian republic, notwithstanding the Allied prohibition.

In fact, both German and Austrian parliaments supported unification. Provincial plebiscites in the northern Tyrol—which was still part of Austria—and in Salzburg confirmed the rising popular interest in Austria for merging with Germany. In April 1921, 98.6 percent of the electorate in the province of Tyrol voted in vain to join Germany. One month later an overwhelming 99.3 percent of voters in Salzburg indicated their preference for annexation to Germany.[1]

As Austria struggled through the depression, so did Schwammberger. Finally, after being out of work for fifteen months, he found temporary work as a salesclerk with a firm specializing in bankruptcy auctions. It was a true sign of the times. At last he had a job, but he was hardly on the fast track.

There had to be a way out, a door to something better, some hope. Like thousands of others, Schwammberger, a man of average ability, little experience, and limited promise for success, turned to the man who seemed to offer the key. On April 18, 1933, Josef Schwammberger swore an oath of allegiance to Adolf Hitler and became a member of Hitler's burgeoning internal security force, the Schutzstaffel, or SS.

Hitler's Nazi program did offer hope. Even more, with his mesmerizing oratory and mystical fascination with ceremony and symbol, the wild-eyed Austrian ex-corporal offered Germany and Germans throughout Europe a sort of redemption. Hitler extolled Germanness in every imaginable expression: German folk myth, German opera, German literature, traditional German dress, and, of course, German ethnicity itself.

Hitler defined Germanness and the political aspirations of the greater German nation at a time when millions of ordinary Germans just like Schwammberger were especially vulnerable. Whether Austrian, Prussian, or Bavarian, the Germans were a defeated people. They had been separated from the source of their once-imperial strength and humiliated by the shackles imposed by the Allied victors. In a time of chaos and despair, Hitler represented order and a restored hope for greatness.

The Nazis' appeal grew rapidly. Throughout the 1920s the Austrian offshoot of the Nazi party had been just one of a number of right-wing German nationalist, or Pan-German, parties.* During this time there were no more than 5,000

---

*The term *Nazi* comes from the official name of Hitler's organization, the National sozialistische Deutsche Arbeiterpartei, or the National Socialist German Workers' party.

Nazi party members in the entire country. But in the 1930 national elections the Austrian Nazi party drew some 110,000 votes and established itself as the third major party in the country alongside the conservative Christian Socialists and the more liberal Social Democrats. By January 1933, when Hitler claimed the chancellor's post in Germany, the ranks of the Austrian Nazis had increased more than eight-fold, to some 40,000 dues-paying members.[2]

Hitler's anti-Semitism reinforced his drive to give Germans a sense of sharing in a grand design, of belonging to a noble cause. Building on the deeply ingrained traditions of mistrust and even loathing, Hitler transformed a religious distinction into a racial one to serve his political objectives. As one prominent Holocaust historian noted succinctly, "Modern German anti-Semitism was the bastard child of the union of Christian anti-Semitism with German nationalism."[3]

The German nationalist movement cast Jews not only as not-German but as a vile and dangerous enemy. Poles, Gypsies, homosexuals, and other groups targeted later for wide-scale maltreatment and even murder were never viewed as so dangerous a threat. For whatever the distinction is worth, they were not considered enemies so much as forms of human rubbish that the (supposedly) more highly evolved Germans eventually would have to clear away.

Loyalty to the nationalist movement and self-awareness as a German were even more intensely bred in the black-shirted members of the SS. Founded in 1922, the SS originally was named the Adolf Hitler Shock Troops. Hitler's idea was to have a highly disciplined, absolutely reliable, elite corps of armed bodyguards. As the name suggested, this paramilitary force was utterly committed to Hitler's personal defense. The group's ultimate name, Schutzstaffel, which means "protection squad," preserved this idea.

In its early years the SS was responsible simply for security, for the personal safety of Hitler and the security of Nazi party meetings and functions. Under Heinrich Himmler, who took the helm of the SS in 1929, the concept of security was expanded in two important ways. The SS became the self-appointed guardian of racial purity for the Aryan nation. The agencies of the SS also were responsible for all internal police and security functions in the expanding Nazi state.

Under Himmler, the SS became a monolithic, all-powerful police power whose reach extended to every corner of German life and death. As Himmler increased the scope of his influence and as Hitler stepped up his anti-Semitic campaign, the SS assumed primary responsibility for operating the vast network of Nazi concentration camps, for managing the euthanasia campaign against hundreds of thousands of mentally retarded Germans, and for implementing the "Final Solution."

Himmler's first step toward making the SS the preeminent police power in Nazi Germany was to enlarge its membership. There were just 280 SS members when Himmler assumed the position of *Reichsführer, SS* (state leader, SS). By mid-1932 Himmler had added some 30,000 men to the SS rolls, mostly, of course, in Germany itself.[4] The wave of recruits rose even higher in 1933, when Hitler successfully captured power.

Former military officers, down-and-out aristocrats, and unemployed workers like Schwammberger rushed to join the SS in the early 1930s. In addition to the promise of a job, recruits were drawn in droves by Himmler's compelling propaganda pitch. In theory the SS was to become the elite vanguard of the entire Nazi movement. Not only were SS members supposed to be the most loyal defenders of the Nazi cause, but they were expected to represent the best of German manhood.

According to Himmler's racial fantasy, his SS men possessed the purest Aryan blood and the strongest and most beautiful Nordic features. Bearing pure Aryan seed and the ruthlessness to combat infectious elements in society, such as Jews and Slavs, Himmler believed, the SS would cleanse Germany and lead the German people to greatness.

In practice these standards were extremely flexible. After all, Schwammberger's dark hair and below-average height hardly cast him as the picture of Himmler's Nordic prince. As one SS historian noted, if the SS chief had imposed his racial qualifications strictly, he "would have had to dismiss the best part of half the SS, for they were mostly simple middle-class citizens, bearing little resemblance to [Nazi racial theorist] Walther Darré's picture of glorious Germanic men."[5]

All SS men were bound by a strict code of conduct and, more important, attitude. Discipline was ordered and intense. In addition to swearing an oath of allegiance to Hitler, SS men were taught to be loyal above all else. The regimentation, the ritual songs and dress, and the elite status conferred by the SS uniform all bound the SS men to one another and to Hitler's movement.

With all that is known today about what the SS later became, it is easy to suspect that the typical SS man was a rabid anti-Semite who was drawn to the organization for that reason. But few Germans in 1933 had any understanding of the treacherous and violent path down which Hitler was then leading them.

Instead Schwammberger and many of the thousands of new SS recruits clearly viewed the blackshirt uniform as an attractive answer to their dismal economic and professional prospects. Just as with Arnold Susskind and the other brownshirted members of Betar, the SS provided Schwammberger with a sense of place and purpose and self-esteem. The SS was promised a spirit of camaraderie and a more encouraging outlook toward the future.

In fact, as important as anti-Semitism was to Hitler's world view, it was only one factor that drew Germans by the millions to the Nazi party. The party did not win legislative seats in the late 1920s and early 1930s because it was advocating the Nuremberg Laws that followed in 1935 or because its leaders promised to kill all the Jews. In fact, Hitler had toned down his anti-Semitic rhetoric to win votes in the 1928 German elections. As a historian of German voting patterns during this period concluded in her seminal study of German attitudes toward Hitler and nazism:

> Many Germans hoped Hitler could pull Germany out of the depression and others thought he was the only man capable of restoring dignity to the nation after its humiliating defeat in World War I and the Treaty of Versailles. . . . In short, there was a myriad of reasons for joining the Nazi party or voting for Hitler. Anti-Semitism was only one and not necessarily the most important one, and it was apparently not a major determinant of Nazi success at the polls.[6]

Still, even if the SS recruits did not enter with fully formed anti-Semitic views, they were certainly indoctrinated in ways that prepared them to carry out the crimes of the Holocaust. Schwammberger and the other SS recruits were instilled with a virulent arrogance and ruthlessness. "The SS man learned that: his basic attitude must be that of a fighter for fighting's sake; he must obey unquestioningly; he must be 'hard'—not only inured to but impervious to all human emotions; he should be contemptuous of 'inferior beings' and arrogant towards all those who did not belong to the Order. . . ."[7]

As popular support for the Nazis and the SS continued to grow in Austria, the Austrian government became increasingly displeased. In May 1933, two months after Schwammberger had been fitted for an SS uniform, the Austrian government outlawed the Nazi party and its affiliate organizations.

This action against the Austrian Nazis was the culmination of a bitter feud that had developed between Hitler, then newly installed as chancellor in Germany, and Engelbert Dollfuss, the diminutive Austrian leader who was attempting to solidify an authoritarian regime modeled after that of Italy's Mussolini. Dollfuss, who had come to power just one year before, resented Hitler's sentimental calls for German unification. Under Dollfuss, Austria turned its back on its more powerful cousin. Instead the Austrian leader looked south for support from Mussolini, who was then interested in projecting Italian influence in the Mediterranean and Balkan countries. Austria, as a gateway to that region, was a key element of Mussolini's vision.

Dollfuss, however, did not enjoy the popular support at home that Mussolini found in Italy and that Hitler was exploiting in Germany. Dollfuss was vulnerable, especially considering the earlier expressions of support among the Austrian electorate for Hitler's nationalist policies. Pan-German sympathizers carped from the right. And the left wing, stifled by Dollfuss's increasingly authoritarian regime, cared no more for him.

When Hans Frank, then Hitler's minister of justice, made a blatant propaganda visit to Austria in May 1933, Dollfuss became fearful that the Nazi party would tap into the widespread discontent and encourage unrest. Soon after Frank crossed the border, Dollfuss had him expelled.

Hitler reacted angrily to this slight by imposing a thousand mark tax on Germans visiting Austria, a move designed to starve Austria's tourist industry. One month later Dollfuss declared the Austrian Nazi party illegal. Ironically, the Austrian chancellor decided there was one strong-arm political tactic among the many popularized by the Nazis that he admired enough to imitate. In March 1933, five weeks after taking power, Hitler had established a concentration camp prison in Dachau, a quaint artists' community north of Munich. A few weeks later Dollfuss established a similar camp south of Vienna, where he imprisoned Nazis and other political opponents.

These developments caught up with Josef Schwammberger on July 25, 1933. On that day, for the first of what would be many times over the course of his life, the twenty-one-year-old SS recruit was forced to flee. Slipping across the border into Germany, Schwammberger joined up with the newly formed Austrian Legion, a ragtag SS fighting force then training in several camps near Munich.

Schwammberger spent two years in rigorous military training. Years later, one of Schwammberger's fellow legionnaires, Karl Adolf Eichmann, looked back proudly on the experience. "The drill was hard and at times almost beyond endurance," according to one historian's account. "Later he used to display with pride the scars on his elbows, the visible consequences of exercises crawling through barbed-wire fences. It was there that he acquired the power to master his body and the ability to control his emotions."*

Eichmann later climbed the SS ladder to one of the most powerful and deadly positions in the Nazi state. But in those early months of SS service, like Schwammberger, he was just another lowly foot soldier.

By 1934 the ranks of the SS's Austrian Legion had swelled to some ten thousand.[8] In that time the legion served as a way for Hitler to maintain political pressure on Dollfuss.

*Gideon Hausner, *Justice in Jerusalem* (New York: Harper & Row, 1966), p. 31. Hausner's account of Eichmann's early life is based on evidence presented at Eichmann's 1961 trial in Israel, at which Hausner, as Israel's attorney general, was the lead prosecutor. The biographical material comes from Eichmann's own lengthy statement to prosecutors and from transcripts of a series of interviews Eichmann gave to a Nazi journalist in the 1950s, while Eichmann was hiding in Buenos Aires. The interview was to have been used in the preparation of a book—which was never published—arguing that the Holocaust never occurred.

The presence of the SS units so close to the German-Austrian border was a warning, like a vulture sitting on a tree waiting for a hobbled animal to fall.

Exactly one year after Schwammberger left Austria, he was drawn into one of the most dramatic of Hitler's early diplomatic confrontations. Back in Vienna, Dollfuss had been struggling to shore up his political strength amid increasing opposition from both the left and the right. The Austrian leader did have the support of the Catholic Church, the army, and the conservative Christian Socialist party. The loose coalition of these forces was enough to allow him to cling to power. Perhaps Dollfuss's most important asset, however, was his link to Italy's Mussolini.

On July 25, 1934, a band of Austrian Nazis, frustrated after spending more than a year under cover, revolted against the Dollfuss regime. Government police managed to put down the rebels but not before a handful of conspirators had located and mortally wounded Dollfuss. The Nazis also managed briefly to control the state radio station and to broadcast news of the uprising across the country, which touched off minor skirmishes in all the major Austrian cities.

Hitler claimed that the coup attempt was not his doing, despite the incessant barrage of anti-Dollfuss propaganda the German Nazis had been sending across the border through radio broadcasts and airplane leaflet drops. Especially when he saw the revolt was failing, Hitler had to deny his involvement.

The Austrian Legion members, meanwhile, had been waiting anxiously for the news from Vienna. When it finally came, eager to assist in what they expected to be their glorious return home, the exiled SS men hustled across the border. Soon, however, it became clear that the coup plotters had failed and were being rounded up and that Mussolini had responded to the uprising by positioning Italian troops along Austria's southern border. With this news, the soldiers

of the Austrian Legion, Schwammberger among them, scur-
ried back to their base camps in southern Germany.

Officially Hitler distanced himself from the Austrian
debacle, not wanting to upset Mussolini any further. But
after Austria had been finally incorporated into the Reich
a few years later and Hitler had strutted triumphantly along
the grand boulevard that rings Vienna's historic quarter,
the upstart Austrian rebels were hailed as heroes of the
Reich.

Then Austrian Legion alumni Schwammberger and Eichmann, among many others, could return to posts in the
German province of Austria, having seen the day when the
vision for one nation of Germans was finally—if only temporarily—realized.

Marcel Tuchman was born in Przemysl in 1921, the year
before the birth of the SS. Through the years that the SS
developed into an all-dominating instrument of terror and
torture, Germany and the rest of Europe became an increasingly hostile environment for millions of European Jews.
Nowhere was the anti-Jewish fever more powerfully felt than
in Poland. Through the years of his growing up, Tuchman
experienced firsthand the violent anti-Semitism that the SS
came to represent so ferociously.

A stately man who learned to choose his words carefully,
Tuchman came from a more privileged background than the
Susskinds and the Nussbaums. His father was in the export
lumber business, along with Marcel's grandfather and uncle.
Lumber had become one of Poland's most successful industries and one in which Jews had prospered. But the worldwide economic depression in the early 1930s hit Poland
hard, and the Tuchman family business was not spared.

"They were exporting railroad ties for the coal mines,"
Tuchman recalled. "Then in 1932, when the depression occurred—we used to call it the crisis, that was the Polish or

European term for the depression—my father realized that the firm could not support three families. Since he was quite able and educated in business, he left Przemysl and went to Krakow to work as a director of the Suchard chocolate factory. Then he became director for the [company's office] in Warsaw, and we stayed there until the outbreak of the war."

Most ethnic Poles did not weather the economic drought as well as the Tuchmans. In the early 1930s the country's economy was still largely backward, with a population predominantly engaged in farming. The impact of contracting agricultural markets fell most heavily on Polish families, who dominated this sector. Some 60 percent of all Polish families worked in agriculture, while only about 4 percent of Poland's Jews were in farming.

A relatively high percentage of Jews tended instead to go into commerce and the professions. More than a third of all Jewish breadwinners were engaged in some form of business, compared with only 3.4 percent of Poles. And in 1931 one-third of all lawyers and more than half of all doctors in the country were Jewish.[9]

These statistics aside, it can by no means be said that Jews were living in luxury while their fellow Poles starved during the economic crisis. Some Jewish families were comfortable, it is true. But hundreds of thousands of Jews were impoverished well before the Great Depression fell upon Europe. According to some estimates, more than a million Jews, or about one-third of the Jewish population in Poland, were living below the poverty line in the 1930s.[10]

Even more significantly, Poles had all the political power. The Polish majority controlled the state government, and increasingly during the 1930s government measures led to restricted Jewish economic participation. Jews were barred from the civil service. Quotas were imposed to limit Jewish access to public education at all levels. Polish employers were discouraged from hiring Jewish workers. One by one Jews were pushed out of the formerly free professions. Merchants were required to post certificates with the shop owners' names as they appeared on the birth registries, a way of identifying the Jewish-owned shops for boycotting Poles.

Violent anti-Semitism in Poland did not begin all of a sudden in the 1930s, just as Hitler was not Germany's first anti-Semite. Poland had been reconstituted in 1918 without regard to the tremendous ethnic tensions trapped within its borders. The majority and stridently Roman Catholic Poles, the self-superior ethnic German minority, and the ardently nationalist Ukrainians all pursued their independent ethnic interests. If there was one thing on which these groups could agree, it was a fierce antipathy to the Jewish minority.

Poland's Ukrainian minority, especially, was violently anti-Semitic. Militant Polish Ukrainians, unhappy with being separated from their republic to the east, agitated in Poland, especially in Galicia, where their numbers were considerable. In 1919, for example, during the first full year of Poland's newfound existence, Ukrainian nationalists killed some sixty thousand Jews in a wave of pogroms.[11]

Even that number boggles the mind, yet it represented but a sampling of what was to come. When Soviet Russia launched its unsuccessful attack on Poland in 1920, Jews were widely accused of being Bolshevik sympathizers even though many Jews fought with distinction in the Polish Army. Bands of Poles and Ukrainians waged smaller-scale pogroms all over the country in frequent outbursts of anti-Jewish violence during the first years of Polish independence.

Anti-Semitism in Poland, of course, was not a universal phenomenon, just as it would not be true during the Holocaust to come that every Pole was a Nazi collaborator. Many Poles were friendly to their Jewish neighbors before the war, just as many Poles, at tremendous personal risk, later gave shelter and other comfort to their Jewish friends, not to mention complete strangers faced with certain death.

But anti-Semitism in Poland, if not universal, was without doubt pervasive. Economic stresses heightened the sentiments already deeply ingrained in the Polish consciousness. Marshal Józef Piłsudski, a World War I hero who came to power in a coup d'etat in 1926, rallied Poles behind a nationalist banner that further exacerbated anti-Semitic strains even though the marshal himself opposed the more strident anti-Jewish measures.

The so-called Jewish question had been an issue in Polish politics for centuries, but from the moment of Poland's recreation in 1918 it became one of the most prominent national preoccupations. "At times, it seemed as if most, if not all, of Poland's social and economic problems—and there were many in an underdeveloped country, freshly re-united after one hundred and fifty years of partition—could be ascribed to the presence of a large Jewish population and could not fully be solved until the 'Jewish problem' had been solved," observed one Polish-born historian, whose mother is Catholic and whose father is Jewish. Most Poles understood a very simple formula: Pole meant Roman Catholic. "Jews, all Jews, were finding themselves excluded from the Polish nation by virtue of definition," this historian concluded.[12]

Jews reacted, understandably, with terror. Between 1921 and 1937 nearly four hundred thousand fled the country, many to Palestine, some to the United States, Germany, Austria, France, and elsewhere.[13] But many more were without the means to leave or faced other obstacles to emigrating. And the greater the urgency became over the years leading to the Second World War, the more countries in the West lost interest in absorbing the refugees.

The British cut back severely on the numbers of émigrés allowed into Palestine. Other countries of Europe as well as the United States opposed increasing their immigration quotas to accommodate the increasingly frantic Polish Jews. For most of Poland's Jewish population there was no alternative to staying and praying for conditions to improve.

Marcel Tuchman spent his boyhood in this atmosphere of ethnic hatred and violence. As he grew older, he began to understand the impact of the worsening relations between Jews and Poland's other ethnic communities. During the 1930s Tuchman was but a schoolboy, first in Krakow and then in Warsaw, but he encountered the venomous bite of anti-Semitism again and again.

"A kind of red-neck patriotism revived, and the first thing they did was start beating Jews," he recalled. "Because Jews, being somewhat cautious, sensitized by history, would go to the banks and remove their savings during a crisis like this, knowing that next day their funds might be unobtainable. They were singled out from the row of many people taking their money out, and these Fascist students with bamboo canes and razor blades on the end would attack Jews and cut them up and so on."

One day in 1936 Tuchman was touched directly by this anti-Jewish violence. The incident occurred during a parade of students marching to lay a wreath at the grave of the unknown soldier at the presidential palace in Warsaw on the first anniversary of Marshal Piłsudski's death. In recognition of his academic distinction, Tuchman was given the honor of being one of the wreath bearers.

"One of the students, a Pole, a non-Jew, resented that, very badly resented it," Tuchman remembered. "And he was a stupid, very primitive guy, son of a sergeant in the legion, so he thought that it polluted the patriotism if a Jew was carrying the wreath. And all the way along the parade route he would step on the back of my shoes and bait me. 'You Jew, you Jew, you dirty Jew.'"

The Polish boy continued his taunts all the way back to the school. Finally Tuchman struck back. "I took the back of my arm, and I was rather strong and athletic, and I knocked him out with a blow on the face. As I walked into the school, I was informed by my friends, Poles, that if I come out again, I'll be lynched. So they kept me inside under the protection of teachers for a few hours until things quieted down. This was a small incident of anti-Semitism."

In the year Adolf Hitler assumed power in Germany and Josef Schwammberger enlisted in the SS, nineteen-year-old Arnold Susskind continued his work as a political organizer. Susskind thrilled at his work, the nonstop meetings, the traveling, the writing for the *National Tribune*, Betar's newspaper. "My parents were very happy because my picture was always in there," he recalled. "They were proud. I was a short time on the executive board. And they used to send me to conventions. I was very active. They knew me in all the towns."

Susskind's involvement in Betar satisfied a number of different impulses. Certainly he believed in the cause of Zionism, of claiming and building a national home for Jews in Palestine. The political work was also rewarding socially. As charming as little Przemysl may have been in the years before the war, it was nonetheless a small town.*

Susskind's political activities gave him a ticket to the outside world, to the cultural and intellectual offerings of Krakow, to Jews in communities throughout southern Galicia, and to a feeling of purpose, all the same sorts of reasons

---

*Nearly every survivor interviewed for this book spoke of Przemysl as if its beauty were surpassed only by Eden itself. They praised the gentle hills, the smooth waters of the San, the quaint plazas and cosmopolitan boulevards. To the modern visitor, it is extremely difficult to appreciate what the city must have looked like more than half a century ago, let alone that it was nearly as lovely as nostalgic ex-Przemyslites describe. Like many Eastern European cities, the city today is filthy, crowded, and decrepit. The farm country surrounding the city, on the other hand, is still quite lovely, and it is easy to imagine the Galicia of seventy-five or one hundred years ago as one drives the back roads and through the small villages sprinkled about the fertile landscape.

why anyone, anywhere, in any age is drawn to politics at the community level.

Politics for Arnold Susskind, as for thousands of Polish Jews, was also a key to self-identification during a time of tremendous upset and confusion. In 1917 Poland did not even exist. In 1918 it was born again. In 1917 Galicia was part of Austria. In 1918 it was part of Poland. In 1918 and again two years later Jews fought alongside Poles against the Bolsheviks of Russia. In 1919 Poles were chasing Jews through the streets, waving sticks and worse.

The situation was disorienting and raised many disturbing questions. Could a Jew really be a Pole and a Jew? Should the Jews stay or leave? If they stayed, should they assert their rights as ethnic minorities, or should they assimilate and attempt to bury the issue all together? If they left, where would they go? If they went to Palestine, how would they get there, with what means? And what would they do once they got there?

The Jews of Poland were not of one mind on any of these difficult questions. A proliferation of social and political organizations attracted followings for every conceivable variation of sentiment. Women's groups, religious groups, Zionist groups of many different stripes, cultural groups, sporting clubs, political parties—these groups served as a uniform does, as a badge, an identity.

"The majority Jewish youth was very active for Israel," Susskind remembered. "Because anti-Semitism was always so strong, in Poland especially. They used to drive us to it. This was the only place you felt home."

ENDINGS AND
BEGINNINGS

In the Austrian provinces, where small numbers of Jews
had lived in more than seven hundred towns and
villages, almost every one of the seven hundred raised a
white flag to tell the world that no Jews remained.
—Martin Gilbert[1]

n 1935, one year after the failed Nazi insurrection in
Vienna, Josef Schwammberger was discharged from the
SS fighting force, the Austrian Legion. A severe gallbladder attack forced his withdrawal from the combat troops in
waiting and left him unfit for any active military post. (He
had gallbladder surgery the following year.)

Following his release from the legion, Schwammberger
was assigned to the Reich Labor Office in Berlin, where he
worked for several months in the employment department.
His position was low-level. But at least he had a job.

For Schwammberger the Berlin assignment marked a return to his former professional status. He was still a member
in good standing of the vaunted SS and the powerful Nazi
party. But he was no longer a promising young SS soldier
on the brink of overthrowing the government of his homeland and fulfilling the Führer's vision of a unified German
nation. Instead Schwammberger was once again on a barely
promising path toward certain obscurity within the labyrin-
thine Nazi bureaucracy.

Opportunities for advancement in the SS and elsewhere in
the government structure certainly existed. Schwammberger
simply did not, or did not know how to, take advantage of
them. He was one of a multitude, part of the indistinguish-
able middle.

At the end of February 1936 Schwammberger was transferred again, this time to the Baltic seaport of Warnemünde,
where he served as a security guard at the Heinkel aircraft
factory. The development of an air force was a top priority
for the fledgling Nazi regime. After all, without a powerful
fighting force behind him, Hitler's adversaries might not
have taken his belligerency seriously. The threat of another
costly European war would not have been so compelling,
and Hitler would not have been able to bluff and browbeat
Britain and France into submission. A mighty air force was
also key to the development of the lightning-speed attacking
power that ultimately made the German Army invincible in
the early months of the blitzkrieg.

Schwammberger's arrival in Warnemünde came at a critical moment in the development of this vital fighting capabil-
ity. Just a few months earlier Hitler had shocked the world
by revealing that Germany had been quietly assembling an
air force for more than a decade. Ernst Heinkel, one of the
pioneers of German aviation, had opened his first aircraft
factory at the Warnemünde site in 1922. Shortly thereafter
he began designing and building planes secretly for the
German military, in direct violation of the international bans
on German rearmament that had been in effect since the
end of the First World War. Heinkel continued as one of
the primary contractors for Hermann Göring's *Luftwaffe*, the
German Air Force, through the end of World War II.*

---

*Heinkel was born in a village near Stuttgart, a city that figured so
prominently in Schwammberger's life. After World War II Heinkel returned there to build motorscooters before dying in 1958 at the age of
seventy.

But as central as was Heinkel's role at this juncture in the life of the Nazi state, Schwammberger's part was utterly peripheral. In a handwritten "life history" he penned several years later as part of his SS marriage application, Schwammberger characterized his duties at the Heinkel factory as dull, noting that his "job as a guard failed to satisfy" him. After a short while he was able to ingratiate himself with the chief of plant security and landed a job "as a specialist in the Special Tasks A section," as Schwammberger described it, which meant simply that he was a security agent in the factory's personnel department.[2]

Clearly Schwammberger was not blazing a trail through the party or SS ranks, unlike his erstwhile confederate in the Austrian Legion Adolf Eichmann. Eichmann had left the SS Bavarian military camp in 1935, the same year as Schwammberger. But Eichmann had been resourceful as well as physically fit. And he had well-placed connections, including Ernst Kaltenbrunner, a veteran Nazi and the future number two SS official, who had personally enlisted Eichmann in the Nazi party.*

When Eichmann left the Austrian Legion training camps, he joined the SS security police unit, the Sicherheitsdienst, or SD. Eichmann took an enterprising approach to his position as head of the SD's office on Jewish affairs. By then it had become clear that the fate of Germany's Jewish population was going to be a continuing preoccupation of the new Nazi leadership. In fact, Hitler's issuing of the Nuremberg Laws shortly after Eichmann settled into his new job was as sure an indication as there could be that the Nazis had lethal designs against the Jews. So Eichmann took it upon himself to become an expert on Jewish customs and religion, on Jewish history, and on the politics of Palestine.

*In 1942 Kaltenbrunner succeeded Reinhard Heydrich as head of the Reich Main Security Office, the most powerful post in the SS under Himmler. In 1948 Kaltenbrunner was hanged at Nuremberg.

Eichmann excelled at the Nazi power game. His genius was his facility for organization, his meticulous attention to detail, and his relentless pursuit of efficient completion of the task put before him. He was the consummate Nazi yes-man, the mastermind as bureaucrat, the mad scientist as paper-pushing functionary. And he anticipated the bigger picture within which to apply his passion and skills. He understood Hitler's aims and devoted himself cold-heartedly to advancing them.

Schwammberger exhibited none of these abilities. Where Eichmann tamed the many-tentacled Nazi organization, Schwammberger was overwhelmed by it. Clearing up a clerical snafu involving his Nazi party membership records, for example, required months of pleading on Schwammberger's part. After a lengthy correspondence with party officials in Munich, he finally arranged to have his membership transferred from Innsbruck to the Nazi party office in Rostock, a medium-size city where Schwammberger lived while he worked at the Warnemünde aircraft factory a few miles away.*

Schwammberger's chances for advancement may well have been limited by his medical infirmity. But while his disability surely kept him from a military posting, it ought not to have kept him from more significant assignments elsewhere in the SS hierarchy, such as those that Eichmann and thousands of lesser bureaucrats were finding for themselves.

With Himmler's fanatical emphasis on Aryan pedigree, the Nazi establishment was forever rife with rumors about this or that person's Aryan credentials. Schwammberger, whose physical bearing belied the Nordic stereotypes, was not spared such gossip and such talk may have slowed his

*In 1992 Rostock grabbed headlines around the world as the site of deadly neo-Nazi violence against immigrants seeking asylum and citizenship in Germany.

advancement. But the same was true of many of the leading Nazi figures, including Eichmann's boss and the head of the SD, Reinhard Heydrich. Besides, in spite of how common the whisper campaigns were within the SS, in most cases the SS looked after its own. "Towards others the utmost cruelty was permissible," one SS historian observed, "but within the fold the weaker brethren were protected."[3]

The best explanation, then, for Schwammberger's evident inability to progress beyond clerk status during this period of his career was a certain taste for the clerk's life. He had a decent job, he had German citizenship as of 1935, he had the uniform of the elite SS, and he was alive to witness the revitalized German nation. For the first time in his life Schwammberger was experiencing a moment when Germans were starting to feel good again about being German.

Schwammberger stayed in Rostock for nearly three years. Later in his SS career he met up again with Heinkel's expanding industrial empire, but first he had to find his way back home to Innsbruck.

By 1938 Hitler had already significantly consolidated his powers at home. Germans were thrilled with many of the steps their leader had taken in the mid-1930s, including the plebiscite that returned the industrial Saar region to Germany in 1935, the commitment to remilitarization, and even the anti-Jewish measures codified in the 1935 Nuremberg Laws. These political successes emboldened Hitler to make a second attempt at overthrowing the Austrian Republic. After months of propaganda, diplomatic posturing, and outright bullying, Hitler finally had his way with the weakened Austrian government.

Kurt von Schuschnigg, who had succeeded the murdered Dollfuss as Austrian chancellor, simply did not have the political strength to withstand Hitler's maneuvers. Schuschnigg hardly commanded the military muscle to oppose the full-scale assault Hitler was threatening. And Mussolini, once the power ensuring Austrian independence, by this time had been wooed into Hitler's camp.

In the end Hitler realized his lifelong dream without a fight. On the evening of March 14, 1938, the Nazi leader waved triumphantly from his motorcade to the cheering, adoring throngs of German Austrians along the road to Vienna that gathered to welcome him and the Third Reich. In contrast with the failed coup four years earlier, Hitler had triumphed this time and had realized the Anschluss—the German word for the joining of Austria to Germany— bloodlessly. (There were, however, minor scuffles associated with the SS campaign to round up and imprison thousands of anti-Nazi agitators, critics, and Jews.)

History had dealt a cruel irony to Austria, a country that had dominated Central Europe for so long. Overnight seven million Austrians became junior members of the new Germany. Vienna was downgraded from a former imperial capital to a provincial outpost. And Austria itself simply ceased to exist. As one eyewitness and World War II chronicler described it, "Austria, as Austria, passed for a moment out of history."[4]

For Austria's nearly two hundred thousand Jews, the absorption of Austria into Germany was no cause for celebration. Many still had fresh memories of progroms in the east, memories of the villages of Poland and Russia from which they had fled. The shock was particularly great in Vienna, where the vast majority of Austria's Jews had concentrated and where Jews made up fully 10 percent of the city's population. (By the end of the war there were only a few thousand Austrian Jews left.)

As in other parts of Europe, Jews felt a tremendous sense of betrayal when the Nazis entered and began to wreak havoc on their communities. For generations Jews had been an integral part of Austrian life. Many considered themselves "Austrians of the Mosaic Faith," just as some Jews in Poland thought of themselves as "Poles of the Mosaic Faith," and as many Jews in Germany had assimilated thoroughly and had come to regard themselves every bit as much German as a Protestant German or a Catholic German.

Thousands of Austrian Jews had devoted themselves not merely to blending as best as possible, even while maintaining their cultural and religious identity, but to contributing to the artistic, political, and commercial wealth of the nation. In Vienna, during the period between the two world wars, composers Gustav Mahler and Arnold Schönberg, psychoanalysis founder Sigmund Freud, and satirist and editor Karl Kraus were but a few of the city's Jewish luminaries.

Michael Hellman experienced firsthand the violence Hitler brought to Vienna, once one of the most civilized and cultured cities in the world, immediately after the Anschluss. Hellman's mother had gone to Vienna from Przemysl as a young woman during the First World War. She had left behind her entire family in Poland to join the tens of thousands of Jews fleeing in all directions in hopes of escaping anti-Jewish attacks, especially from the Czar's troops that during World War I had briefly occupied her hometown.

"In retrospect it seems ironic that the Jewish population of both Russian Poland and Galicia looked on the Germans and Austrians almost as liberators, but at that time their great enemy and oppressor was clearly Tsarist Russia," observed Hellman, now a retired bookkeeper in London.[5]

Once in Vienna Hellman's mother met her husband, a watchmaker who had come to Austria from the Slovakian town of Žilina, near the Polish border. In 1931, when Michael was just eight years old, his forty-four-year-old father died from kidney failure.

The diversity of Jewish life in the struggling Austrian Republic of the 1930s made a lasting impression on young Hellman. As was true of the Jewish communities in Poland, the Jews of Vienna were enthralled with politics and formed political groups of every imaginable description. There were Zionists and anti-Zionists, assimilationists and socialists. In secular politics Jews tended to vote for the more liberal Social Democr..s because "they were the only party which did not have an anti-Semitic plank in its program."

There were many opportunities for cultural diversion in Vienna, too, Hellman recalled:

> Everyday life was brightened by occasional visits to the amusement park in the Prater [one of Vienna's many public parks], watching the impressive May Day parade of the Social Democrats (the Austrian Communists were a negligible force), and also watching the Spring Parade of the Army.
>
> Then there was my newly discovered interest in soccer football and following, in particular, the fortunes of the Jewish soccer club, Hakoah, who gave a much-needed boost to Jewish self-esteem when they won the championship in 1924 (when I was one year old) but in my time usually hovered around the bottom of the League's First Division.

There were many other diversions, too, such as the annual religious festivals and the Yiddish theater, and there was almost an outdoor concert in one of Vienna's manicured public parks.

Hellman was eleven years old when Dollfuss came to power and began to turn the Austrian Republic into "an authoritarian, Christian, Corporate State with no parties, only the Fatherland Front." The Fatherland Front was Dollfuss's idea of a single replacement for all of Austria's political parties. It might well have been called the Dollfuss Front. That same year Hellman joined Betar, the same organization for which Arnold Susskind was organizing back in Przemysl and other villages near Krakow.

Hellman was too young, too inexperienced to sort out

the political differences between the various Zionist organizations. He was drawn to Betar's fervent commitment to a Jewish state in Palestine. And there were other attractions. "I was just impressed by the military-style uniform of Betar, drilling to Hebrew commands, and could identify with their aims of imbuing Jewish youth with some pride and fighting for a Jewish State."

Hellman's mother and his legal guardian—a family friend appointed to be legally responsible for the boy after the death of his father—were less impressed. They worried about the negative attention Michael might draw to himself, especially considering the worsening political mood of the city. They appealed to him to leave those "Jewish fascists," as Hellman remembered them describing the organization, and finally he agreed.

He left school in 1937, but after he had spent some time looking for a job, his guardian suggested postponing his battle with the bleak job market. Since there seemed to be no great urgency to start a career anyway, Hellman decided to spend a few months studying at a yeshiva, an Orthodox religious academy. Together with several other boys, he went off to the land from which his father had come, Slovakia. It was his very first trip abroad. He and several friends boarded with Jewish families while they studied at the school. "None of us had any inkling of what we would come back to," he recalled.

What they came home to was the frightening aftermath of the Anschluss. In fact, Hellman arrived back in Vienna exactly one day after Hitler's victory parade through the city. "We came back to a city full of swastika flags flying from windows, slogans painted everywhere, 'Ein Volk, Ein Reich, Ein Führer!,'* practically all passersby in the streets sporting swastika badges, police wearing swastika arm bands,

*The Slogan *Ein Volk* . . . means "One People, One Empire, One Leader."

and the previously illegal SA [Sturmabteilung, or storm troopers], SS and Hitler Youth all walking about in uniform," Hellman remembered vividly. "It was like a nightmare come true."

The abuses and deprivations to which Germany's Jews had been introduced over a period of several years were unleashed overnight on the Austrian Jewish community and with unprecedented ferocity. Rabbis were taken out from their synagogues and forced to wash toilets with their prayer shawls. Jewish shops were marked so that Austrians would know to stay away. Every right and every life were in jeopardy. Within a month of Hitler's conquest some five hundred Jews had committed suicide.[6] The entire Jewish community was in a state of panic.

Time has faded memories of specific conversations from this time, but Hellman did recall his mother's anxiously discussing the situation with friends and neighbors:

They talked about the "scrubbing parties." That first weekend groups of Jewish men and women had been rounded up and forced to scrub pavements (sidewalks in American) to remove the Schuschnigg slogans and Fatherland Front symbols painted there in previous weeks. They were surrounded by jeering mobs, including children, who were enjoying this "fun." Another thing people talked about was the spate of suicides reported gleefully in the Nazi papers. The impending "aryanization" of Jewish stores and businesses was another topic being discussed.

Adolf Eichmann arrived in Vienna three days after Michael Hellman returned home from the Slovakian yeshiva. Eichmann's assignment was to coordinate the expulsion of Austria's Jews in what became a rehearsal for the massive forced transfers of all of Europe's Jews, first into ghettos and then into the death camps. Eichmann later coordinated the latter effort as well, all under the auspices of the Central Office for Jewish Emigration, which he established during those first few days back in Vienna.

Within a year nearly one hundred thousand Jews left Austria, most after having been completely stripped of their money and property. In retrospect, those who managed to get out—even if with only the clothes they were wearing—were clearly the lucky ones.

And then came *Kristallnacht* (night of broken glass). It was November 9, 1938, the very night Hitler and his buddies from the early Nazi party days in Munich were celebrating the fifteenth anniversary of the so-called Beer Hall Putsch.* The unprecedented assault on the German Jewish community was allegedly prompted by the murder of a German diplomat in Paris by a seventeen-year-old student named Herschel Grynszpan. The boy was protesting Hitler's decision to expel en masse eighteen thousand Polish Jews who had been living in Germany since the end of World War I. Among the deportees was the boy's entire family. What Grynszpan could never have imagined was that his act would give Hitler the excuse for which he had been longing to initiate a new wave of anti-Semitic violence.

Every act of anti-Semitic violence in Germany up to that point paled in comparison with what was wrought in the course of that one night. Hundreds of synagogues throughout Germany were set aflame. All but one of Vienna's several

---

*The putsch was Hitler's failed attempt in 1923 to overthrow the Weimar government. The plot landed him in Landsberg prison, where he wrote *Mein Kampf*. Mysteriously, other seminal moments in German history, in addition to *Kristallnacht* share the same anniversary. The last German emperor, Wilhelm II, abdicated just days before the end of World War I on November 9. Seventy-one years later, the Berlin Wall, the single most recognized symbol of the cold war and of a divided Germany, was brought down on November 9.

dozen synagogues were demolished. Thousands of Jewish-owned shops were smashed. Houses and apartments were burned and looted. Thousands of Jews were beaten, arrested, and dispatched to concentration camps.

The international community expressed outrage at the Nazi pogrom. But few countries were willing to modify their immigration policies to allow entry to the masses of frantic Jews looking to escape the newest terror campaign in greater Germany. Fewer still were willing to do anything to try to stop Hitler before matters became much worse.

Finally, on December 14, just one month after the Nazi rampage, British Prime Minister Neville Chamberlain agreed to admit ten thousand Jewish children as long as Jewish relief agencies in Britain agreed to assume responsibility for their care. Out of deference to the wishes of the British territory's Arab population, he denied a request to permit increased emigration to Palestine. The outbreak of war the following September brought an end to the so-called *Kindertransport* (children's transport) rescue operation.

Among the thousands of German Jewish and Austrian Jewish children who were called up on one day's notice and forced to leave their families and friends behind was fifteen-year-old Michael Hellman. On only his second trip abroad, he boarded a train carrying 130 other Viennese Jewish youngsters who were leaving behind their families to travel alone across the Continent to Britain.

For a while Hellman received regular letters from his mother back in Vienna. Then the war started and Austria's Jews were rounded up and sent to camps in Poland. And then the letters stopped.*

---

*After the war Hellman investigated his mother's fate. From Vienna she had been sent to the Lodz ghetto in western Poland. From there she was moved to the Chelmno death camp. "It is well documented how people were killed in Chelmno," Hellman noted.

. . .

Michael Hellman left Austria, the country of his birth, with the nightmare images of the Nazi take-over still careening in his mind like the jolting and jerking of the train carrying him to safety in Britain. That same month Josef Schwammberger came home to Austria, the country of his birth, with Hitler's nationalist dream for a united German people finally on the way to being realized.

Through contacts back in Innsbruck, Schwammberger managed a transfer home and into a job with the regional office of the German Labor Front. In December 1938 Schwammberger, then nearly twenty-seven, moved back in with his parents. Once again he could look up at the snow-capped mountains that surrounded the city. He could walk the few blocks from his parents' home and look down on the crisp waters of the Inn River. Only now he was home in Germany. His SS uniform no longer labeled him a rebel or an outcast in Austria. He was one of the chosen, the elite. Josef Schwammberger belonged.

Although he certainly was part of a distinguished group as an SS man, his position in the ever-expanding SS universe by no means reflected his presumed special status. Schwammberger's rank, after four years with the blackshirts, was only *Rottenführer*, which in U.S. military terms is comparable to a corporal. Eichmann, by contrast, had entered the SS at the same time as Schwammberger but was already a commissioned officer, an SS lieutenant.

Nor was Schwammberger able to land as plum an assignment as Eichmann had attained. Once again Schwammberger held a job that relegated him to an obscure and inconsequential corner of the burgeoning Nazi bureaucracy. Schwammberger himself described his job with the German Labor Front as "a personnel sub-section chief and statistician."[7]

For the time being the hapless SS Corporal was still a

nobody. Nothing about his position or prospects suggested that he was working his way toward becoming a leader who would be feared by all his charges and would hold in his hands the power of life and death. Josef Schwammberger was home, but he was still a small-time, small-town clerk, just as he had been when he last lived in Innsbruck.

The German Labor Front itself had become an important institution since Hitler had abolished all labor unions in Germany on May 2, 1933. That day had been one of the classic moments in the history of Hitler's rise. Only the day before, the new German chancellor had lectured one workers' rally after another on the Nazi party's commitment to the German worker. May Day would always be a national celebration of work and workers, he had vowed, his voice no doubt contorting with affected passion.

The next day Hitler occupied and then closed down the offices of every single one of Germany's major unions. Every important labor leader within reach was sent to the nearest concentration camp. Hitler then tapped Robert Ley, an alcoholic Nazi leader from the Rhine city of Cologne, and put him in charge of creating the German Labor Front.

Ley's Labor Front became the country's one and only union and grew to be the largest of all the many Nazi party organizations, with twenty-five million members. Wages, hours, even vacations were coordinated and controlled by Ley's enormous bureaucracy. The magnitude of the job was awesome. And the extent to which his agency was critical to the success of Hitler's regime was equally significant. Hitler took away from the workers of Germany their political freedoms, such as their right to collective bargaining, but he gave them what they had craved so desperately: jobs. In return, the historically well-regimented German workers gave back to Hitler what he needed: a disciplined labor force on which to rely for the production of war goods. Although reduced to "industrial serfdom on subsistence wages," the German worker "had a job again and the assurance that he would keep it," according to one prominent World War II historian.[8]

By February 1939, just a few weeks after his return to Innsbruck, Schwammberger began hustling to obtain and fill out the forms and applications he was required to complete to qualify for official SS approval to marry. The woman whom he had chosen for his bride was twenty-five-year-old Katherina Anna Seib, a slender woman with poker-straight blond hair.

There was nothing particularly romantic about the wedding plans. As an SS member Schwammberger was forbidden to have a religious ceremony. It was one of the quirky inconsistencies in the ideology of the SS. Himmler expected his men to declare themselves "believers in God" but to renounce ties to a specific religious faith. The SS demanded a simple civil proceeding. Schwammberger complied, even though the rest of his family retained their affiliation with Catholicism.

The months before the wedding were filled with anxiety for Schwammberger and his fiancée. They really did have to complete the paper work in a hurry. After all, the SS did not make it easy for an SS man to get married. And Kathe was already pregnant.

Both Schwammberger and Seib had to submit to rigorous medical examinations. The SS wanted to be assured that the couple were physically qualified to bear Aryan children. Himmler and racial theorists at the SS Race and Resettlement Main Office (RuSHA*) were implementing as literally as possible Hitler's well-documented vision. "If the fertility of the healthiest bearers of the nationality is thus consciously and systematically promoted," Hitler had written in *Mein*

*RuSHA is the acronym for Rasse-und Siedlungshauptamt.

Kampf back in 1923, "the result will be a race which at least will have eliminated the germs of our present physical and hence spiritual decay."[9]

Some of the questions the SS doctors were required to ask during the review sounded logical enough, but others were outright bizarre. Kathe Seib had to document her menstrual cycle, for example. Schwammberger had to answer whether he had ever been a bed-wetter and in what quantities he used alcohol and cigarettes.

The medical questionnaire, filled out by an SS doctor, was exhaustive. The application asked for common enough details, such as Schwammberger's eye color (dark brown), hair color (brown), height and weight, and a brief medical history. Other questions revealed the SS leaders' obsession with eugenics. The doctor measured the size of Schwammberger's skull (56.5 centimeters), described his overall build (muscular and slim), diagrammed his teeth to show cavities (Schwammberger had six fillings), and examined his eyes, lungs, urine, and reflexes, among other body parts and functions. On the last page of the questionnaire the doctor assessed Schwammberger's overall physical condition (average) and indicated whether he believed the couple was "desirable for reproduction" (yes).

At one point in the survey the doctor asked Schwammberger if he was capable of giving the Reich Aryan children—that is, if he and his wife-to-be were fertile. In a jocular reference to Seib's already enlarged condition—she was past her first trimester by this point—Schwammberger answered that they had already demonstrated their reproductive abilities.

Another major component of the SS marriage application was the requirement for a detailed account of the family histories of both bride and groom. The SS race masters were determined, at least as a matter of policy, that only those with the most unassailable Aryan pedigrees should be allowed to marry and procreate. This meant, of course, that one could not have any Jewish or other non-Aryan blood. And the SS took the concept of mixing blood not only seriously but literally.*

In order to prove one's Aryan purity, therefore, the SS preferred to have candidates document their family trees back at least four generations. This requirement caused a great deal of trouble for many applicants. Germany did not even exist as a unified country until 1871. According to Nazi rhetoric, a German from Moravia (now part of the Czech Republic) or Ukraine or Austria or Danzig (now the Polish city of Gdansk) was every bit as much a Reich German as a German from Hamburg or Munich. But it was not always easy to obtain the necessary documentary proof, birth and death records especially, to satisfy the bureaucrats in Berlin, the arbiters of German pedigree.

Schwammberger had a very difficult time with this part of his application, which included several different multipage forms on which to list all family members and their vital statistics, as well as a family tree grid on which the candidate again had to provide detailed histories of parents, grandparents, and so on, going back four, five, six generations, depending on how much information he was capable of—or interested in—providing.

In several places Schwammberger was unable to complete even the basic required data. He did not offer any information at all about his paternal grandfather's family. He did not even provide the name of his paternal grandfather. Either attempting to conceal information or else behaving obtusely, Schwammberger on one form scrawled that his grandfather's name was "not applicable."

On another biographical form he indicated simply that

---

*The Race and Settlement Main Office did more during the Third Reich than just check genealogy trees. The "settlement" part of the agency, for example, "Germanized" conquered territory to the east; that meant replacing non-German landowners with certifiable Aryans.

his father's side of the family came from the *Ostmark*, the German name for "eastern territory" and the way nationalist Germans referred to Austria. On his mother's side, Schwammberger was unable to trace his roots beyond his maternal grandparents. Again, he simply indicated with sweeping slashes of his pen on the SS family tree form that this side of his family came from Bohemia, the province of the contemporary Czech Republic that includes Prague.

By July 1939 Schwammberger had pulled together all the materials for his marriage application and had sent them off to the RuSHA officials in Berlin. But the SS race masters were not satisfied with Schwammberger's shoddy documentation. Letters from Berlin chastised him for the sloppiness of his application. One official wrote to demand additional evidence detailing the cause and age of death for his maternal grandmother. This official also insisted that the Race Office could not tolerate answers such as "unknown" for such questions.

Schwammberger's shifty approach to the marriage application minimally raised eyebrows back in Berlin and may have even raised more serious questions about the quality of his Aryan stock. If he was covering up evidence of Jewish traces in his bloodlines, he could be thrown out of the SS or, worse, imprisoned.

Schwammberger certainly understood the dangers. Meanwhile, his fiancée, now only a few months from delivering their first child, had moved in with her future husband, his parents, and his three unwed sisters. Schwammberger was sending frantic letters to Berlin, pleading for the necessary official blessing. Finally the Race and Settlement Main Office signed off on the marriage, and Schwammberger and his bride hurried down to city hall to pick up their license.

Josef and Kathe were married on September 2, 1939, one day after the German invasion of Poland had launched the start of World War II. Their first son, Wolfgang, was born shortly thereafter.

. . .

Meanwhile, Arnold Susskind had also met the woman he wanted to marry. One of the communities he had helped organize for Betar was the town of Mielec, located about fifty miles northwest of Przemysl. After he had given a speech there one evening, Sally Tytryn, a petite young woman with dark eyes, approached him. She reached for his handkerchief, plucked it from his breast pocket, and said she wanted it as a keepsake.

Six months later they met again when Susskind returned for another political function in Mielec. They courted by letter. In 1937 they married.

The Susskinds settled in Mielec. Sally's family was fairly prominent in the town of less than five thousand or so residents, about half of whom were Jewish. At the turn of the century Jews had made up 57 percent of the total, but that number had fallen following widespread Jewish emigration after the First World War.[10] Sally's uncle, like the Tuchmans back in Przemysl, was in the lucrative timber business. Sally's father was also well-to-do.

"My in-laws, they weren't millionaires, but I can say wealthy people," Arnold reflected. "In those days in Poland they had three buses and two car taxis. That was a big deal over there. You didn't see too many cars."

With the financial support of his father-in-law, Arnold went into business for himself, opening a stationery store. "In Europe they used to buy for the bride and groom a gold watch as a gift. But I didn't want a gold watch. So after we got married, my father-in-law called me in. He said, 'You don't want a gold watch; what do you want?' So I said, 'I like to own my own business like my father.' So he said, 'How much you need?' They were like parents to me."

Arnold and Sally lived comfortably, even as the storms were gathering in Europe. In some ways the lives of the Susskinds and the Schwammbergers took similar turns. The Susskinds, too, had a son, Emmanuel, right around the start of the war. In far more significant ways, their experiences could not have been more directly opposed. Before long they would find out just how violently different the wartime experiences of an Austrian Nazi and a Jewish family could be.

CHAPTER 5

HELL

Through me the way into the suffering city,
Through me the way to the eternal pain,
Through me the way that runs among the lost.
—Dante, *Inferno*, Canto III

A s Germany fired the first shots of the second world war of the century, German soldiers painted slogans on the side of cargo trains that would carry them to the battle lines deep inside Polish territory. One read: "We're off to Poland to thrash the Jews." Down to the lowliest recruit, the members of the mighty German fighting machine were well aware of the twin aims of the lightning strike: to add Poland to Hitler's expanding empire and to settle the so-called Jewish question.

Hitler had made no effort to disguise his intentions toward the Jews. Nine months before the attack on Poland, he had declared in a speech in Berlin that war would bring about "the annihilation of the Jewish race in Europe." Not the wholesale transfer to Madagascar. Not the resettlement of hundreds of thousands of families. Hitler had been explicit: annihilation. In no uncertain terms that was exactly what he meant.

Little Mielec, where Sally and Arnold Susskind were then living, fell quickly before the indomitable advance of German tank divisions. The thrashing of Mielec's Jews followed immediately.

Following the Nazi practice of selecting Jewish holy days for acts of especially harsh abuse, the Germans waited until September 13, the eve of Rosh Hashanah, the Jewish New Year, to begin the brutal first phase of their first campaign against the Jewish population in Mielec. On that evening German soldiers set fire to the town's main synagogue. The twenty-five people forced inside the crumbling building were burned to death. That same day thirty-five Jewish women were arrested at the *mikvah*, the ritual Jewish bathhouse. The women were paraded through the streets naked and led to a nearby slaughterhouse, where they, too, were burned to death.

Those who were not killed outright often were tormented and humiliated. One eyewitness observed how the German soldiers "gathered 200 Jews in the street, made them stand against a wall with arms raised, and after a few hours announced that they were going to shoot them. In an agony of fear, the Jews remained standing against the wall, expecting that any moment would be their last."[1]

Religious Jews were persecuted with exceptional brutality. Men were forced to cut their beards or actually had them yanked from their faces. Religious books, prayer shawls, and other symbols of Jewish religious and cultural life were desecrated. Jews were forced to carry rubble from bombed-out buildings, to clean toilets with their prayer shawls, and to hand over all valuables, including wedding rings and other heirlooms.

The rampage in Mielec, as well as the countless other places just like it, was plotted, choreographed, and set in motion by the armchair schemers in Berlin, men like Eichmann and Heydrich. But in the field these designs were implemented with a ruthless improvisation by innumerable willing and eager participants. When it came to attacking the common enemy, collaborating Poles and Ukrainians welcomed the chance to join the invading Germans, with whom neither group had been exactly friendly over the centuries. Thousands of Poles, especially Catholic priests and members of the Polish intelligentsia, were also singled out for harsh and often murderous treatment. Just as he had made no secret of his plan to rid Europe entirely of its Jews, so the Nazi leader had openly proclaimed his intention to install Germans as lords over a battered and enslaved Polish people, who, like the Jews, Hitler had argued, were racially inferior.*

There are numerous documented cases of Poles' assuming tremendous personal risks to aid their Jewish friends and neighbors. But the vast majority of Poles either offered no resistance or openly assisted the Nazi soldiers and security police in their attacks on Jews. Many of the same Catholic priests who were targets of Nazi violence eagerly stirred up anti-Jewish passions. Poles looted Jewish homes and businesses, and many jeered and cheered the terrible fate of their Jewish neighbors.

It is tempting to describe the scenes of Nazi terror during the first weeks of that fateful September as ones of unimaginable violence. It seems that it must be impossible, even to a generation exposed to graphic depictions of violence in the movies and on television, to fathom the true depths of what really happened. Hollywood has created robot cops and android terminators that kill dozens of men in the opening five minutes of a film. But even the most twisted scriptwriters

---

*See Richard C. Lukas, *The Forgotten Holocaust* (Lexington, Ky.: University Press of Kentucky, 1986). By war's end the Nazis had killed an astounding three million Poles. Lukas argues that the extent of the Polish suffering under the Nazis has not received due consideration.

could not craft a story more depraved than what happened in the first few weeks of World War II. Beyond the sheer numbers of people victimized, which were indeed staggering, the level of human cruelty still confounds the human imagination many decades later.

The Nazi Holocaust, however, was not and is not beyond description. If the Nazi nightmare is to make any sense or if, for that matter, any moment in history is to be understood and be seen as real, then it must be imagined, it must be described. The words must be found.

For many people any understanding of the Holocaust has been reduced to a number of images: the number six million, the train tracks at Auschwitz, the piles of emaciated bodies, the frightened eyes of the ghetto child. But there was so much more. The full extent of the tragedy can be appreciated only by accepting one disturbing truth: The Holocaust was a mass movement made up of individual acts of cruelty and hate, inflicted one after another after another, one human being against another.

Adolf Hitler was not the devil. He was a man. Adolf Eichmann had warm, not cold, blood in his veins. As for Josef Schwammberger and the thousands of other SS men and the Gestapo police and eager Wehrmacht boys and the hate-filled Poles and angry Ukrainians and club-wielding Lithuanians, their acts were indeed monstrous, but not one of them was a monster.

Likewise, the Jews who were herded into ghettos were not cows or sheep or any other animal. The thousands who were shot, the millions who were gassed were not one faceless mass, one mind-numbing statistic. They were men and women and children and babies. They were each and every one a human life destroyed.

"We had to sweep the streets," Arnold Susskind said, recalling the first few days after the Nazi occupation of Mielec.

"That time wasn't too many cars, only horses, and horses do something, and we had to sweep that. The Polacks used to say, 'See that you Jews have to clean! We used to do, and now you have to do.' It was very downgrading. Imagine if here today they said you have to sweep the street, you have no more rights, you know, you're not an American, you just a Jew. That's what happened."

Overnight many of Susskind's former classmates turned against him. "Every day in school I had in my class Polish students, friends, and they were invited to my house, because we were well off, not rich, average middle class," he recollected. "We had a good business. Everybody went to school. And a nice apartment. One friend's father was a regular worker, you know, and when the Nazis came, he became my enemy right away. Next day."

Where could one run? The dangers were everywhere, from all sides. But it soon became clear that Arnold, at least, could not stay in Mielec. Soon after the German invasion of Poland and just before the worst of the anti-Jewish violence began in the town, rumors swirled that the Germans were taking young Jewish men into forced labor on the front. "All the young men ran away," Arnold related.

So Arnold and his brother-in-law left together, leaving Sally and their infant son behind to stay with her parents and the rest of her extended family. The situation would surely calm down soon, they figured, and then they could be together again.

As they set out into the countryside, they witnessed a Poland in complete chaos. The Polish Army, with its hopelessly outdated hardware and technology, was overwhelmed by the superior and highly trained German units. And the attacks on the civilian populations, Jewish and Polish, created havoc and massive displacement. Entire families were fleeing, not knowing in which direction to run.

The Polish-Romanian border was closed when Susskind

and his brother-in-law reached it. So they turned north again and began walking toward the Russian border. "People there didn't even know there was a war because the war was mainly in the middle of Poland." On Rosh Hashanah, the very day the Nazis were burning down the Mielec synagogue, Arnold slept on the floor of a flour mill owned by a Jewish man in a hillside village overlooking the Polish-Russian frontier.

Weeks passed, but the two men remained under cover. "We were having sandwiches, and we were discussing what to do," Susskind recalled. "What's the next step? This is the end of the world, we thought. Then we saw three airplanes flying from the Polish border to Russian border. Messerschmitts. And we said, 'Aha, it's going to be war between the Germans and the Russians.' But these were the three planes, the German foreign minister went to see Molotov. At that time they split Poland."*

The next day the Russians advanced across the border and took control of Szumsk, the village in which Arnold had been hiding. After several weeks of lying low and with nothing to be gained from staying, Arnold decided to return home. Sally's brother decided to take his chances as far away from the Nazis as possible and headed off in the opposite direction toward the Russian interior. Arnold and Sally never heard from him again.

Arnold decided to stop off in Przemysl to check on his parents before continuing on to Mielec and his wife and infant son. When he arrived in Przemysl, he found that the San River, which divided the city in half, had become the new German-Russian border. At that border point tens of thousands of Jews crossed the river in Przemysl, fleeing from

---

*On September 28, 1939, Foreign Ministers Joachim von Ribbentrop and Vyacheslav Molotov met in Moscow and signed the German-Soviet Boundary and Friendship Treaty, an extension of the nonaggression pact reached the month before. The result of the new treaty was the division of spoils from the invasion of Poland. Once more Poland ceased to exist.

the German-occupied part of Poland into what was clearly, if only temporarily, the safer side. At night Arnold could hear the German border guards drinking beer and singing rowdy tunes on the other side of the narrow waterway.

Susskind's parents were unharmed, but they were not so well by the time he returned from his hideout in the hills. "My parents they had no food. Everything was terrible. The Russians had nothing to give. The women they bought nightgowns and they thought these were elegant dresses."

The Susskinds lost their candy store when the Russians set up large cooperative markets and installed local Communists as managers. As a result, the family had no means of earning income. All they could do was sell or barter what they already had. Making matters even worse, soon after Arnold arrived back in Przemysl, the Soviet police initiated a wave of arrests of Zionist activists.* Arnold was no sooner home again than he went back into hiding, this time for two months.

One day during this period he went to the movies. It was dark in the theater, and he figured no one would recognize him. "I was sitting in the movie and next to me sits this guy, his name was Chaim. And I saw he was wearing a Russian policeman's uniform, and my heart starts pounding. I am thinking he knows me and now I am finished."

But Chaim also remembered that Arnold had tutored him when they were younger and that Arnold's father had been generous with his own father. "So he says to me, 'Susskind, don't worry, I know how your father was to my father, how nice he was. And you taught me how to write. So don't worry, I am going to help you.'"

*Hitler believed that world Jewry and bolshevism were twin prongs of an international plot to pollute and rule the German people. At the same time, ironically, Stalin considered Zionism incompatible with the goals of communism and sent many Jews to labor camps in Siberia during and long after the war.

Chaim helped Arnold get a menial job, sweeping floors or clearing rubble. (Arnold can no longer remember anything about the job or for whom he worked.) The work allowed him finally to buy food and to help support his parents. "This was the beginning of living with the Russians under occupation."

Meanwhile, Sally Susskind was with her family back in Mielec on the "Aryan," or German, side of the newly established Russian border. Through a friend Arnold arranged both for false identification papers for his wife and a cousin and for a courier to take the documents to her in Mielec.

But Sally was all but trapped where she was. For her to wander too far from familiar turf, let alone set out across the German sector of rural southern Poland even with false papers was simply too risky. Jews on the road were in nearly certain peril. Besides, she was afraid to leave her parents behind. Neither Arnold nor Sally could say when or even if they would be together again.

Shortly after the start of the war Josef Schwammberger entered the abyss, and in so doing, he abandoned all hope of remaining apart from the evil work of the Holocaust. Ostensibly Schwammberger was going to war to serve the fatherland in Poland. He was also stepping through the gates of hell.

Up to that point, for the first twenty-seven years of his life, the young Schwammberger had found for himself the most innocuous, the most unremarkable of assignments, in life, in work, and in the SS. For twenty-seven years he had been a speck on the planet, hardly the sinew and seed of the vaunted *Übermensch*, German philosopher Friedrich Nietzsche's ideal of the German superman.

That autumn, as the world again faced the specter of war and the Jews of Europe faced the prospect of their utter annihilation, Josef Schwammberger joined his fate with Germany's, with the fate of all Germans then and for generations to come. That fall an unremarkable man in an SS uniform joined thousands of other nobodies, other druggists and bakers and salesclerks and farmers and soldiers, in a march across an extraordinary threshold to a brink from which there was no return.

Before 1939 the world existed on a different plane, in a sense, in a different quantum. Hitler was no less a dictator in the early years of the Third Reich, but he was certainly not the only member of that club. Franco and Mussolini and, for that matter, the United States and other Western governments had never been shy about using military muscle to pursue political and economic interests.

Up until 1939 there had been ample reason for the Jews of Europe, especially in greater Germany, to feel an awful foreboding about their future. Jews had already been shut out of economic life in Germany through boycotts and the deprivations of the Nuremberg decrees. They had been subjected to harangues and dislocations following the Anschluss and *Kristallnacht*. And the country was in the hands of a man clearly committed to a dangerous and destructive anti-Semitic program.

But up until that fall no one really believed Hitler would go to the ultimate extremes he had promised in so many fiery warnings. Jews in the pre-1939 era could reflect on the many anti-Semitic persecutions throughout their difficult history. They had been expelled from England in the thirteenth century, from Spain in the fifteenth century. Jews had long borne the brunt of ethnic unrest in Poland and the Russian states. France, the model of modern liberalism, had given Jews the Dreyfus affair.* And Hitler had already estab-

---

*Alfred Dreyfus, a captain in the French Army, in 1894 was falsely accused of espionage and treason. The incident became a national scandal and a symbol of deep-seated anti-Semitic sentiment.

lished concentration camps as early as 1933 and been sending Jews there in great numbers. Many had never returned.

Still the persecution was recognizable, knowable. Jews had survived past persecutions. Surely, most figured, they would survive this one. The pain of those who suffered directly, those who lost livelihoods or loved ones, could not be dismissed. But to the community as a whole, to the world, the violence was on a comprehensible level.

There had not yet been a program to "euthanize" tens of thousands of Germany's mentally retarded and mentally ill. There had not yet been a massacre at Babi Yar.* There had not yet been a Josef Mengele to conduct his vile experiments. There had not yet been death camps in places named Auschwitz and Treblinka and Belzec and Majdanek. But Hitler's road signs had clearly marked the path. The many thousands of Schwammbergers among the Nazi crusaders had no reason not to take their Führer at his word.

After 1939 everything changed. Beginning in that year, thousands of Germans just like Schwammberger—average, unremarkable, regular men and women—joined in an unprecedented crusade. They had to have been as clear about the purpose of their mission as the Germans soldiers who went to war knowing they were attacking Poland to thrash the Jews. The legions of Schwammbergers who went to Poland to conduct the Holocaust could not have helped knowing what they were doing in hell.

Schwammberger's bride was preparing to give birth to their first son when he made his move to enter the world of death. On November 13 he left his family and his sheltered and scenic Tyrolean home for the combat branch of Himmler's rapidly expanding empire, the Waffen-SS. Because of

---

*Babi Yar is the name of a large ravine in the woods outside Kiev where SS mobile killing units in 1941 massacred 33,771 Jewish men, women, and children, all in two days.

his gallbladder disability, he was assigned to a replacement training battalion of the Eighth SS Infantry Regiment and stationed near the Silesian city of Breslau.*

Following Germany's swift conquest of Poland in 1939, the formerly Prussian territories were annexed to the Reich. A separate province, the so-called General Government, was created out of the rest of Germany's share of the defunct Polish state. The territory of this district stretched from Warsaw to the new German-Russian border, then south to the Slovakian border and west to include Krakow, which became the new entity's administrative, military, and SS headquarters.

When Germany later attacked the Soviet Union in June 1941, the hunk of eastern Galicia, including Przemysl, that had been part of Soviet-occupied Poland, was annexed as part of the General Government. The rest of what had been Soviet-occupied Poland was carved up into various administrative districts.

Following the German attack against the Soviet Union, Schwammberger was transferred back to a desk job, this time in the office of one of the most powerful men in the General Government, SS and Police Leader Julian Scherner. Scherner was one of an elite cadre of SS commanders Himmler placed throughout the Reich so that he could manipulate his operations without having to negotiate the civil or military chains of authority. Each SS and police leader was given a certain geographic domain within which to supervise all SS operations.†

Specifically these commanders were charged with over-

---

*Silesia is in the southwestern part of modern Poland. Germany, and Prussia before it, had long eyed the area for its wealth of natural resources, especially coal and iron. Breslau, now in Poland, is known as Wroclaw.

†That Governor-General Hans Frank and Himmler's SS deputies were constantly feuding over turf fitted perfectly with Hitler's modus operandi, which was to make sure no one subordinate became too powerful.

seeing what the SS euphemistically termed the resettlement of Poland's Jewish population. This process involved relocating Jews to the larger villages and cities, which then served as vast holding areas. From these collection points Jews could be easily moved to extermination centers.

After a year spent attending to administrative tasks in Scherner's office in Krakow, Schwammberger was finally given his first independent command. His assignment was insignificant in global terms, a pinprick on the map compared with the massive "resettlement" operations already under way in Warsaw and Lublin. In those places thousands of Jews were being "processed" every day at such killing camps as Treblinka and Belzec.

However small, the assignment was Schwammberger's opportunity for greatness. Up to that point the thirty-year-old Nazi had been either a paper pusher or a uniformed bench warmer. He had been a nobody. Now, at last, he had a chance to become somebody.

In September 1942 Schwammberger became a whip-toting commandant. In a Polish town called Rozwadow, he joined his SS blood brothers in the extermination of European Jewry.

Sam Nussbaum was only nineteen when the Nazis invaded Poland and quickly overran Przemysl. On the first day the Nazis were in his town five hundred Jews were marched to the Jewish cemetery at the edge of town and shot there. One of those five hundred Jews was a young man Nussbaum's age who had worked for the same Jewish plumber to whom Nussbaum was apprenticed. "He was strong as a bull," Nussbaum recalled. "They shot him. Five hundred of them. This was in 1939."

Soon after the Nazis arrived, Nussbaum heard the same rumor Arnold Susskind had heard in Mielec. To avoid being taken into slave labor for work at the battlefront, Nussbaum and his father set out on foot from Przemysl, but they only

managed about sixty miles when they stopped. "The German
Army looped around and cut off the Polish Army, chopped
them in chunks. We were about one week with the Germans.
They would get us to work, beat us up. It was terrible."

The new German-Soviet border ran along the San River,
cutting directly through Przemysl, so the German forces
retreated back behind that line. Nussbaum and his father
walked with the Russian troops as they marched toward
the new frontier, to the formerly Polish, formerly Austrian,
formerly Polish again, most recently German town of Przemysl.

In June 1941 the border collapsed in the face of the
attacking German troops, and Przemysl again came under
Hitler's control. Deportations to the death camps did not
begin until the following year for Przemysl's Jews. In the
meantime and for the remainder of 1941 they were steadily
pummeled into submission.

The Jewish communities on the German side of Poland
had already suffered terrific abuses, following the pattern of
ever-intensifying restrictions and attacks that had been well
tested in the other Nazi-occupied lands. Their businesses
and property were stolen. They had been forced to wear
armbands and carry ID. They were organized into increasingly dense, unsanitary, food-starved ghettos. Jews from
smaller villages were rounded up and forced into these collection points, creating further crowding, disease, and mal-
nutrition. The onslaught was so violent that many were
simply too stunned to resist.

One of the most important instruments the Nazis used to
implement their extermination plan was the Judenrat (Jewish
council), which every Jewish community was obligated to
organize. The Judenrat's reason for being, according to the
Nazi design, was to facilitate and coordinate the Nazi administration of Jewish life until it was time to administer the
community's death.

Typically, prominent members of the community served

on the councils, helping enforce curfews, organizing cultural events, and managing social services, to the increasingly limited extent services were even available. As the Nazis applied an ever-tightening vise on the Jewish community, as the time came to read the rolls of those called to board the cattle cars, the Judenrat was placed in an ever more compromising position.

Often, especially during the first months of the Nazi occupations, these Jewish community leaders were completely unaware of the true significance of their actions. The entire Nazi system, after all, had relied heavily on mass deception from the very beginning. In the early and mid-1930s Hitler had screamed himself into a lather about uniting the two German states, Germany and Austria, but then insisted he had no intention of interfering in Austria's affairs. All the while he had plotted Austria's incorporation in the Reich.

Similarly, Hitler had vowed to rid Europe of its "Jewish problem" but then spoke reassuringly of "resettlement." Throughout the first years of the war, many Jews wanted so badly to believe they were simply being relocated that they chose not to believe Hitler's other warnings about their fate. And so Jews by the trainload were sent from all over Europe to points of concentration and then, still unsuspecting, finally to points of death. There the deception continued as the gassing victims were told they were merely being sent to the showers.

The deception was intended to secure the maximum cooperation with the minimum resistance. To ensure order in the carrying out of the extermination, it was essential that the Jews remain in the dark for as long as possible. Millions of Jews indeed did not or were unable to fight back as they were led to their demise. Many others battled overwhelming odds and died fighting.

Still others were perhaps less noble and attempted to save

themselves and their families any way they could. Especially toward the end of the war, when there were no longer any delusions about the true meaning of the Nazi resettlement operation, saving oneself involved the greater risk of selling one's soul.

The banks of the San River protected the Jews of Przemysl from the Nazi's anti-Jewish campaign in the west only until June 1941. From that time the struggle for life and survival began in earnest. That was when Sam Nussbaum received his first taste of the conflict so many Jews endured during the Nazi Holocaust. Nussbaum was forced to help the very people who had already shot friends and members of his family and whose stated reason for being was the extermination of every last Jew in Europe.

The Gestapo unit assigned to Przemysl in 1941 took for its headquarters the Jewish high school, just around the corner from Sam Nussbaum's house. From the start of the war the building had fallen into disrepair, along with the rest of the city. But the Gestapo and other Nazi brass wanted hot showers and demanded that the building's leaking pipes be repaired. So Dr. Ignatz Duldig, a prominent lawyer who had been appointed to lead the Przemysl Judenrat, was ordered to deal with the problem. Duldig called in the only plumber he knew who was still around: Nussbaum.

Nussbaum took his teenage brother with him to the former school. In the basement they found stashes of potatoes, which they stuffed into their pockets for later. Then Nussbaum set about fixing the pipes. "It took me time to fix up the plumbing because they didn't have copper tubing, what I could have done easier, but that galvanized pipe, iron pipe, and I had to cut up sections and replace them and so on. So the Gestapo was complaining about me."

The Gestapo was hardly known for showing patience with its Jewish laborers. If Nussbaum could not work faster, he might get himself and his brother killed. He could hear the police upstairs complaining about how long his work was taking, but he was already working as fast as he could.

Finally a Gestapo officer named Breuer came downstairs, his heavy black boots pounding ominously on the wooden stairs. As it turned out, Breuer was coming to their rescue. "He was a nice guy," Nussbaum recalled more than fifty years later. "He said, 'How come it takes you so long?' Nicely. So I said, 'Come with me, and I'll show you.'

"And I took him and showed him all the sections of pipe, four or five feet long, all split open. I said, 'Take a look. This was all here. See the pipes? I replaced them. It takes me time. I'm the only one here. We don't have any other plumbers. Just me.' I told him that. So he said, 'I can see. I appreciate what you're doing.' Just like that! 'Keep it up, and let me know when you get closer so I can tell those guys over there.' "

Nussbaum paused and smiled to savor his own story. "That was Breuer. He saved my life."

CHAPTER 6

THE LIQUIDATOR

My father said to us, "If any of you survive this, never forget this scene."
—Anna Unger Weinberg, Przemysl survivor[1]

The most destructive year of the Holocaust was already well under way when Josef Schwammberger took command of the small forced labor camp in Rozwadow in September 1942. Schwammberger, by this time a thirty-year-old SS *Unterscharführer* (sergeant), had plenty of models to follow for someone in charge of liquidating an entire campful of Jewish prisoners.

Special commando units of the SS, called *Einsatzgruppen*, had already swept through eastern Poland and into Soviet territory, following on the heels of the German Army as it pressed toward Moscow and Stalingrad. The members of these official murder squads often consumed bottles of alcohol before being able to go about their assignment: the systematic "cleansing" of one village after another.

Some became so sickened by the work that they braved the mockery they knew they would face from their comrades and asked for transfers. Contrary to the claims of many Nazi

91

defendants and Nazi apologists, there were ample opportunities for avoiding this type of "service." As one historian observed, "In none of the vast literature on the Holocaust is there, so far as I know, the record of a single case of a German policeman or member of the SS having been severely reprimanded, imprisoned or sent to the front—much less shot—for his refusal to participate in mass murder."[2]

Most remembered their SS motto—"Loyalty is thine honor"—and dismissed their Jewish victims as nonhuman. The SS mobile killing units rounded up men, women, and children, forced them into forests or open fields, ordered them to dig massive pits, and executed them by the hundreds and thousands. The *Einsatzgruppen* units were responsible for an estimated two million Jewish lives.

By the time Schwammberger reached Rozwadow the first fixed centers of mass killing were also fully operational. Hitler had created the first concentration camps in 1933. But these and the others that were added to the network, including Auschwitz in June 1940, were primarily for political prisoners. Jews certainly were prominent among the camp populations, but there were also Polish priests, French socialists, German unionists, homosexuals, and others.

By the winter of 1941 SS chief Himmler was ready to begin building on the experience gained during the infamous T-4 initiative, the euthanasia program, in which lethal injections and poison gas were used to eliminate tens of thousands of mentally retarded and physically disabled people during 1939 and 1940. State institutions and hospitals all across Germany had helped the SS compile a list of racially undesirable "patients" for what came to be known as "special treatment." By the end of the summer of 1941 nearly one hundred thousand German children and adults had received this treatment.

On December 7, 1941, the Japanese launched a devastating surprise attack on Pearl Harbor, and U.S. President

Franklin Roosevelt in a speech to the nation the next day declared December 7 would "live in infamy." On the same day, at the place called Chelmno, in a small town outside Lodz, one of the largest cities in German-annexed Poland, the gas chambers were being readied for the first transports of Jews.[3] Within months death camps were operational at Majdanek, Belzec, Treblinka, and Birkenau, a massive extension of the Auschwitz facility.

With the death camps on-line, the process of human extermination became far more efficient and the capacity for killing became gargantuan. In August 1942, the month before Schwammberger arrived in Rozwadow, more than four hundred thousand Jews from all over Europe were gassed to death in the death camps in Poland.[4]

The engines of the Holocaust, then, were in full use by the time Schwammberger, armed with a pistol, a horse whip, and a black-haired German shepherd, arrived in Rozwadow. Located about one hundred miles northwest of Przemysl, Rozwadow was significant only because of its proximity to a modern munitions plant about three miles away at Stalowa Wola.

In 1939 the Germans had occupied the facility, which at the time was considered one of the most modern steel facilities in all of Europe. Stalowa Wola was then incorporated into the vast network of industrial plants that made up the Hermann Göring Works, named for Hitler's longtime deputy.

To supplement the plant work force of several thousand Poles, the SS had established a small concentration camp at Rozwadow to house about twelve hundred Jews from nearby villages. Every day, under the watch of a corps of Ukrainian guards, the Jews were marched from the barbed-wire camp to the bustling steel plant and then back at the end of the day. Josef Schwammberger became their commandant.

He was responsible for their work and also for living

conditions at the camp. But these conditions might better be described as dying conditions. Rozwadow had abominable sanitary facilities and inadequate food. Schwammberger was known for taking the already starvation-level rations intended for the camp inmates, selling them on the black market, and pocketing the proceeds.

As the weeks went by, more and more inmates found themselves too weak to work. That was precisely the point.

Joseph Wellner was twenty-five years old when he was taken from his hometown, a small village north of Krakow. On Saturday morning, the Jewish Sabbath, one week before Rosh Hashanah, the Jews in Wellner's village were "evacuated," as he described it nearly five decades later.[5] Women and children were sent to the gas chambers at Belzec. The men were farmed out to various labor camps like Rozwadow all across Poland.

Within a few days Wellner found himself at Rozwadow and working for Josef Schwammberger. Every morning Schwammberger assembled the camp prisoners and selected people for work in the factory nearby. The young SS man carried his whip menacingly and always wore crisp white gloves, remembered Wellner, who now lives in quiet retirement in Queens, New York.

Trained as a watchmaker, Wellner worked in the steel factory, carrying loads of ore to the giant smelting ovens. The Jewish workers toiled twelve hours a day. Ethnic German taskmasters kept them moving. The Polish laborers taunted the Jews, who were reduced to slaves.

Dr. Edmund Goldenberg, a doctor living in Binghamton, New York, was also at Rozwadow during Schwammberger's tenure as camp commandant. Born in Theresienstadt, the town outside Prague that the Nazis later picked as the site for Czechoslovakia's main concentration camp, Goldenberg grew up in Krakow, where he studied medicine before the German invasion in the fall of 1939. After escaping from a concentration camp in Lwow, an ancient Galician city now part of Ukraine, Goldenberg ended up in one of the villages that, like Wellner's, was emptied of its Jewish population in the fall of 1942.

As they arrived in camp, Schwammberger greeted his Jewish prisoners with the demand that they turn over all valuables and money. The newly installed SS chief promised that any Jew who refused or was unable to work, for whatever reason, would be killed.

Memories of the harsh conditions of the camp have not faded even after so many years. The inmates lived on soup and bread, which was brought into camp every day in a wheelbarrow that doubled as a cart for removing the bodies of those who succumbed to typhus, dysentery, or a Ukrainian guard's pistol. Prisoners were denied access to the latrines at night, so the barracks soon became filthy. Bedbugs and lice were rampant.[6]

On Yom Kippur, the holiest day in the Jewish calendar, a day traditionally given to prayer and reflection, the Jewish labor crew marched the few miles from the camp to the steel mill, the same as every day. On that September evening Schwammberger assembled the Jewish workers in a large clearing beside the factory. Standing on a podium, the SS man called for a Jew named Frankel. Three men stepped forward. Schwammberger indicated he wanted the one who was Rabbi Frankel.

The rabbi, Schwammberger announced, had been accused of sabotage. Several Poles from the steel factory apparently had denounced the rabbi for refusing to work because of the holiday. Schwammberger had the rabbi brought up to him on the podium and in front of the entire gathering of dismayed prisoners shot the man in the head.

Rabbi Frankel was not the first person Josef Schwammberger had shot, and he would hardly be the last. By mid-November dozens of Jews had already died in the Rozwadow camp. On November 14, 1942, some three hundred of those inmates who had managed to survive that long were selected to be moved to a new, smaller work camp right on the grounds of the steel factory. Schwammberger's corps of Ukrainian guards shot the remaining hundred or so prisoners and buried them in the nearby forest.*

The Jewish population of Rozwadow was thus completely liquidated.

Sally Susskind will never forget March 12, 1942. When she recalled it fifty years later during an interview, she slipped into a kind of delirium, a state of visible panic. Her thoughts became fractured. Her voice rose to a pitch.

March 12 was the day when Mielec became *Judenfrei*, as the Germans called it. The word means "Jew-free." The town where she was born and raised, the place where she fell in love with a bright-eyed political organizer, the home of her parents and their parents and generations of family and memories became Jew-free.

"So was a relocation, and they sent us; they took all the Jewish people at three o'clock in the morning," Sally related, her swollen, arthritic hands shaking. "They knocked on the doors; they knocked on the windows; they knocked all over. They pushed us out into one place, children, women, old people, young people. At that time I was young. And they started to separate us. My grandfather they took away right away. They sent us first, was about ten kilometers [six miles] from our town, and over there was a big hangar for planes, so they put us over there and kept us. It was still cold, March the twelfth. At the time it was a little snowy, and they kept us a few days over there."

There had been killings before. No Jew still alive in 1942 could claim to have been sheltered from the sights and

*With no surviving eyewitnesses to the mass execution, Schwammberger's direct participation could not be established with sufficient certainty to warrant conviction on charges related to this incident at his later trial. Numerous witnesses, however, did testify to having heard about Schwammberger's direct involvement.

sounds of Nazis killing Jews. People had grown accustomed to the fear, to the uncertainty about the future. They had prayed for some force to intervene. But they had not imagined violence on this scale.

"We didn't know, every day was a different segregation," Sally continued, her voice becoming more frantic. "They took out the Jewish men; then they took us around; they took out again all the people who were middle-aged, and some people were sick, some men, so they took us a few days over there. They didn't give us nothing to eat."

The "segregations" were called *Selektionen* (selections), another malevolent Nazi euphemism. At these selections people were separated into two groups: those who would work and therefore live and those who would be sent to death. Over the course of those snowy March days some 400 elderly and sick people, as well as children, were shot in large groups in the forest beside the airplane factory just outside town. About 750 others were taken to a nearby forced labor camp. And the remaining Jews who had been gathered in Mielec, all those who had come from Mielec itself and from the surrounding villages, about 3,500 people in all, including Sally and her parents, were taken to Lublin, en route to the death camp at Treblinka.[7]

Before they reached Treblinka, Sally and her cousin realized they could not wait a moment longer if they had any hope of ever escaping alive. With her infant son in tow and carrying the false identification papers Arnold had smuggled to them, Sally and her cousin disguised themselves as nuns and jumped the train carrying Mielec's Jews and the rest of Sally's family. Traveling at night, the two women walked the narrow country back roads to Przemysl. Sally had not seen her husband in more than two years.

Life for Arnold and his family and the other Jews of Przemysl, meantime, had grown steadily worse in the months since Hitler had attacked the Soviet Union the previous June. In the first weeks of the Nazi reoccupation the

German Army had restored order, which included putting a stop to the looting of Jewish homes and businesses by Poles and Ukrainians. But with the arrival of the SS and Gestapo, the killing program had begun in earnest.

In June 1942 the Jews of Przemysl received the order to relocate themselves and only those possessions they could carry into a tiny quarter of the city that soon became a walled-in ghetto. They were given twenty-four hours to pack and to move. Through the Judenrat the SS slowly but steadily squeezed the Jewish community. In the ghetto the Jews were denied food, access to the city's markets, medicine stocks, and any work other than that which was coordinated by the SS.

A small but solid and robust man, Susskind recalled the long months he spent in the ghetto with an emotional detachment. Unlike his wife, Arnold seemed perfectly comfortable discussing the time during which he lost his entire family, almost as if he were referring to someone else's experiences. As he recalled his ordeal, the words came easily, if not always with absolute precision.

"Then, systematically, one day they said that all Jews have to bring all fur coats," he related. "Next day Jews have to bring all jewelry, if not they'll be shot. Next day it was the Jewish Committee has to deliver ten thousand dollars, or so much in [Polish] zlotys, and if not, they take a thousand Jews and shoot them down. That was their system."

Life in the ghetto became increasingly desperate. There was no food; there was no space. The sight of Gestapo and SS uniforms often meant death was on the way. Children were designated as sentries. When they saw a Gestapo officer coming, they called out, "*Shesh,*" the Polish word for the number six. In the Przemysl ghetto that became the signal for everyone to hide.

"It was dehumanizing, this plan," Susskind remembers. "People were dying in the streets, and you just passed by and didn't pay attention to it. You got used to it." The dread of death was constant. "Every day was important day to live. You never knew what tomorrow bring. If you saw ten Gestapo marching into the ghetto, you knew something was going to happen, but you didn't know if you going to be next or if someone else."

Work was the key to survival. If you were healthy and resourceful and lucky, you were given work. If you had work, you might avoid being "selected" for death. Susskind remembered working briefly for an Austrian officer soon after the ghetto was formed. In exchange for performing odd jobs, whether it was fetching something or shining the officer's boots, Susskind received a piece of bread or something else to eat.

"He was always nice to me," Arnold recalled. "I don't know how he was to other people. Only I did what they told me to do exactly. I was a servant."

Interjecting, Sally added, "In order to survive, you had to get that piece of bread."

Revealing the feisty rapport between himself and his wife of more than half a century, Arnold insisted on sounding as if he were disagreeing or correcting her comments when really he agreed completely. "No! I couldn't say no. Besides, sometimes I was glad, because I knew I would come home with something."

Sally ignored her husband and underlined her own point: "A piece of bread. *This* was the most important thing."

Arnold noted that the officer was a "lieutenant or something" and even resembled Schwammberger a bit. "Maybe he was Schwammberger, very possible. He looked like him. Only I tell you in ghetto your mind didn't work right. You couldn't be normal."*

Driving her point home, Sally added, "When you hungry,

*The Austrian officer Susskind mentions could not have been Schwammberger. If he worked for the officer soon after the ghetto was created—a point about which he is confident—then he is referring to a time that predates Schwammberger's arrival at Przemysl by more than eight months. As there were many Austrians in the SS, Susskind's confusion is not surprising.

when you cold in winter without shoes, without clothes, you don't think about nothing else but that, how to get this piece of bread."

The alternative to work was idleness and the far greater risk of being selected for deportation. "If you couldn't do something, you are nothing, they don't need you," Arnold explained. "Why should they feed you if you don't do nothing for the German Reich? Only in ghetto, ghetto was one of the worst things what could happen."

Life in the Przemysl ghetto became deadlier as the Nazis stepped up their liquidation program. There were two major deportation *Aktionen* (actions) in the town in 1942, each lasting several days. In the months leading up to that summer Jews had been gathered up from the surrounding villages and corralled in the Przemysl ghetto. As was the case with the other collection points all across Poland, Przemysl was picked in large part because of its access to rail lines. The villages fed into urban ghettos, and the ghettos in turn fed directly to the death camps.

On July 27, 1942, the SS began the first major liquidation effort in Przemysl. In the several days that followed more than 1,000 Jews were sent to a nearby forced labor camp and 12,000 to the gas chambers at Belzec. Those 12,000 joined some 150,000 Jews from other collection points in Poland who were gassed at Belzec during the month of August. During the first *Aktion* hundreds of other Przemysl Jews were shot in the street or were marched to the woods outside town to be shot. In November, during the second *Aktion*, another 4,000 Jews were sent to Belzec.

Before the first shipment of Jews was moved out during the first selection, the Judenrat was given five thousand work permits to distribute. These permits were the functional equivalent of temporary stays of execution. Those without the permits faced two choices: certain deportation to a killing center or hiding.

"In a time like that the ingenuity is unbelievable," Arnold Susskind recalled. "What a person can do from nothing! A lot of buildings were destroyed from the air force attacks during the war. Some bombs made big holes in the ground. I remember I had a friend who was studying for a doctor. His name was Mandy. He died. The Germans killed him. We used to go to same school, only he went to Italy to study medicine. He came back. He should have stayed there. Anyway, we went in a bunker under the ground. It had a little opening to the outside."

Arnold, his wife, Sally—who had made it safely back to Przemysl before the ghetto was created—and the others in hiding had constantly to worry about being discovered. In one bunker Arnold and Sally used, there were nineteen other people hiding. "We used to see through the opening the SS go by with the German shepherds, so we used to have a little pepper, and I used to put there so the dogs would sniff and they couldn't feel it."

And there was the constant struggle to find food and water. Prowling Gestapo and SS police officers frequently shot at Jews trading valuables for scraps of food with Poles who came to the wall of the ghetto. Nor was there access to potable water. "We digged a little well for water, but it had too much iron in it, so people started losing their teeth," Arnold remembered. "They used to look like monkeys, you know; everybody had lost three, four teeth in the front."

One time, on a search for something to eat, Arnold had a frightening encounter. "We had no food, so we tried to go out once in a while, take a chance, to organize some food," he related. "One time I went to a place away from the city. I knew it used to be there a pharmacist, Lauffer was his name, and the pharmacy was on the ground floor, and he used to live upstairs. And I went there to look for food. I thought they were rich people, and I figured maybe I'll find something there. And I found two carrots, something else,

too, but I don't remember. All of a sudden I see myself. I
didn't know. I didn't realize. I looked in a mirror. The closet
was open. And there was a mirror on the door. I had a beard,
a red beard. I didn't shave for weeks. I got scared. I thought
somebody else was in there."

With the senses so seared from the slow death that was
life in the ghetto, it seems impossible that one man could
have left an impression that endured more prominently
than all the others through more than five decades. But
Schwammberger did just that. The SS man's eyes, in particular, left a lasting impression, just as they had on Dr. Tuchman. "His eyes was electrifying. His eyes could kill. He was
a very good-looking, handsome man. And his eyes was just
terrible."

Having liquidated the work camp at Rozwadow,
Schwammberger's next assignment from the SS regional
headquarters in Krakow was to bring his experience to bear
on the remnants of the ghetto in Przemysl. By the end of
1942 the area of the ghetto had already been reduced to few
square blocks as the SS had reduced the population to a final
few thousand souls. Those who remained had nothing, no
food, no money, no possessions, and very little hope. Those
fortunate enough had a good hiding place.

Upon Schwammberger's arrival in February 1943, the
ghetto was divided in half, one side for those still providing
slave labor, the other side for the nonworking Jews. Those
in the working ghetto received meager rations of food to
keep them barely functional. Those stuck in the nonworking
half of the ghetto received nothing, except what they could
trade, steal, or share with someone from the working ghetto.

Although officially Schwammberger's authority was limited to the working ghetto, he stalked both sides at will,
looking for any opportunity to crash his whip down on
someone's back or to unleash his German shepherd, a dog
trained to tear human flesh. Sometimes Schwammberger

simply shot at anyone who happened across his path. He also took it upon himself to administer personally the punishment for anyone caught trying to escape the ghetto confines: death by hanging or by a pistol shot to the back of the head.

By the time of Schwammberger's arrival in Przemysl, many hundreds of thousands of Europe's Jews had already perished. Arnold and Sally, too, had already withstood extreme hardships and suffered personal losses. Arnold had lost his parents and both his brothers. His sister had been shot by the Nazis in Holland, but he did not know that then. He believed until the end of the war that she must surely have been safe there. Sally knew nothing of the fate of anyone in her family except her grandfather, who she knew had been taken and shot in the woods outside Mielec with hundreds of other elderly Jews and children. She assumed that the rest of her family had since been killed at Treblinka.

But Arnold and Sally still had each other, and they still had their infant son, and that was saying a lot for a Jewish family in Poland in 1943.

That spring Arnold had his first encounter with the new commandant of the Przemysl ghetto. "So, this was in the middle of '43," Arnold recounted. "And they used to, how you call it, they used to send out Gestapo and Jewish police and grab anybody they could get a hold of, mostly women and children, older people. So the Jewish Committee picked up twelve or twenty people in ghetto, and in the beginning we didn't realize this was for other purposes, and we digged a hole and the hole covered me. The hole was about two feet higher than me, and it was sandy, the ground was very sandy. It was about eight by twenty feet."

All of a sudden Arnold heard the sound of trucks, and he scrambled to climb out of the hole. "Yeah, I ran out the hole, and over there were old broken houses, the homes that were bombed before, so, you know, there were places where we could hide." He looked back and saw Schwammberger marching toward them in full SS uniform, obviously in charge of a number of Ukrainian guards and a large contingent of Jewish prisoners. "I heard machine guns, and I understood what was going on. Then I was hiding underneath something, I don't know, an old car or a building, I don't remember. Anyway, I was laying on the floor and I heard, I saw the guys shooting like that, the screaming babies. That time they killed about four hundred people."

After fifty years some details were foggy in Susskind's memory. He admitted, for example, that he could not be positive that Schwammberger was actually doing the shooting or if it was only the security forces under his command. "I saw Schwammberger," Susskind said. "I don't remember if I saw him shooting. I know he was giving out orders."*

Arnold managed to escape that day. The Jewish workers who were brought along to cover over the dead were then shot themselves when their job was done. Had Arnold not hidden himself among the crumbled buildings nearby, he would have met the same unfortunate end.

Susskind's next encounter with Schwammberger was also nearly fatal. Once again the SS commandant chose an important Jewish holiday to impose a baseless punishment. The occasion, this time, was Passover, when Jews celebrate their liberation from slavery in ancient Egypt. An important part of the Jewish tradition surrounding this usually festive week is the eating of matzo, a flat crackerlike bread. Jews eat this unleavened bread, and have done so for thousands of years, as a symbolic reminder of the haste with which their ancestors left the pharoah's land.

Susskind and six other men had been secretly baking

*The incident Susskind described above was not the basis for any official charge in the indictment subsequently brought against Schwammberger in Germany.

matzo in preparation for the holiday, which had assumed a special poignancy for the Jews held hostage in the ghetto. "The Jewish Committee gave us five pounds of flour," Susskind recalled. "This was like a million dollars. I mean, we would rather make bread, but the religious guys they insisted [on baking matzo], so we tried to help them, and we got caught."

Schwammberger lined up the seven men against one wall of the ghetto. He pulled his white gloves from his belt and carefully slipped them onto his hands. Schwammberger's dog, Prinz, sat threateningly at his side. Taking a step toward the first man on line, Schwammberger raised his gun to the back of the man's head and fired. "Just like that," Susskind remembered.

"I was on the [other] end," he continued. "The situation was just exactly like this. Here was the end of the wall, and we were near a narrow street, and when I saw that, I ran away. The guy after me, they were shooting after us, and he got shot in the shoulder. The third guy after me was shot very badly and died. And this guy was shot in the shoulder, he was a doctor or something. I don't know what happened to him."

During the first few days of September 1943 Schwammberger coordinated the final major *Aktion* in Przemysl. With his dog and his armed Ukrainian guards, he went door to door through the ghetto, rounding up those who had not voluntarily assembled with the others for the last trainload of Jews bound for Auschwitz. Schwammberger used smoke and tear gas to force stragglers to leave their bunkers. In this way many hundreds were rooted out of their hiding places and taken to the awaiting trains or to be shot. Defying the odds, Arnold and Sally and their son managed to remain safely hidden.

Arnold and his family were among the last Jews in the ghetto. Many Jews remained hidden in underground bunkers

or in the attics of sympathetic Poles and Ukrainians. That
didn't leave enough people to serve on the final cleanup
detail, to sort the clothes and valuables of those who had
most recently been shipped off to the death camps. Schwammberger assigned the surviving members of the Jewish police
to root out some "volunteers" from their hiding places.

An acquaintance located Arnold and offered him the
chance to join the work detail. At first Arnold was adamant
about not leaving Sally and his son behind in the bunker.
They had been lucky so far. There could be no assurance if
they separated again that there would ever be another reunion. "She said, 'Go, maybe you'll be able to save us later,' "
Arnold remembered. "I didn't want, but finally she started
begging."

The next day, sure enough, Arnold was able to sneak back
to the spot where he had left his family and smuggle his
wife and son into the barracks where the small group of
workers had been housed. "We paid up a Ukrainian guard
so he would let us in. Then we came with a wagon and a
horse," Arnold related. "We went back to the bunker. I took
my wife and child. Other people started screaming, 'Take
me, too.' But I couldn't."

Officially Przemysl was at that point *Judenfrei*. There still
remained the several dozen workers and the countless Jews
still in hiding. The rest, with very few exceptions, all were
dead.

Strangely Arnold and his family enjoyed some of the best
times they had known in many months during the several
weeks he managed to participate in the ghetto's final work
detail. "They had a shower over there, and we hadn't taken
a shower in weeks. We had lice and things like that. This
was a time we started to have food. We [hadn't had] food
for weeks. And these were the last people. And Schwammberger was in charge."

These last survivors of the Przemysl ghetto could not

delude themselves any longer about what the future might hold. They knew too much about what had already happened to believe that the present condition would last long. They had come a long way since the days when Polish soldiers, living in the same barracks they now occupied, frequented the Susskind family's candy store before the war.

Now the scene in the cramped quarters was surreal. "Young kids, fourteen years old, sex, things like that at night, because people knew that tomorrow is not tomorrow. Everybody was enjoying as long as he was alive."

Whatever drop of promise Arnold and Sally may have sensed during this period soon evaporated. On February 1, 1944, after only a few weeks in the barracks, the men were suddenly rounded up and shipped out to join what was left of the forced labor brigade at Stalowa Wola, the steel plant near Rozwadow, the village Schwammberger had wiped out the previous year. In Stalowa Wola Arnold joined the remaining members of the forced labor brigade, including Joseph Wellner, who had been among the three hundred Jews spared the final liquidation.

Arnold tried to make the best of the situation, tried to focus on staying alive. Somehow or another he would find Sally again. In the meantime, he had to keep moving, keep working.

The day after the Przemysl men were sent away, Schwammberger organized the remaining women for a final transport. The only ones remaining, other than those in hiding, were the women who had been part of the so-called cleanup detail. And amazingly enough there were a few children who had managed to survive the ordeals of the last few months in the ghetto.

But what happened next Sally could hardly bear to discuss. "When they took us away from Przemysl, they took away the children," Sally began, her voice quavering. "There were seven children still left over from our people. They took away the children, three year old, two year old. They took them from us away. We didn't know nothing about what they would do with them. And you know what? We still didn't believe that this would happen, the killing. We didn't want to believe or we were so naïve or we had never heard of this. We didn't want to think."

Stepping in for his wife, Arnold found the words that Sally was unable to articulate. "The small babies they picked up by the legs and hit the head against the wall. They didn't want to waste bullets. My wife didn't want to give the child, and finally friends said, 'You're young, if you live through the war, you'll have another child.' So they took away, and all the [older] children were shot."

That day Arnold and Sally lost their four-year-old son, Emmanuel. Sally remembered that it was Schwammberger who not only coordinated the roundup but personally joined in the killing. Before Schwammberger could round up the women and send them on to Plaszow, a concentration camp just outside Krakow, three of the mothers who lost babies committed suicide. As much as she desperately wanted to give up and go the same way, Sally concentrated on staying alive.

Arnold and Sally were separated once again. They both had lost their entire families. Now they had lost their son, too. And once again they had no idea if they would ever see each other. If they lasted another week, they would be lucky. For any Jew still alive in Poland, or almost anywhere in Europe in 1944, their situation looked dreadfully familiar.

As a plumber Nussbaum had a lifesaving skill. A Jew with the ability to work, because he either had a specialized skill or had managed somehow to stay healthy and strong, had a much better chance of being the only member of his family not sent to the crematorium.

Scholars, rabbis, financiers, lawyers, and other learned

professionals were almost always automatically marked for death when "selections" were made. "They liked shoemakers, could make good German boots," Nussbaum correctly pointed out in an extensive interview. "A shoemaker had good, and a good tailor had good. The high commanders like a good suit. The tailors made it very well. Tailor was more important than a plumber."

Such tragic life-and-death choices were part of everyday living and dying in the ghetto. The piece of bread eaten by the mother might mean the sister would not live. Then the next day the mother would have nothing more to eat anyway.

Forcing the Jews themselves to make impossible choices about life and death gave the Nazis a powerful tool. As Hitler had demonstrated on *Kristallnacht*, boundless violence could make the cost of any meaningful act of resistance simply too overwhelming. When the mass of Jews in Poland finally began to accept that all the terrible threats were not bluffs, that the Nazis were as ruthless as Hitler had promised they would be, few could find the strength to fight back.

In Przemysl, too, the Nazis demonstrated their ability to leave Jewish prisoners no choice but to submit to death. In the spring of 1943, for example, a young Jewish man named Green escaped from the ghetto into the woods surrounding Przemysl after stabbing a Gestapo officer. The eager SS sergeant responded with a time-honored Nazi tactic in order to impose his will.

Schwammberger stormed into the nonworking part of the ghetto, grabbed fifty hostages, and threatened to start killing them off unless Green returned to face his punishment. Green, who had been imprisoned in the ghetto in the first place and slated for death only because he was Jewish, now had to weigh his one life against the lives of fifty innocents.

When word of Schwammberger's extortion reached him in the woods, Green returned. He was promptly hanged from the ghetto gallows. To reinforce his point, Schwammberger ordered the other ghetto prisoners to witness the execution. In a further act of inhumanity, the SS commandant ordered the young man's trousers pulled down around his ankles just before kicking out the chair. Schwammberger laughed as Green breathed his last and lost control of his bladder.

Jews were frequently placed in such no-win situations. Ignatz Duldig, the first head of Przemysl's Judenrat, came to be regarded as a martyr in the town because he finally reached the point where he could no longer continue to act as the Nazis' stand-in executioner. At first, like so many others, he believed Hitler would go only so far as to resettle the Jews. Actual annihilation was simply unimaginable.

When the ghetto in Przemysl was established in mid-1942, several months before Schwammberger arrived, the local Gestapo chief demanded that Duldig supervise an orderly roundup of all jewelry. There were threats. The Jews were afraid. Duldig complied. Then he was asked to organize a collection of all furs and winter coats. Duldig complied again. The Nazis were systematically looting the Jewish population.

But when Duldig was ordered to assist in the roundup of Jewish children during the first deportation, he refused. "He seen what they doing to the Jewish kids, they killing them," Nussbaum recalled. "They asked him to deliver fifty, one hundred, and he said, 'From now on I'm not delivering you any kids anymore. If you want, you take yourself. I'm not doing it.' They shot him right away behind the [Judenrat] building. He was a hero."

Others were not as honorable as Duldig. There was a Jew named Teich whom Schwammberger had brought with him from Rozwadow when he was finished liquidating the Jewish work camp there.* In Przemysl Teich served as Schwamm-

*There do not seem to be any records of Teich's first name. Nor do any of the survivors interviewed remember more than his surname.

berger's unofficial aide-de-camp. Among other duties Teich was known for extorting gold and other valuables from his fellow Jews on Schwammberger's behalf, usually in return for promises of food or protection. Needless to say, Teich never kept these promises.

Nussbaum remembered distinctly one encounter he had with Schwammberger's henchman in the final days of the Przemysl ghetto. The Nazis had converted the old Polish Army barracks (called the Koszary) into the headquarters for the Judenrat. (The same barracks housed the final cleanup detail after the Jewish council ceased to exist.) The building formed part of the perimeter of the ghetto. One day Schwammberger came into the Koszary and demanded to know why the toilets had not been cleaned. Teich looked around the room and noticed Nussbaum.

"So Schwammberger says, 'Twenty-five,' " Nussbaum recounted. "He had a whip, and he had his dog with him. And I lay down, and Teich whipped me twenty-five times with that whip. Believe me, for three weeks I couldn't lay on my back because he wanted to show Schwammberger he does a good job."

Duldig and Teich were extremes. Resistance to the Nazi terror was not limited to grand acts of public defiance. Nor were leading collaborators like Teich the only villains. There was a great and murky middle where, for so many people, the line between saint and sinner was less clearly drawn. In that gray area Sam Nussbaum existed, excelled, and survived the Holocaust.

Many times Nussbaum faced the fate so many hundreds of thousands of other Jews had already met. Each time the diminutive man with the impish smile defied that fate.

Sometimes he was just lucky to have been trained as a plumber. During the first mass deportation in July 1942, for example, he was among the throngs of Jews assembled and waiting to board the death train. Confinement in ghettos meant that Jews all over Europe lived in virtual isolation.

There were many wild stories, rumors of mass shootings and death camps. But no one could distinguish the truth from the fantasy.

At the time of the first mass deportation in Przemysl those who might have doubted the Nazis' intentions wanted so intensely to believe that all would be well that they went along. So the Gestapo and SS officers loading up those first trains relied largely on volunteers to make the massive operation run smoothly.

Many, in fact, jumped at the chance to leave the ghetto, having already known suffering and the loss of family members. Nussbaum's father, who had raised his eldest son to dream of moving to Palestine, now nominated the young man to represent the family on the first transport. If he fared well, he could send back word for the others to follow.

Waiting with the others to be crammed into the freight cars, Nussbaum was plucked out of the crowd by the Gestapo officer Breuer, who was just happening by and recognized the plumber who had done such a good job on the leaking pipes of the Gestapo headquarters the year before. Breuer knew the train was heading for the Belzec death camp, and he grabbed Nussbaum by the collar and told him he was wanted for a special errand.

"I told him I needed to get on the train, but he insisted I had to go for him. That's how I missed that transport."

Nussbaum's reprieve thanks to a Gestapo officer was the ultimate irony. Making Breuer's gesture even more bizarre was the fact that the SS (of which the Gestapo was an affiliate) and the German Army nearly came to blows over the same deportation action. In the entire history of the Third Reich it was one of the most dramatic moments of conflict within the Nazi state.

When the local Wehrmacht (German Army) officials heard about the scheduled roundups in Przemysl, they protested to the regional SS authorities in Krakow, the ones responsible for coordinating the "resettlement" operation. The army commander wanted to make sure that those Jews toiling as slave laborers in the various ghetto workshops, repairing army uniforms, mending boots, sewing shirts, and so on, would be spared, if only temporarily, the deportations. But the SS had its own agenda and was little interested in accommodating the army's interests.

Throughout the war the SS and the military branches bickered constantly over access to vital resources such as gasoline and railway cars. The army was concerned with moving troops, the SS with transporting Jews to the death camps.

In this case the Wehrmacht threatened to blockade the city and its bridges if the SS insisted on deporting the Przemysl ghetto's Jewish laborers. Before the standoff could lead to a mini-civil war, the dispute was resolved at the highest levels of the SS and Wehrmacht leadership.[8] A new policy was drafted whereby Jews would be replaced with non-Jewish workers in all factories and shops throughout the General Government as soon as was possible. But for the time being some Jews with working skills were to be spared.

When Josef Schwammberger arrived in Przemysl in February 1943, Nussbaum's good fortune did not abandon him. Schwammberger soon heard about Nussbaum's abilities and drafted him to be his personal handyman. Only now Nussbaum wasn't simply lucky. Now his survival depended on his willingness to work regularly for the enemy.

Nussbaum was not being asked to serve as an enforcer, like Schwammberger's Jewish kapo, Teich. He was never asked to beat another Jew or to extort property. He was never made to smoke out a family from a hiding place. He never held back the arms of a man Schwammberger shot in the head, as one Jewish kapo reportedly did.[9] Nussbaum simply knew how to fix things and could make himself useful. Being useful meant surviving.

One day, for example, Schwammberger approached him for help with a rather unusual project: The SS man wanted a private source for alcohol. So he had Nussbaum build him a distillery for vodka behind the Koszary. "I didn't know how to do it," Nussbaum recalled. "So he told me to get some copper tubing and bend it in a coil, and we were cooking potatoes in what was like a little swimming pool for children, only it was steel. They were boiling, and we were catching the steam."

Schwammberger enlisted Nussbaum for all sorts of chores. He mended a fence, minded the still, repaired a toilet, patched a leaky pipe. On a September day in 1943 Schwammberger ordered Nussbaum to the train station to make certain the doors were locked on each of the cattle cars about to leave town with their cargo of Jewish deportees.

On that one day some two thousand Jews were sent to their deaths at the Auschwitz gas chambers. There was no longer any need for deception about the so-called resettlement. Nussbaum understood as well as anyone that there was no coming back.

Nussbaum did not want to lock the car doors, but he also knew that if he refused, he would be killed. He had already witnessed Schwammberger shooting Jews with far less provocation. And Schwammberger had a detachment of armed Ukrainian guards at the train station. They would be happy to shoot a defiant Jew if Schwammberger did not shoot first.

"What could I do anyway? What could I do?" Nussbaum asked anxiously. "Ukrainians, they had so many of them with machine guns, and Germans, SS. I couldn't do nothing."

After sliding the train doors shut, the twenty-three-year-old plumber went back into the ghetto, back to the hiding place in the basement of the run-down apartment building where his parents and five younger siblings had been stashed. When he got to the empty bunker, he realized what he had done. "I came over there, and they were gone," he recalled. "So I knew they were on that train." With his own hands he had locked the door on the car carrying his own family off to the gas chambers.

Fifty years later Nussbaum still had vivid memories of the man who sent his family to their deaths. Most people saw the official Schwammberger, the man in the uniform with the horse and the German shepherd and the whip and the circle of Ukrainian guards. Nussbaum often had a unique perspective from which to observe the man.

One day the young plumber was working on a bathroom in the villa Schwammberger had commandeered for his wife and young son. "I was working on his toilet. Schwammberger came home and took his jacket off, and you know what came out? A cross on a chain." Nussbaum laughed as if he had just told a joke. "I was so surprised to see this. It fell out underneath his shirt when he was bent over washing himself. Killing Jews with a cross around his neck! To him it was normal, see?"

From behind a rickety fence he had built to shelter Schwammberger's vodka still, Nussbaum had a secure place to witness what was going on in the ghetto. Often he saw more than he wished to see. On a couple of occasions, for example, he saw Schwammberger lead a group of Jews to a wall and with his own pistol shoot them all dead.

Once he saw Schwammberger leading a column of thirty bedraggled Jews, men, women, and small children. Schwammberger led the group into a tiny cell just inside the building that housed the Jewish council. He then pushed the beaten-down captives into the room until they were practically one on top of the other. A few hours later, when panicky screams had softened to low moans, Nussbaum walked past the door and saw steam coming from the small window in the door of the cell.

As close as he often was to Schwammberger, Nussbaum

today says he is no better able to explain the SS man's behavior. "A beast kills when it is hungry," Nussbaum observed. "But I couldn't call him a beast because I wouldn't want to embarrass the beast. He just killed because he wanted to kill."

CHAPTER 7

SURVIVORS

The prisoner who had lost faith in the future—his
future—was doomed.
—Viktor E. Frankl[1]

osef Schwammberger completed the liquidation of
the ghetto in Przemysl by the end of 1943. Just
after the start of the new year he was transferred—
of all places—to Mielec, the village where Sally Susskind
had been born, the place she would never see again. One
last time Schwammberger was given command over a small
group of beleaguered Jews in an insignificant corner of the
war-ravaged Continent. For a final few months Schwammberger was allowed to be master.

In the course of 1944 the Russians steadily pushed back
the exhausted German forces. On the other front the Western allies launched a decisive invasion at the craggy beaches
of Normandy. That year marked the beginning of the end
for Germany, the year Hitler's troops stopped advancing and
started retreating.

But the war against the Jews proceeded without regard to
the obviously worsening military prognosis. The SS contin-

ued the mass killing of Jews, in fact, without interruption until the very last possible moment.

With the Red Army less than a hundred miles away and advancing, Schwammberger accomplished his last assignment. The Soviets eventually did overrun Mielec but not before Schwammberger had finished eliminating the last remnants of yet another centuries-old Jewish community.*

Schwammberger's actual domain was a small forced labor camp adjacent to the town's aircraft assembly plant. The Polish government had built the factory complex just before the war, just in time, really, for the Germans to take it over for their own purposes. Of the several thousand Jewish prisoners held captive there, no more than a handful survived Schwammberger's vicious reign.

The camp functioned much as the Stalowa Wola facility had, much as the dozens of other forced labor camps administered by the SS all over occupied Europe. At Mielec Jewish slaves supplemented the factory's mostly Polish work force. The Mielec plant manufactured—of all things— bomber aircraft and was managed from afar by—of all people—old Ernst Heinkel, who was still churning out the wings for Göring's Luftwaffe. What a coincidence that after so much time Schwammberger was still in charge of security for Heinkel. But how much the job description had changed.

The Polish employees at the factory worked for wages, while the Jews worked in order not to be shot. Conditions at the camp were hardly better than the worst of the concentration camps. Food was scarce, medical care was nonexistent, and Schwammberger ruled with terror.

Loew Chiel, a mechanic born in Mielec, was only eighteen when Schwammberger took command of the forced labor

*Schwammberger was not charged for crimes committed during his tenure at Mielec. See Chapter 14.

camp. Chiel had worked in the factory since the March 1942 resettlement action that had cleared the nearby village of Mielec entirely of its Jewish inhabitants. At first conditions at the work camp had actually made life there almost bearable. Certainly prisoners at the factory work camp were better off than the hundreds of thousands of Jews who had already been shot or "processed" through one of the killing camps.

Conditions in the camp changed drastically when Schwammberger assumed control. Fifteen people were dying at Mielec every day from starvation, overwork, and abuse. Schwammberger did not tolerate illness. Anyone who became sick was shot.

Chiel recounted Schwammberger's actions in a statement to Austrian police in 1946:

> Schwammberger's first act was to order the Jews to surrender all their gold and jewelry. Severe punishment and even death was [sic] threatened for failure to surrender such objects. Understandably, a large number of Jews chose not to reveal their possessions of gold and jewelry. Subsequently, one day Schwammberger conducted an inspection and search in which he discovered about 50 Jewish men and women who still had valuables. He shot these 50 people outside of Mielec and buried them in a mass grave. I, personally, had the opportunity to observe this execution.[2]

Salamon Balsam, who had been a farmer in Mielec before being rounded up for forced labor in the Heinkel factory, had a more direct encounter with Schwammberger following one of these jewelry inspections. "Once, he personally pulled my three gold teeth with a pair of pliers," Balsam told Austrian police.[3]

In the dining room of his modest brownstone house in

Queens, New York, Nathan Fortgang pulled up his trouser leg to reveal pasty white flesh and a scar near his knee. One day during Schwammberger's term at the Mielec work camp he had called on Fortgang, the resident locksmith, to open the door to a warehouse. "It took me a few minutes to open those locks," Fortgang recalled in an interview. "I was so afraid, I was shaking." Covering up his leg, the elfin man related how Schwammberger gestured to his German shepherd, the same animal he had had with him at Przemysl. "The minute he put up his hand this dog caught my knee, tore my pants."[4]

In the years since Schwammberger joined the SS, he seemed to have developed a genuine appetite for cruelty. Today war is waged or threatened with weapons of mass destruction, with infrared sensors on long-range cannon or with Scud missiles carrying poison gas or biological weapons. A killer today no longer need look into the face of the victim, see his expression, hear his plea, smell his last breath. But Schwammberger did. Schwammberger looked in the faces of his victims again and again.

By summer the Red Army had advanced into Poland, liberating Przemysl and other small towns in Galicia on its drive toward Krakow and beyond. Schwammberger evacuated Mielec on August 24. Most of the remaining ragged prisoners there were shipped to other camps deeper inside Germany. A few escaped to the woods in the confusion.

Schwammberger rejoined SS and Police Leader Scherner's office in Krakow for a few weeks after clearing out of Mielec. According to the ethic of the organization he had served and according to the will of the leader to whom he had sworn his undying allegiance, Schwammberger had finally triumphed in his life. He had done his job well. After a life spent in mediocrity, he had proved himself a standout commandant and liquidator of Jews. He had asserted the superiority of the German race with a passion. Had Hitler won the war, Josef Schwammberger might well have been a minor battlefield celebrity.*

Instead by this point Hitler had driven himself and his country to madness. The Allies were closing in on both fronts. Germany was on the brink of defeat. The SS would forever be a dirty word. And Schwammberger would be held up as a criminal, not a hero.

In the fall of 1944 the Russian push through Poland was irreversible. By the end of the year the Poles had reclaimed from the Nazis their revered university and ancient castle atop Wawel Hill in Krakow. In January 1945, the following month, the Soviets liberated Auschwitz.

Schwammberger had long since left Poland and the ruins that were his handiwork. Many German soldiers and officers refused to carry on the fight, seeking instead to save themselves from the imminent military collapse. Feeling especially urgent about the need to make arrangements for Germany in the aftermath of defeat were the members of the SS. The SS men understood that for them retreat was insufficient. They had to escape.

After stopping briefly in Hamburg with a unit of Waffen-SS men just evacuated from Poland, Josef Schwammberger began the rest of his life. Once again his SS uniform branded him an outlaw, this time in the eyes of the advancing Allied forces. Once again he was on the run. Twelve years earlier he had been running to Germany. This time he was running in the other direction.

After receiving false papers from a senior SS officer, Schwammberger's unit dispersed. The British and Americans

---

*We take for granted the implausibility of this. Had Hitler concentrated his forces in the west and saved himself for an all-out attack on the Russians, or if he had waited to attack Britain and devoted his resources to the eastern front, then he might have bought several more years. Perhaps that would have been long enough for his scientists to catch up with the Americans in the development of the atomic bomb.

were fast approaching from the west. Meanwhile, Jews and other prisoners were led on foot by the thousands and transported in rickety trains from locations in the east to camps in the interior of Germany. Once again Europe was in a state of chaos and mass dislocation.

Amid this mad scrambling of refugees Schwammberger made his way home. Traveling south from Hamburg by bicycle, he continued on foot for a short while after his bicycle was stolen. In a small town near the Elbe River west of Berlin, Schwammberger bought another two-wheeler from a sympathetic *Hausfrau*, and he rode along the back roads through central Germany and down into Bavaria, past the training camps where he had begun his SS career, up the foothills of the Alps, and around the winding mountain roads to Innsbruck.

When Schwammberger arrived back in his hometown, he immediately went to the house of a friend. He figured Innsbruck was safe, at least for the moment, at least long enough for him to catch his breath and to plan his next move. There was no other obvious place to go. If he stayed clear of his family for a while, perhaps he could hide out successfully and "avoid capture as an S.S. man," as he himself later explained.

But the Allies were marching rapidly through Germany in the weeks following Hitler's suicide on April 30 and Germany's surrender on May 8. Only four years earlier the SS had followed behind the German Army invading the Soviet Union and had wiped out one Jewish village after another. Now the Allies were sweeping up hundreds and thousands of Nazis suspected of responsibility for those and other atrocities.

Ultimately the tiny house of Schwammberger's friend in Innsbruck could offer no protection. The SS man was arrested on July 20, 1945.

Sam Nussbaum survived the Holocaust because he was good with his hands. The rest of his family, his mother and father

and brothers and sisters, were not so fortunate. And in the end even the special favor he enjoyed as Josef Schwammberger's personal handyman was only temporary.

This was true for most of the Jews who bought themselves time by cooperating, even if not outright collaborating, with the Nazi masters. The reprieve in most cases was strictly for the moment. Those who avoided being shot with the masses because they shoveled the earth for the grave pit almost always went the same way in the end, only they endured the horror of having seen everyone else go before them.

Nussbaum was a rare exception. For him temporary was always just long enough.

One afternoon in September 1943, shortly after the last large-scale deportation from Przemysl, Schwammberger caught Nussbaum napping by the makeshift vodka still. Schwammberger, then at the height of his power, could have killed Nussbaum on the spot when he came upon his dozing fix-it man. Instead the SS man ordered Nussbaum to be on the next transport out of Przemysl. Deportation rather than execution, a moment's respite from annihilation, that was Josef Schwammberger's gift to his former plumber.

In the first week of October 1943 Nussbaum was on a train to Szebnia, a small concentration camp about thirty miles west of Przemysl, near Krakow. There, to his utter amazement, Nussbaum found his father. At the last moment during the final deportation from Przemysl, Nussbaum's father had been pushed from one line into another. After Nussbaum himself had locked the train compartment doors tight, the rest of the family had been sent directly to Auschwitz and to the gas chambers. Nussbaum's father had made it onto another train.

After a few weeks together at Szebnia, Nussbaum and his father finally were transferred to Auschwitz, too. Most people were sent directly to the gas chambers. Some, including Nussbaum and his father, were sent to the worker barracks.

Life and death, for many people during the years of the

Holocaust, often followed such a serendipitous course. For brief moments lives intersected at a camp, in a ghetto, on a transport. The faces of brothers, friends, cousins thought to have been lost restored faith, renewed hope, reawakened memories. But when the miracle of chance did inspire a reunion it was too often short-lived. After several days there was another good-bye. Or, as was more frequently the case, there was no time for good-bye.

Sam Nussbaum and his father were separated before they could both pass again beneath the iron gate at the entrance to the camp, the one that bears the words *Arbeit Macht Frei,* which means "Work makes you free."

"They were picking out people to go to another camp," Nussbaum recalled of that fateful day around the beginning of 1944. "And so they asked me to read an instrument. You measure ten hundred millimeters. It's an instrument to measure the thickness of something. And I knew how to read it. But my father didn't. They kicked him back to Auschwitz, and I went to a coal mine. That's how I lost my father."

Once again the father's decision to push his son into a trade had saved the son's life. That training, combined with Nussbaum's willingness to work for the Nazi masters, more than came in handy, however. It was the light that led him through the final hellish months of the Holocaust.

The coal mine to which Nussbaum was shipped from Auschwitz was near the industrial city of Katowice in southern Poland. When he arrived, the German supervisor in charge of the brigade of Jewish slave laborers to which Nussbaum was assigned assembled the haggard prisoners and asked if any among them had plumbing experience. What an unbelievable stroke of luck! Nussbaum and two others eagerly stepped forward, hoping the German officer had a special project to offer that would be a way out of the dank and dangerous mine shaft.

The German supervisor looked over the three volunteers. " 'Before I take you over there,' " Nussbaum later remembered him growling, " 'I want you to know: If you are not a plumber, I'll bring you back and you will be shot right here on the spot.' Just like that. That was his speech. 'But if you a plumber,' he says, 'then I need you.' "

The other two men standing with Nussbaum put their hands down and went back to the group. Now he stood alone in front of the grim-faced German. "And I stand there, and he said, 'You a plumber? What do you know about pumps?' Just like that. I say, 'Pumps? What kind of pumps? They got electric pumps, they got gasoline-driven pumps—' He said, 'Come with me, you're my man.' "

Nussbaum was brought through the bowels of the mine to the place where the facility's water pumps were located. He was assigned to work with a young Polish man named Yascov who had no experience whatsoever in plumbing. Nussbaum was experienced enough for the both of them. He recognized the problem immediately and quickly repaired the system on his own. Yascov was so grateful that Nussbaum had made him look good, indeed, that Nussbaum had almost certainly saved both their lives, that the next day he brought a gift. "That Yascov was so happy he brought me doughnuts," Nussbaum related.

As far as Nussbaum was concerned, the doughnuts were a luxury he was incapable of appreciating. It was like giving a glass of fine burgundy to a man dying of thirst in the desert. But the pastries smelled delicious, and he had to restrain the urge to stuff his mouth with them. Instead he gave them to one of the camp kapos.

At all concentration and forced labor camps the Nazis enlisted certain inmates, called kapos, to help police or administer the facility in return for special, if temporary privileges.* Often Jews were made kapos, on the theory that

---

*The word kapo probably derives from the French military rank, caporal. Another possible derivation is the Italian capo, which means "boss" or "chief."

actions could be carried out in a more orderly fashion if the Jewish victims believed they were following the instructions of fellow Jews. Sometimes the kapo became a real friend, a protector to the camp prisoners. Often he felt he had to be as ruthless as his Nazi masters in order to save his own neck. And sometimes the kapos, even the Jewish kapos, became intoxicated with their own power and went out of their way to be vicious.

Nussbaum's German kapo was so grateful for the sweets that he asked how he could return the favor. "What the hell am I going to do with these doughnuts anyway?" Nussbaum told the German. "I need soup, I need bread. I don't want doughnuts."

The kapo managed to slip Nussbaum a brand-new shirt, which did nothing for an empty stomach but was plenty valuable nonetheless. Nussbaum took his commodity to his friend Yascov back at the water pump station. Yascov, a Polish civilian who worked at the coal mine as his job and not because he was imprisoned there, was thrilled with Nussbaum's offering because shirts, like so many basic goods and services, were in very short supply. If you could find your way to the black market, vodka was easier to find than a crisp new shirt in the Polish city where Yascov lived.

The final payoff for Nussbaum came when he presented a bottle of vodka Yascov brought him to the camp kapo and his buddies, who proceeded to drink themselves into a blissful and boisterous stupor. At first Nussbaum was concerned. The kapo and his guard friends were carrying on without seeming to care that the entire camp could hear them. If they enjoyed themselves too much, Nussbaum worried, he might be found out and punished. In the end, however, their revelry was his salvation.

"The thing is, what I want to tell you is, I didn't eat the doughnuts and I didn't drink the vodka," Nussbaum explained, drawing to the punch line. "But that kapo was giving out soup. And they never mixed up the kettle. On the top was water, and on the bottom had a piece of meat sometimes, some peeling from the potatoes, and he went right away to the bottom and, 'Plumber, where are you?' And I came over, and he took the best stuff and put it on my plate. No soup, just the good stuff. And it kept me going."

Nussbaum's doughnut tale suggests one of the most troubling and least discussed realities of the Holocaust: Sometimes the victims were afforded a say, directly and indirectly, in deciding who among them would live and die. By virtue of Nussbaum's ability to seize an opportunity, he was able to win exceptional treatment. This favored status allowed him to overcome forces to which hundreds of thousands of others were forced to surrender. Hundreds of his fellow Jews at the coal mine were worked to death or starved. But Nussbaum found a way, at least for the few months he was there, to keep out of the way of the whips and to receive enough food to survive.

The dark side to Nussbaum's success, the tragic opposite result of his actions, was the fact that in saving himself, he assured that others would suffer or perhaps even die. Nothing Nussbaum ever did was intended to hurt anyone else. But the fact that he received a plate filled with meat at the soup line meant that some number of others received only the watery broth from the top of the kettle. Perhaps some of those deprived of the meat became too weak and were killed because they could no longer work hard enough. Or perhaps they succumbed to disease or exhaustion.

Another of Nussbaum's survival stories further illustrates this conflict. At the same coal mine he met another kapo, another German who had heard Nussbaum was something of a handyman and approached him with a special request. The kapo had a beautiful pocketknife he wanted repaired. Through his years of learning the plumbing trade, Nussbaum had picked up a basic understanding of blacksmithing. He managed to fire and temper the steel blade, reshape and sharpen it, and re-create the knife as if it were new.

The kapo was pleased and promised not to forget that Nussbaum had performed such a service. A few days later all the prisoners were lined up in the courtyard near the barracks for a head count. A prisoner had escaped from the camp the night before. The German overseer directed his kapo to "handle" the situation. "The commander tells that German I made that knife [for] to bring two guys and bring them out there," Nussbaum remembered. "So help me God, he grabbed me and another guy. And I called him by his name. And he said, 'Ah!' and he pushed me away. And he grabbed another guy. Pulled him out. And they fought, but he was strong, and they were weak. He cut them down, and they were laying there for ten days. It was ice cold, and that's why they were left laying there. See what a chance I had? I'll never forget that."

Again and again Nussbaum's life was spared, and someone else therefore suffered or died in his place. But why Sam Nussbaum? The key to his survival was not that he was more clever or more fortunate. Sam Nussbaum survived the Holocaust because he found ways to win privileged treatment, and he won privileged treatment because he was able and willing to hold the enemy's hand.

Was Nussbaum then a hero because he found the means to set himself apart, to find a path through the death maze, to overcome the impossible odds? Or was he a villain, a lesser-grade version of the thousands of collaborating Poles and Ukrainians and others who killed Jews all too willingly for the Nazis?

The Holocaust would certainly be a great deal easier to explain if it were true that all Germans were Nazi killers, all Poles were vicious collaborators, and all Jews were unfortunate and innocent victims. But human actions are rarely so neatly understood. Many Germans resisted Hitler in a variety of ways. One of the more colorful methods of subtle protest was used during the Nazi salute. Instead of hailing Hitler, some Germans said under their breath, "The snow was piled up this high." And large numbers of Poles did risk their lives to shelter or assist Jews. And some Jews did aid the Nazis in the murder of their fellow Jews.

Still, even if there can be no absolute standard for evil, there must be a range. Where do Sam Nussbaum's actions fall, then, on the spectrum of Jewish behavior during the Holocaust?

First, there is the question of intent to consider. A man who intends to kill is judged more harshly than one who kills inadvertently. There is also a qualitative difference between a man who shoots another voluntarily and a man who shoots another because he himself has a pistol to the side of his head.

Or is there? Hitler could never have carried out the Holocaust alone. Without the thousands of people following his orders, the murder of millions could never have taken place. Just as Hitler relied on his generals to make his war and his deputies to implement the "Final Solution," he relied on willing Poles and Ukrainians and Lithuanians and Croatians and others to serve as bullies and guards and snitches and executioners. The success of the extermination plan in key areas also often relied upon Jewish assistance. Every one of the Holocaust murderers, from the unarmed Eichmann down to the whip-wielding Schwammberger to the Jewish police who helped round up the ghetto stragglers for deportation to Auschwitz bears some share of the responsibility. The only real difference is one of degree.

In Nussbaum's case the question is extremely sensitive. Clearly he was not a kapo. His actions were not nearly on the order of the outright atrocities committed by the henchman Teich and other Jews who helped Schwammberger extort jewelry and other valuables, who assisted in the roundups of Jews for deportations, who actually collaborated with the Nazi police. In fact, the young plumber never harmed anyone directly.

Sam Nussbaum simply did what he was told and hoped he would not be shot. How could he have done otherwise? Who would have done differently in the same situation? This was the terrible conflict Josef Schwammberger and thousands like him forced on those fortunate—and on those unfortunate—enough to survive to the last days of the Holocaust.

Arnold Susskind spent the last year of the war being shuttled from one camp to another as the Germans were forced into a steady and ultimately decisive retreat ahead of the driving Red Army. His first stop after being evacuated from the steelworks at Stalowa Wola was, amazingly, Plaszow, the same camp outside Krakow where his wife, Sally, had been sent from Przemysl.

"And who do I see there? My wife!" Arnold recounted in an interview, beaming at this point in his story. "My wife was working over there in the garment center for the military, so she brought me a pants, a shirt, a jacket. So I said, 'I'll see you in the evening.' In the evening they took us away. She went to Auschwitz. I went to Gross-Rosen."

From Gross-Rosen, a work camp about sixty miles east of Dresden, Susskind was transferred to a succession of camps, sometimes by train, sometimes on foot. After a few weeks the Nazis moved him again, always deeper into the heart of Germany. Susskind's life had become a purgatory. He did not know where he was being taken or for how long. He was starving. He had been beaten, worked nearly to death. He had seen his family sent to their deaths.

On this nightmare trek that ultimately led him to Buchenwald, Susskind recalled that some people were so exhausted that they simply lost their weakened grips on life. Others, so numbed by all that had happened, could no longer manage even the most basic human emotions.

"One time they loaded us up in wagons for beef or cattle, cattle wagons, and in each wagon twenty or thirty people, I don't know," he related. "It was wintertime, and I was talking [to] a guy like that, we were just talking. Most of the time we talked, 'Oh, a piece of bread, today in my house we would have, oh, the memories.' I talked to him, and all of a sudden he died. With open eyes and open mouth. It was cold. So we took the body behind us to warm us. That's the way you became. Like animals. You just tried to help yourself. In a wagon like that, fifty percent died. People were like a sculpture, all of a sudden dead."

In April 1945, with Germany just days away from losing the war, the Nazis continued their anti-Jewish campaign without relent. Susskind arrived finally at Buchenwald, a massive concentration camp near the historic city of Weimar.* The facility was swollen with prisoners brought in from the freshly evacuated camps in Poland and elsewhere in the east.

On April 13, 1945, Arnold Susskind at last became a survivor.

"It was sunny," Susskind said of the day he will never forget. "It was very breezy. We were sitting in the barracks. They called us out to the assembly place and gave everyone a half loaf of bread, some marmalade, and some cheese. And we know right away something is wrong. And they said, 'Whoever wants to go with us, marching with us, can go. If not, you can stay here.'

"All of a sudden American planes start flying around very low, so they were very confused SS men. They screamed,

---

*The constitution that defined the German state between 1919 and 1933 was drafted in Weimar.

'Everybody in the barracks.' Finally the planes stopped flying. They called us out again. 'Who wants to go?' And one of my close friends, we were together eleven months, he said, 'Arnold, I'm going.' And I said, 'If they have to shoot me, let them shoot me.' "

Even if Arnold had believed that this time, after so many deceptions, he could trust these SS men asking him to leave the camp with them, he was far from certain that he was physically capable. He weighed only seventy pounds. He could barely walk. He was so weak with hunger he felt that being shot while eating a last piece of bread might not be such a terrible way to go if that was to be his fate. Many inmates, however, did go with the SS men. Half an hour later Susskind heard the all-too-familiar rattle of machine-gun fire.

"An SS man came over me and called me in German, 'You shitty man,' or something like that, 'are you still alive?' And he hit me with the lower part of the gun, the butt. In my face. I started bleeding. Next to me was a poor Czechoslova-kian, not a Jewish man. And he [the Czech] laughed and kicked me and said, 'Finally you are dead.' I make believe I'm dead. I plopped down on my face. An hour later I was liberated."

After spending a few weeks recuperating at Buchenwald, which had come under American military control, Susskind set about trying to track down his wife. Once again he found himself not knowing exactly in which direction to move next. Europe was in bedlam. The chaos felt familiar, but the sudden rush of freedom was overwhelming.

The feeling of displacement was also reminiscent of Po-land immediately after the Nazi invasion in 1939. Then Poles who had been his friends and former schoolmates overnight became his enemies. Now the Germans, who one week before would have turned him in to the Gestapo, were smiling politely and offering him clothes and food.

A few weeks after the formal surrender, when Germany was carved into four military occupation zones, Buchenwald fell under Soviet control.* Susskind again found himself on a plot of land that had changed hands several times in quick succession. Once more he faced the decision of whether to go east or to go west.

During World War I Polish Jews had welcomed the Germans as liberators from Soviet domination. During World War II Jews had felt much safer being east of Germany, away from the threatening Nazis and toward the friendlier Soviets. Now most Jewish survivors wanted nothing more than to be as far west as they could go. The trauma of forced mass migration once again defined the Jewish experience on the European continent.

There were many reasons Jews were not eager to return to the lands coming under Soviet control. Among the most compelling was the fact that for so many Jewish survivors there was nothing but graves to return to in Poland or Russia or Romania. All their property had been stolen. All their families had been killed. To the west there was at least the promise of a new start.

In spite of the risks involved in returning to Poland, Arnold was determined to find out what had happened to Sally. He had last seen her at the Plaszow work camp near Krakow. She had been strong enough to work there, so perhaps she kept up energy enough to last until the end. One way or another Susskind had to know, so he turned back toward Poland. In the confusion surrounding Buchenwald's transfer from American to Soviet hands, Arnold managed to grab

*Britain took administrative control of the northwest sector, including Hamburg; France occupied the southwest region; the United States took the central and southern regions, including Stuttgart; and the USSR took eastern Germany. Berlin, although deep in the Soviet zone, was itself divided into four zones. Austria was similarly divided into four zones of occupation.

some sheets of leather from the camp stockroom. When he got to Krakow, traveling mostly on foot, he sold the leather for gold.

In Krakow Arnold learned that many Jewish women had ended up at Bergen-Belsen, an enormous concentration camp just south of the northern German industrial city of Hamburg. Arnold didn't even bother going back to Przemysl or Mielec. He already knew there was no one left of his family there.

The gold Arnold had acquired helped him buy passage back to Germany through Czechoslovakia. He had to bribe his way across the military borders and pay for guides through the unfamiliar territory. After several months he finally made it to the gates of Bergen-Belsen. Immediately he recognized some people he had known in Poland.

Susskind was ecstatic when he heard that his wife indeed was still alive. It was nothing short of a miracle. And then he heard the bad news. Just a few hours before he had arrived, that very morning, Sally had left the camp to return to Poland to look for him. They had just missed each other. "I came in on the railroad on one side; she left for Poland on the other."

This time Arnold stayed right where he was, deciding it was best to wait for Sally at Bergen-Belsen. He could only hope that once she got to Poland, she would run into someone who had seen him there when he had passed through and that she would realize he was waiting for her back in Germany. That is exactly what happened.

Anna Unger Weinberg was one of the women at Bergen-Belsen who broke the news to Arnold Susskind that his wife, Sally, was still alive and that she had gone back to Poland to look for him. After resting up herself, Anna went back to Poland, as the Susskinds each had done. Unlike the Susskinds, twenty-one-year-old Anna was not going back to look for anyone in particular. She had her own reasons for going back to Przemysl.

"I fulfilled the promise I made to my father by going back to Poland after the war," Anna explained, the sound of defiance still firm in her voice. "I showed them they couldn't destroy me." The "them" Anna referred to were not Nazis. They were Poles.

Anna's father had fought in the Polish Army during World War I and had been captured and held prisoner in Tashkent, the capital of the former Soviet republic of Uzbekistan, just north of Afghanistan. Upon his return to Przemysl Anna's father had started a family and managed the family farm.

Anna was the eldest of four children. She was bright and attractive. At the Hebrew academy, which her father helped establish, she studied "bookkeeping, sewing, dietetic cooking, Hebrew, mathematics, everything." Because she was a good student, other kids would sometimes steal her homework.

More than forty-five years after her return to Przemysl, Anna recalled her childhood home with a longing. In her comfortable home in suburban New York she wept when she spoke of the home that was lost forever.

"We lived on property that had been in my family for several hundred years," she related, explaining that her family lived in the part of Przemysl called Zasanie, which means "on the other side of the San." "We had twenty cows. We had maids. We had Polish people who would help us with the harvest. It was green fields. A mountain was on one side, a river on the other."

Just before the German Army invaded Poland in 1939, her father received a warning. "Before the Germans came, there was one Polish guy, and he said to my father, 'The Germans are coming, and they're going to kill the Jews,'" Anna recalled. "My father hit him over the head. Then the Germans came and said all the Jews have to go to the other side, to the Russian side."

Anna and her family were given no time to pack. They had to leave almost everything they owned. Her father tried to stay behind the rest of the family to protect their belongings; but a Pole notified the Gestapo, and her father was forced to leave. As Anna and her family evacuated their own property, they witnessed the looting. "The Poles were over there, grabbing the cows and all the things from the house," Anna remembered tearfully. "They were some scum, taking all of our possessions."

Through the terrible years that followed, Anna watched as her three brothers and her parents were taken away to the gas chambers. She survived, sometimes hiding, sometimes just being lucky. She even worked for about one month as a housekeeper for Schwammberger. Like Sam Nussbaum, she had been forced at gunpoint to help load the trains bound for the death camps.

Shortly after she ran into Arnold Susskind at Bergen-Belsen, Anna set out for Przemysl. Traveling in Germany was relatively safe since the Allies had come in and the German forces had been decimated. But traveling in Poland for a Jew was still plenty dangerous. There were numerous incidents of anti-Jewish violence, even killings long after the last Nazi crematorium fires were extinguished.

The most infamous incident occurred in the Polish town of Kielce on July 4, 1946, when forty-two Jews were murdered in a rampage of hysterical violence triggered by a false rumor that a Polish boy had been kidnapped by two Jewish men. The dead, killed by axes, stones, and gunshots, included two children and one man who could be identified only by the tattoo on his forearm, a number that indicated he had been at Auschwitz.[5]

Tens of thousands of Jews, those who had been taken in by Polish and Ukrainian families, those who had hidden in the woods or in the sewers to survive, took the pogrom at Kielce as a clear sign that they could not stay in Poland. They had clawed their way to survival, but their connection with the country their families had known for centuries could not endure the Holocaust.

When Anna arrived in Przemysl, she went directly to the police station. "I went to the chief of police and told him I wanted my cows back," Anna said. "I wanted to give them to an orphanage." Actually she would have given them to anyone as long as she could have had the satisfaction of reclaiming them from those who had stolen the animals from her family six years before. The police chief thought she was kidding, but when she refused to leave, he finally agreed to send several police officers along with her.

Anna went to the homes of those she suspected of having taken the cows, with the police officers following behind her. She collected four of the animals with little resistance. One woman put up a fight. "The woman said she had paid my father and had a receipt. I said, 'What receipt?' She said to wait for her husband to come home. So we're waiting there, me, seven policemen, the cows tied up outside, and this woman."

Suddenly several scowling young Poles came into the house. They had heard that Anna was there and of the reason for her visit. Anna recognized the men as having been active collaborators during the Nazi occupation. "One says to me, 'You? You still alive?' And I say, 'You can see it.' I was young and childish then. I should have realized."

Anna could see she was in trouble. But there did not seem to be a way out at this point. "And then this woman comes in and says she is a friend of my father's. She says she must tell me a message before anything else happens. She takes me into the other room, closes the door, and opens the window. She says, 'Have you ever run for your life?' "

CHAPTER 8

ZERO HOUR

On this eighth of May, let us face up to the truth as well as we can.

—Richard von Weizsäcker, president of Germany[1]

In the days following Josef Schwammberger's arrest in Innsbruck, Austrian police began the process of gathering information on the captured SS sergeant. Working under the auspices of the French military authorities who occupied the far western part of the country, the local police interrogated Schwammberger's friends and family members. In their possession they found and confiscated eight large cloth sacks filled with gold, coins, and jewelry. Schwammberger had smuggled the loot into the country over the course of the several years he was on assignment in Poland.

The Nazis had appropriated and extorted from the Jews since Hitler came to power in 1933. Thousands of businesses had been "Aryanized," meaning they were simply taken away from Jews and given to Germans. When a Jewish family was deported, a German or Polish or Hungarian family moved into the vacant dwelling.

The Nazis conjured up the most barbarous taxes ever

conceived. After Nazi thugs ransacked the Jewish communities of Germany and Austria on *Kristallnacht* in 1938, the Nazi government levied a one-billion-mark payment from the Jewish community to pay for the damage inflicted on it. Later Eichmann's elaborate organization for deporting Jews from all over Europe to the death camps in Poland relied on funds appropriated from Jews to cover the cost of the transports. Over and over again the Jews paid an enormous victim's tax.

The stolen property in Schwammberger's possession—which the Austrian authorities at the time valued at more than fifty thousand dollars—represented a tiny fraction of the Nazi plunder of the Jews. But the sacks of valuables were graphic evidence of the human destruction Schwammberger had brought to the Jewish communities he had liquidated. Each gold watch had belonged to a human being; every coin had been part of someone's life savings; every wedding band had symbolized a promise, a future, a love.

In a signed statement to police, Schwammberger acknowledged that he had been a member of the Waffen-SS, not the German Army, as he claimed when he was first taken into custody. He also described in detail the contents of the bags of property. One sack, he told the Austrian police, contained "cigarette boxes, a gold watch, fine gold, 2 American $20 bills, 2 small gold pieces, pearls, a cravat pin, a watch, 2 gold rings."[2]

But Schwammberger insisted that he had done nothing wrong to acquire the stash of valuables. He told the police that various Jews had given him their belongings as gestures of gratitude for being taken out of the nonworking ghetto—he was clearly referring to the ghetto at Przemysl—and for being moved to the workshops in the so-called Ghetto A, where life was marginally safer.

"He kept to his story," the Innsbruck chief of police reported in a memo to the local district attorney, "that the jewelry was forced on him, particularly by camp inmates or their relatives, because they apparently thought that acceptance amounted to a tacit agreement [that they would] receive better treatment."[3]

Schwammberger had other explanations for the jewelry. One of the sacks, he told police, contained gold pieces and other valuables he had found "in an abandoned house, once occupied by Jews." Another sack contained valuables he claimed to have found buried in the cellar of a village farmhouse.

Perhaps Schwammberger figured that none of the many Jews who saw him demanding the gold and jewelry and those from whom he had actually stolen the property could possibly have survived the war to challenge his version of events. Perhaps he did not believe that people like Salamon Balsam from Mielec would live through the camps and death marches and deprivations to show up in Innsbruck one day and point to the gaps in their jaws where Schwammberger himself had used pliers to yank out gold-filled teeth.

In cold and direct terms Schwammberger also admitted to police that he had killed thirty-five escaped prisoners during his tenure as commandant of the Przemysl labor camp. In the statement Schwammberger wrote:

From February 1943 until February 1944, I was in charge of a labor camp in Przemysl, which had been created from a section of the ghetto by barbed wire and declared a labor camp. Jews were working there repairing Wehrmacht clothing and shoes.

There were frequent escape attempts [and] in most cases the escapees were brought back by the Security Police. The penalty for attempted escape was execution. The Security Police turned to me and told me that it was my responsibility to carry out the executions. Although initially declining, the Security Police served me with a written order signed by a superior, S.S. Police Leader Scherner, stating that I was duty bound to carry out the executions. From there I understood that escapees brought back by the Security Police were to be shot. I do not know if any actual legal proceedings preceded execution.

Altogether, I carried out executions on 35 individuals, shooting them in the back of the neck with a pistol from a range of 10 centimeters (about four inches). If they showed any signs of life, I then shot them in the temple. Workers from the camp were then called to bury the bodies on the spot. No clergymen were brought in, nor was there any medical attention.

Schwammberger admitted his involvement in two additional killings. In these two instances, he maintained, he was acting in self-defense. "A prisoner from one detail was handed over to me by the S.S., who informed me that they would be coming back for him," Schwammberger asserted in the confession. "He attacked me and went for my weapon. In the ensuing struggle, the gun went off, killing the attacker. A man in the same detail had been hiding in a ghetto house. When he rushed out, I shot at him, and he was killed."

Schwammberger's confession is important because it remains the most detailed public account of his own actions that he has ever given. Of course, in the statement he made no mention of his leading role in the roundup of Jews from the ghetto during the final deportation from Przemysl in September 1943. Nor did he mention at all the other two villages whose Jewish populations he had exterminated, Rozwadow and Mielec. In the statement Schwammberger made no reference to the many random shootings he had committed, to the tortures and other acts of violence for which he was responsible, or to the mass executions he ordered and in which he actively participated.

The confession, in fact, was an exercise in self-exoneration. Schwammberger made it sound as if he were a mere pawn, swept along by events, forced to execute a few escaped prisoners by order of his superior officer, forced to kill a couple more to defend himself.

Schwammberger detached himself from the killings in another way. He described the incidents as if he had been merely a witness to events rather than responsible for them. In the course of his struggling with one prisoner, the gun simply went off, and then, somehow, the prisoner was dead. With the second prisoner, Schwammberger admitted firing the shot but distanced himself from the result by noting that the prisoner "was killed," as if the death were not connected to his own action.

The captured SS man could not deny what had happened. He had been there. He could only shrug off any suggestion of blame. He could only hope to escape the truth about his past.

But Schwammberger could not escape, for in the end the Holocaust was not about extermination but survival. Enough people did survive the attempted genocide to tell of what really happened. As many documents as the SS destroyed, enough survived to support many of the claims of eyewitnesses. Between the paper and the memories there was enough proof to indict those responsible, including Josef Schwammberger.

While Schwammberger awaited his fate in an Innsbruck jail, Austrian prosecutors began to assemble materials for a case against him. Polish authorities, too, were gathering evidence and statements from eyewitnesses in preparation for a case against him. If the Poles were able to win custody of Schwammberger, he would stand trial in Krakow. If that happened, he would likely be sentenced to death and hanged.

After a few weeks in the municipal jail Schwammberger

was transferred to a detention camp for suspected Nazi criminals located not far from Innsbruck. The French-administered camp was called Oradour, named for a small town in central France, Oradour-sur-Glane. There in the summer of 1944, the SS had waged a terrible massacre in which all but 10 of the 652 village residents—men, women, and children—were herded into a barn and into the church and burned to death.

The French later moved Schwammberger to another prison just a few miles away in Kufstein, a scenic mountain town near the German border and not far from Berchtesgarten, Hitler's favorite Alpine vacation retreat. In Kufstein Schwammberger was held in the tower of a thirteenth-century castle that still sits on a hill overlooking the sleepy resort town.

Schwammberger had come full circle. Out of the dislocation and disorder that had defined his youth following the First World War, he had finally found his place among the smartly dressed, proud-stepping SS men. Now, in the chaos that consumed Europe in the wake of the Second World War, Schwammberger was home again. And he was lost again. The order of yesterday was gone, along with the millions who had died at the hands of his comrades.

As Schwammberger contemplated his fate, he could look down from the stone tower of the Kufstein castle to the people below, then desperately trying to restore their lives to normal. They could do so. The end of the war also marked the chance for a new beginning, a reawakening for Germany. Not so for Josef Schwammberger. For the rest of his days he would be branded, as clearly as the blood tattoo under his arm.* Although he might come very close, he would never escape from his Nazi past.

*Each SS member was given a small tattoo under one armpit that identified his blood type.

. . .

As the Allies assumed control of Germany, the realities of the Holocaust and of six devastating years of war in Europe came painfully into focus. Hitler had fought long past the turning point and had led his country and the rest of the Continent to ruin. Germany itself had become a wasteland and would have to be rebuilt completely. There were no social or political institutions, no economy, no services but those provided on an emergency basis by the occupation powers.

Once again the Continent was swarming with displaced civilians. Refugees, Jewish and non-Jewish, poured into camps in Germany and Austria and France and Italy by the hundreds of thousands in hopes of obtaining visas to Palestine and South America and the United States. Many fled from the Soviets. Many were simply homeless for one reason or another.

The Allies set about the extraordinary task of rebuilding Germany in two main areas. First, the country's infrastructure had to be restored. The occupational powers, therefore, set about providing basic services and administrative authority until the Germans could reconstruct their own political system.

The second part of the recovery effort proved much more challenging. It became clear, even before the conclusion of the war itself, that in order to rebuild Germany, there had to be some radical structural changes imposed on the German people. The Allies had learned an important lesson after the First World War: It was not enough simply to disarm the defeated enemy. The enemy must be forced to undergo a conversion. The forces that had led to the aggression had to be cleansed from German society.

The Allies' concept of cleansing, however, had a far different meaning from the one the Nazis had given the term. Cleansing now had nothing to do with actually exterminating individuals. It had everything to do with eradicating nazism.

Immediately after the war, then, the Western Allies set about attempting to re-create Germany in an image that would better serve their political and economic interests, as well as the interests of long-lasting peace. The judicial system was slated for overhauling, and Nazi judges were purged. School textbooks were rewritten, with references to Aryan racial theories removed, and Nazi teachers were pulled from the schools. Every stratum of society was marked for similar therapy. The Allies called this overwhelming undertaking denazification.

Perhaps the most important element of denazification was the plan to prosecute and punish the major war criminals and the perpetrators of the Holocaust. The point was not simply to round up as many criminal suspects as possible and shuffle them through a makeshift judicial system. The Allies actually hoped the trials would provide some lasting guidance on democratic values.

This aspect of denazification was considered as vital as the longer-term efforts to redraft Germany's constitution, rewrite its textbooks, restaff its schools and lower courts and municipal bureaucracies. The trials, it was hoped, would reorient the very way Germans thought. Officials at the highest levels of the American political and military establishment envisioned the Nazi trials as a means just as much as an end. As one historian of the war crimes trials program has noted:

> To many influential Americans, particularly President Roosevelt and Treasury Secretary Henry Morgenthau Jr., the Germans' apparent preference for militarism and authoritarianism had already led to two world wars and the murder of millions of innocent civilians. To avert a recurrence, they had concluded, the Germans needed to

be democratized. As part of this program, these officials decided to use the trials of war criminals to not merely bring the perpetrators to justice, but to demonstrate the evils of totalitarianism.[4]

Most Germans were relieved that the war was over at last and were eager to make a new start. Those in the western zones of the defeated country, moreover, were especially thankful not to be under the thumb of the Soviets. But many also resented denazification as the imposition of victor's justice.

Many Germans fretted that accepting the Allied war crimes trials program meant accepting the idea that all Germans were guilty of the crimes of the Nazi era. The unprecedented scope of the denazification effort indeed made many Germans believe that the Allies blamed all Germans, not just the Nazis. And although there were a number of Germans duly horrified as the concentration camps were opened and the extent of the Nazi Holocaust was revealed, there were not many receptive to the notion of collective guilt.

In fact, the reaction of many Germans was to turn away altogether from any serious reflection about the Nazi past. From the moment Germany's defeat became official, they began to consign the past to the past. The Allied reeducation efforts served only to harp on the atrocities committed in the name of Germany and the humiliation of defeat. Germans, in general, wanted to start over, to regard the day of Germany's capitulation, May 8, 1945, not as a day of mourning but as a day to mark the start of a new Germany, a renewed Germany.

The challenge of denazification, then, was to satisfy the desire to reorient German social and political thought without going so far as to touch off a counterproductive reaction among the German people. But this was not easily done. The Allies faced monumental difficulties in deciding who should be denazified—that is, who should be fined or jailed or punished even more severely. The question was where to draw the line, which, again, was a question of degree.

But striking this balance was a nearly unattainable goal. The Allies firmly believed that hundreds of thousands of Nazis should be punished, but the idea that all Germans were responsible was flatly rejected. That left open a treacherous middle ground. Would an armed camp guard in charge of shooting Jews trying to escape the gas chambers be held less accountable than the one who flipped the switch to turn on the gas? Would the young SS men who snuffed out thousands of innocent lives in the course of an afternoon's work be excused simply because they were following orders?

What about Josef Schwammberger? He had a lowly SS rank, *Oberscharführer* (technical sergeant), so he had many superiors giving him orders. But he also killed with his own hands, under his own independent authority, of his own free will. He was not at any of the major camps, such as Auschwitz or Dachau. Was the relevant measure, then, the number of people killed or the size of the facility or camp he commanded? Would everyone assigned to every small village in all of occupied Europe be held responsible for the Holocaust? There were thousands and thousands of members in the SS. Would they all go to jail?

These were then and remain today difficult questions. Certainly, as far as the pursuit of justice is concerned, as far as the prosecuting of an individual for Nazi crimes, there is an obvious and significant difference between someone who cheered Hitler on the radio but otherwise went about his business and someone who served in the SS Death's-Head Battalion.* But distinguishing the bystanders from the vil-

---

*Members of the Death's-Head Battalion, or the Totenkopfsturmbann, were specially trained SS troops whose particular domain was the administration and guarding of concentration camps.

lains was not always so obvious, especially in the postwar turmoil in Germany.

Naturally these debates raged most intensely among Germans who were not all of one mind about what they had just been through. On one extreme were diehard Hitlerites who vowed to carry on their Führer's campaign, to fight from the hills if necessary. Then there were those who refused to accept the fact that the positive aspects of Hitler's vision for a proud and respected Germany could have become so perverted. Many retired into a state of despair as they understood that again Germany had been defeated and was humiliated in the eyes of the world.

One of the most difficult aspects of the denazification program for the Germans themselves was the notion that justice could be dispensed after the fact. Many argued that it was not inconsistent to argue that what happened under Hitler had indeed been evil, but after all, it had been the law.

Although today it seems inconceivable, it was indeed the law of the land in Germany to discriminate against Jews, to strip them of all rights, to deny them access to schools and business and professions, to steal from them, to move them forcibly into ghettos, and finally to shoot them. The Holocaust, moreover, did not take place overnight. The process of extermination was a progressive one, and every phase was authorized at the highest levels of the Nazi government.

And although there may be those who can legitimately claim they did not realize that Jews were being gassed and cremated by the trainloads at Auschwitz and Belzec and Treblinka, every German, from the youngest to the oldest, knew full well that the law of the land, that the will of the Führer had come to dictate a "final solution" to the "Jewish question." These were not alien concepts. These were freely and widely, if often euphemistically, discussed. If Hitler had won the war, those who were rounded up for prosecution would instead have been lining up for national honors as German heroes.

So rather than judge those whose actions were in the past, before the so-called zero hour, before the start of the new Germany, many Germans believed it would be much better to get on with the business of the present. Of course, there were some nasty times under Hitler, many Germans argued. But the present was plenty challenging, and the future was calling.

The denazification program both challenged and supported this popular impulse. On the one hand, trying thousands of Nazi criminals forced Germans—and, indeed, the world—to focus on the past, to listen to the facts, to hear the truth about atrocities so terrible they would scarcely have been believable otherwise. In fact, many Germans did not believe the stories of death camps and mass graves and gassing vans. The trials lifted the veil on the past and made it real.

On the other hand, by creating a system of judging actions on a relative scale—some crimes were more heinous than others; therefore, some Germans were more guilty than others—the Allies created a means for separating the past from the present. Individual Germans were encouraged indirectly to see their own conduct as distinct from "those Nazis," the ones really responsible for the crimes of the past.

Many Germans, like Schwammberger in his confession, practiced denial to greater and lesser degrees. They said they had not known or understood what was going on. Perhaps one could argue that they should have known. (How could the residents of the town of, say, Dachau, for example, *not* have known what was going on behind the barbed wire of the concentration camp in their small town?) Certainly many did know and simply closed their eyes and their ears and their noses.

After the war many continued to protest ignorance. "The

major concern was for individual survival: for self-justification, a whitewashing of the past," one historian of the period has observed. "Most Germans now attempted to represent themselves as always having been (at least secretly, whatever their outward behavior) 'against it,' and as having had the best of motives for having done, or belonged to, whatever they did. Some observers bitterly commented that, the way Germans were talking now, Hitler must have been the only Nazi in Germany."[5]

Not every German practiced denial, of course. There were many who were shocked and overwhelmed as the truth about the Holocaust became more and more clear. To some the shame and guilt were psychologically crippling. In their eyes, no matter what one might think about collective guilt, Germany had become a nation of criminals. The impact was devastating, even for those who could not have had anything to do with the Holocaust because they had not yet been born. One German writer, born the year after Germany's defeat, captured powerfully the feeling of personal shame:

[Germany is] a country trapped in unaccepted guilt where the Nazi past covers the natives like an adhesive coat of corrosive material that makes you want to peel your skin off. . . . You watch TV, it can be 1965, 1972, 1989. You see footage of Auschwitz and the liberation of Dachau, your eyes fill with tears, your stomach contracts, you look at your father if he happens to be sitting next to you, and if not, you think of him—and you curse your relationship to him. You want to scream, hide, tear your genes out, burn your passport, be a Martian instead of being part of these terrible people, but all you are is a helplessly German daughter with nowhere to hide.[6]

The extent to which the goals for the denazification program became muddled did not ease the overwhelming confusion of feelings over the question of responsibility. Today the term "war crime" is very familiar, but in 1945 the idea of prosecuting another country's leaders for war crimes was still very new. There was no unanimity over who should be denazified, who should be prosecuted, or even what exactly a war crime was. No country or group of countries had ever attempted such a program before, let alone one on so enormous a scale.

As far back as the early Greek societies there were attempts to devise "rules of war." Efforts to codify guidelines for the "humane" conduct of war continued throughout modern history, leading in the mid-nineteenth century to the first international agreements on the treatment of prisoners of war and related issues. But until the 1940s there had never been established any sort of international mechanism for enforcing these agreements, let alone any precedent for the victors in a war occupying the losing country and putting the defeated nation's former leaders on trial.

The Allies had contemplated trying German war criminals after the First World War, too. In the months following Germany's defeat in 1918, the Allies debated the idea of trying members of the German military who were believed to have committed so-called war excesses. But Germany protested strenuously, and the Allies conceded finally to allowing it to handle the matter itself.

German courts did hear a number of cases of alleged war crimes and in one proceeding actually convicted several German soldiers charged with mistreating Allied prisoners. Their sentence, however, was lenient, and overall, the German government proved it was not much interested in making a sincere effort.

In October 1943 Allied leaders meeting in Moscow set in motion the process of making certain that Germany would not escape judgment a second time. The Allies agreed that all Nazi war criminals would be punished to the fullest extent

possible and began making plans to try the most important
Nazi criminals. Later it was decided that there should be a
joint Allied tribunal to prosecute leading Nazi figures.*

The Moscow Declaration, which came out of that summit
meeting, further stated that other Nazis and German officers
involved in "atrocities, massacres and executions will be sent
back to the countries in which their abominable deeds were
done in order that they may be judged and punished."[7]

On March 24, 1944, President Roosevelt proclaimed,
"None who participate in these acts of savagery shall go
unpunished. All who share in the guilt shall share in the
punishment."[8]

Such bold promises were unprecedented. In sweeping
rhetoric the Allies had declared hundreds of thousands of
Germans to be war criminals. Part of the confusion that
resulted from the imposition of war crimes prosecutions was
the scope of the war crimes concept, which encompassed
acts within the traditional understanding of battlefield crimes
as well as those that could only be considered in a new and
separate category called "crimes against humanity."†

The complexity of the Nazi "war" against the Jews raised
some of the most confounding questions. For example, the
Allies debated whether crimes committed before the official
start of the Second World War could be included in the
scope of any Allied-sponsored war crimes trials. After all,
the first concentration camps had not been set up to house
prisoners of war; they had been for political opponents of

*Although France had been taken out of the fighting in 1940, the
French were included among the Allies in important postwar decisions
and were included as the fourth member of the war crimes tribunal at
Nuremberg.

†There were actually three categories of "war crimes" prosecuted at
Nuremberg: war crimes, crimes against humanity, and crimes against
peace, which referred to the planning and waging of a so-called aggressive
war in violation of international treaties.

Hitler and other social and political "undesirables," such as Communists, homosexuals, Jehovah's Witnesses, and especially Jews.

In the end the Allied powers did reach enough of an agreement on prosecution objectives to hold one joint trial of the major Nazi perpetrators. And in keeping with the idea that the trials should act as a means of reeducation as well as a forum for finding justice, the punishment of those convicted at the first Nuremberg trial was handled in a highly symbolic manner.

In the early-morning hours of October 16, 1946, the four-power International Military Tribunal disbanded as the last of the ten Nuremberg convicts sentenced to death was cut down from the gallows. The bodies of the executed Nazis, as well as that of Hermann Göring, who had committed suicide in his cell just hours before, were driven to nearby Dachau, where they became the last bodies to be burned in the concentration camp's crematorium.

For many Germans the drama of Nuremberg undoubtedly bolstered the hope that the Allies were interested in trying to make a point and not necessarily in waging a top-to-bottom sweep of the country. If the Allies were more interested in show than substance, then perhaps they were not so committed to the rhetoric of the 1943 Moscow Declaration and later pronouncements.

But the international tribunal at Nuremberg was not the end of what had already taken shape as a massive prosecution program. Nor had it even been the beginning. The Soviets had been prosecuting those guilty of Nazi atrocities since 1943. Four months after the Red Army liberated the eastern Polish city of Lublin in July 1944, the Poles held their first war crimes trial, in which six SS guards from the Majdanek death camp were convicted and sentenced to death.

Britain, too, had moved swiftly to get started with prosecuting Nazi criminals. Even before the four-power Nuremberg tribunal was able to organize and commence its work, the British tried Josef Kramer, the commandant of the Bergen-Belsen concentration camp, and forty-four of his deputies. Kramer and ten others were sentenced to death.

Once the first and only international tribunal had completed its work, the Allies conducted separate trials in their own administrative sectors of the former German state. The British held their proceedings in Italy and in northern Germany. France tried scores of Nazis in North Africa, Germany, and France.

The Americans continued to hold their primary court in Nuremberg, where an additional twelve multidefendant proceedings against so-called major criminals lasted until April 1949. In addition, the U.S. military authorities tried many Nazis at various other locations, including Dachau, which was converted, appropriately, from a concentration camp into a detention facility for suspected Nazi criminals. The Soviets, meanwhile, tried Nazis at home and in their many satellite states.

The denazification program became more controversial and more unpopular the longer it dragged on. One reason for the mounting discontent was the inconsistency of commitment to the program among the Allies and the evident waning of that commitment over time. Generally the Soviets, having suffered more losses on the battlefield and in the POW and concentration camps than any other country, were the most eager to punish their former enemies, and they did so swiftly and severely for the most part.

The Americans, having been the power farthest removed from the hostilities and the greatest of the wartime atrocities, became less and less enthusiastic about denazification as passions over the coming cold war began to boil. The British became increasingly preoccupied with their collapsing overseas empire, and the French were firm in their resolve to prosecute Germans in their custody but were cautious about raising too many disturbing questions of Vichy complicity.*

As soon as the Allies went their separate ways, their prosecutions started yielding widely varying, even blatantly conflicting results. This only advanced the argument that Allied justice in occupied Germany was arbitrary and that there could be no effective standards of international law.

In March 1946, for example, the British convicted two directors of a Hamburg factory that had manufactured Zyklon B, the poison gas used at Auschwitz and other death camps. The British court rejected the defendants' assertion that they had been unaware of how their product was being used and that therefore, they should not be held accountable. The British sentenced the two men to death.

Just one year later the Americans tried twenty-four directors of the industrial giant I. G. Farben, the largest supplier of Zyklon B and a major employer of Jewish slave labor. This time the American court accepted the very similar defense claim that the company executives had not known the gas was being used to exterminate concentration camp prisoners and acquitted the defendants on that charge.[†]

The Allied authorities themselves recognized that the denazification mission entailed certain hazards. And these political realities ultimately tempered the level of commitment to a sustained prosecution effort. Not only did these realities limit the Allies' ability to make good on their vow to hunt down *all* responsible Nazi criminals wherever they

---

*The Germans occupied northern France beginning in 1940. An unoccupied zone existed in the southern part of the country, with a collaborationist government based in the spa town of Vichy.

†Several of the defendants at that trial were convicted on other charges, including the use of slave labor at Auschwitz and other camps. None of those convicted, however, served sentences of more than a few years, and by the mid-1950s many had returned to prominent positions in German industry.

were hiding, but they prevented a thorough and hard-nosed reckoning with even those Nazi criminals in Allied custody.

One factor that gave the Allies pause was the still-fresh memory of Versailles. After World War I Germany had been made to pay dearly for provoking that terrible conflict. It had been divested of its colonies and territory long regarded (by Germans) as German, including chunks of fertile land that were given to France and Poland and Czechoslovakia. Germany was also disarmed and stripped of its industrial machinery.

Germany had suffered tremendous loss of life and property during the four years of bloodletting. The postwar punishments imposed by the Allies were like salt to the wounds. And Hitler, exploiting the deeply bruised German national ego, had rallied his people against these indignities. The German leader had promised a national redemption.

These lessons were not forgotten as the Allies debated Germany's future in the wake of World War II. If the measures imposed on postwar Germany were again overly harsh, there might be a backlash. If the Allies were not severe enough, there was every danger of angering the Soviets, who, with twenty million war dead, were in no mood to show any leniency toward the Germans. The Allies recognized that the great challenge was to strike the proper balance.

The American commitment to prosecuting Nazi criminals, in particular, further suffered in some specific instances from a direct conflict of interest within the American government. While the American armed forces were rounding up suspected Nazi criminals, members of military intelligence units and the Office of Strategic Services, the predecessor agency to the CIA, were racing the Soviets in the grab for German scientists.

Many of these individuals, perhaps most notably Wernher von Braun and Arthur Rudolph, two of the world's leading pioneers in rocketry science, were spirited to the United

States after the war. They were protected by their military handlers, who spared no effort in making their lives comfortable while they continued their scientific work. U.S. government officials went so far as to doctor personnel records to conceal incriminating biographical data on the scientists, such as evaluations of the fervency of their support for the Nazi cause.

In Rudolph's case, as with many others, there was even strong evidence of participation in Nazi atrocities. Rudolph was a project manager at an underground German missile factory where slave laborers by the thousands were starved and worked to death.[9]

Whose side was the U.S. government on? One arm of the government was rescuing individuals from prosecution as Nazi criminals by another arm of the same government. Not only were the lives of many German scientists spared, but some even went on to become American folk heroes. Rudolph and von Braun, most notably, became pioneers of the American space program and were richly rewarded and decorated for their service.

The factor that most compromised the will of the Western Allies to sustain vigorous prosecutions of Nazi criminals was the speed with which the Nazi threat was replaced by the Soviet threat. Almost as soon as the world war ended, the cold war began. Attention quickly shifted away from punishing the Nazi criminals of yesterday and toward containing the new villains, the Communists, both those abroad and those supposed to be lurking about at home.

As tensions between the West and the Soviet Union became increasingly aggravated, the United States and Europe looked to the western half of the bisected Germany to serve as a buffer against the perceived threat of further Communist aggression and possible expansion. Keeping the West Germans, the anti-Communist Germans, happy and loyal became of paramount importance.

Still, at least in the first few years of Allied occupation in

Germany, these all were merely speed bumps, not road-blocks to the prosecution of hundreds of Nazis responsible for thousands of deaths and other atrocities. All in all, the three Western occupation governments convicted some five thousand Nazis. More than eight hundred were sentenced to death. Some five hundred actually were executed.[10]

There are no reliable statistics on the extent of the Soviet government's prosecution of Nazis, although it is widely known that trials were held all across its postwar (and subsequently cold war) sphere of influence. Many scholars believe that a great number, if not all, of the trials were summary and resulted in death sentences or hard labor. As many as fifty thousand Germans were probably tried by all the victorious powers, according to several estimates.

Meanwhile, no matter how wide the Allies cast their net in the mad scramble to round up and prosecute Nazis, untold thousands managed very easily to slip through the innumerable gaps and disappear into the chaos of postwar Europe. Many Nazis simply adopted false names and returned to their hometowns. Some did not even bother going to that much trouble.

Still other Nazis, including some of the most notorious figures in the SS, escaped the hangman's noose and a confrontation with the deeds of their past by leaving the ruins of Europe far behind. Many joined the throngs inundating the U.S. Immigration Service. Many went to Canada and Australia. One of the most popular destinations, and the destination Josef Schwammberger set his sights on, was South America.

CHAPTER 9

INTO
OBSCURITY

The bloody massacre in Bangladesh quickly covered
over the memory of the Russian invasion of
Czechoslovakia, the assassination of Allende drowned
out the groans of Bangladesh, the war in the Sinai
Desert made people forget Allende, the Cambodian
massacre made people forget Sinai, and so on and so
forth until ultimately everyone lets everything be
forgotten.
—Milan Kundera[1]

O n the second evening of the year 1948 Josef
Schwammberger made his move. Daily life in
war-scarred Europe, incredibly, was already starting to return to normal. Refugee camps had finally begun
emptying; townspeople were digging their cities out of the
rubble; hundreds of thousands of German POWs were returning home to their families. The Allied commitment to
prosecute and, in hundreds of cases, to execute Nazis responsible for Nazi crimes had begun to wane, although by no
means had it dried up completely.

New crises and international concerns were fast becoming
more immediately compelling than those of the past. Even
among Jews the urge to look ahead intensified. Before the
end of the war a Jewish underground had begun leading
illegal transports of Jewish refugees to Palestine. After the
war Britain's policy of refusing increased Jewish emigration
to Palestine fell apart as international public opinion swung

to the side of the convoys of determined Holocaust survivors that confronted Royal Navy ships off the beaches of Haifa. There was every reason to look to the future.

But the past was not quite forgotten. At the start of 1948, only the third full year after the war, American, French, and British courts in occupied Germany were still hearing hundreds of cases of Nazi crimes. Dutch and Norwegian courts were also trying Nazis responsible for atrocities in their countries, as were courts in most of the Eastern European countries.

Meanwhile, Schwammberger continued to sit out these dramatic developments in his prison cell at the castle in Kufstein, Austria. In 1947 he had been transferred back to Oradour, the makeshift French detention camp not more than twenty miles from his hometown of Innsbruck.

Schwammberger then was thirty-five years old, the father of two young boys (his wife had given birth to their second son, Horst, in early 1946, while he was in prison), and a man with everything to lose if he stayed where he was. Life was passing him by, as was a steady traffic of Nazis fleeing Europe through Austria, over the Brenner Pass south of Innsbruck, and down from the Alps into Italy en route to South America.

If Schwammberger did not manage to find a way to join the Nazi exodus out of Europe, he would soon find himself before a judge. The senior federal prosecutor in Innsbruck had finally begun to organize the various materials for a case against him. On December 12, 1947, the prosecutor had sent an urgent memo to the federal police headquarters requesting all documents and records on Schwammberger, strongly suggesting that he was ready to proceed at last. In addition, the prosecutors already had statements from several eyewitnesses to atrocities and murders for which Schwammberger was responsible, as well as the signed confession he had given to Austrian police.

The Polish government, too, was eager for Schwammberger to stand trial. U.S. military authorities headquartered in Munich had already signed off on an extradition request from the Polish authorities, who had collected numerous damning statements from survivors of the labor camps Schwammberger had liquidated. In its extradition request, the Polish government had charged that Schwammberger was "responsible for maltreatment, torturing, looting and mass murder of many Polish citizens" and that the "subject [has a] bestial thirst for blood [and has] killed in this camp [Przemysl] many Polish and Jewish babies."[2]

By the beginning of 1948 Schwammberger's fate had still not been decided. The occupation governments, while certainly concerned with bringing Nazi criminals to justice, had been forced to manage many other crises in the process of restoring order and the foundation for future self-rule in Germany. After two and a half years in prison Schwammberger had been lucky to have lasted as long as he had without having been brought to trial. He could not wait any longer. At any moment he might be called to account for his deeds.

After he had complained of headaches and sleeplessness, Schwammberger's Austrian guards agreed to provide him with sleeping pills. Instead of taking the pill he was given each night, he hoarded the drug. When he had amassed a potent dose, his means of escape was set.

Security at the Oradour camp, like that at many of the makeshift detention facilities holding suspected Nazi murderers all over occupied Germany and Austria, was slack. The Nazis had reinforced ruthless security with terror at their prisons and concentration camps for men guilty of nothing. But the Allies were notoriously deficient in detaining even the most notorious Nazi criminals.

As Schwammberger was practically in his own neighborhood, he was able to coordinate his escape with his friends and family back in Innsbruck. The guard watching Schwammberger, a fellow Austrian, was friendly, and Schwammberger was charming. They shared a drink, and Schwammberger managed to slip him the sleeping pills. As he ran from the camp, he was met by a friend who took him by car toward the Italian border.[3]

Details of this episode are murky at best. Newspaper accounts written four decades after the fact generally misstated the story of his escape from Oradour. One popular version, which was widely retold in different newspaper accounts, had Schwammberger leaping from a train taking him to Salzburg, where U.S. military authorities supposedly were waiting to put him on trial for war crimes.[4]

Even more interesting than the fact that Schwammberger did not escape from a train and that the Americans had no plans to try him was the similarity between this account and a popular fictional story of a fugitive Nazi. Frederick Forsyth in his 1972 novel *The Odessa File* told of an SS man who is being pursued by a dogged German journalist and does jump from a train carrying him to, of all places, Salzburg.[5]

Another account of Schwammberger's escape from Oradour suggested that Schwammberger fled not toward Italy but to Spain.[6] Yet another article credited ODESSA with engineering Schwammberger's escape. ODESSA was one of a number of secret organizations of former SS members widely believed to have given financial support and other comfort to refugee Nazi criminals.* In fact, there is no evidence that Schwammberger received assistance from ODESSA or any such group. In any case such underground organizations surely had their hands plenty full after the war assisting much higher-ranking former officials than SS Sergeant Schwammberger.

With or without the assistance of an SS underground, the

---

*The name is an acronym for the Organisation der Ehemaligen SS-Angehörigen (Organization of Former Members of the SS).

fact remains that it was not difficult even for a major Nazi war criminal to remain inconspicuous amid the tremendous chaos of postwar Europe. And it hardly required any effort to find a means off the continent all together.

From Oradour Schwammberger was driven to Matrei, a small Alpine village less than ten miles north of the Brenner Pass, the border crossing between Austria and Italy.* Schwammberger continued on foot across the mountain passage and down into the Italian-controlled Tyrol. Schwammberger stopped in Bressanone, the village where he was born. He stayed there for three weeks before continuing his journey.

When French officials found out the next morning that Schwammberger and two other former SS men had escaped from Oradour, they demanded from the Austrian police "an immediate and determined search throughout Austria for the . . . war criminals."[7] The Austrian police inspector who had arrested Schwammberger two and a half years before also sent a memo to his fellow police officers involved in the search. The inspector described Schwammberger as "a very dangerous fellow." Police were instructed to check vehicle and pedestrian traffic across the international borders, as well as the Innsbruck home where the Schwammberger family had lived for years. But the efforts were too little too late.

Initially the Austrian police suspected that Schwammberger planned to head north to meet up with his wife, Kathe, who had previously left Austria with their two young sons and was staying with family in her hometown of Eberbach, near the medieval German university town of Heidelberg. Possibly she had arranged to rendezvous with her husband in the town he had known as Brixen before he set

---

*Innsbruck is situated at a very narrow part of Austria. The city is only a few miles south of the German border and perhaps twenty miles north of the Italian border.

out again along the already well-worn Nazi escape route to
Italy. Perhaps her stay in Eberbach was intended all along
as a way of diverting attention away from her husband's real
plan.

For the next year Schwammberger lived alone and worked
as a manual laborer near Florence. Postwar Italy was teeming
with foreigners, so he had no trouble blending in with the
crowd. Refugees from all over Europe had flocked to the
country, hoping to make passage from one of the country's
busy ports.

One day the local police stopped Schwammberger on a
commuter train because he was without identification papers.
At the police station in Florence he was directed to the local
office of the International Red Cross, where he was told he
could obtain the necessary identification documents. There
was no effort to investigate Schwammberger's background.
There was no concern over his lack of identification. In the
tumult of the postwar period, with so many people in flux,
it was nearly impossible to distinguish legitimate refugees
from wanted criminals. Still, the Italian police in effect gave
Schwammberger the key to Europe's back door.

For Schwammberger to get hold of the necessary documents required no great skill. In a formerly top secret memo
describing the status of all illegal emigration movement from
Italy, a U.S. State Department official reported in 1947 that
"although these International Red Cross passports are recognized as perfectly valid identity documents, they in fact
identify nothing." Identification papers were easy to falsify,
the State Department official found after an extensive undercover investigation. These papers then found their way into
the far-reaching Italian black market. "How many dealers
engaging in the traffic in fake International Red Cross passports, who have obtained them by going back repeatedly
under assumed names or aliases, will never be known."[8]

Proving not only that he required no great skill but that
he possessed none, Schwammberger failed to take advantage

of an opportunity to protect himself further by changing his identity on his new false papers. Adolf Eichmann, Schwamm-berger's former comrade from the Austrian Legion, followed virtually the same path to Italy a couple of years after Schwammberger, but he assumed an alias, Ricardo Klement, which he continued to use during his years of hiding in Argentina. Many other fugitive Nazis did the same. But not Schwammberger.*

When Schwammberger left Hamburg after abandoning Poland to the advancing Russians, his SS superiors had handed him forged travel papers in the name of Josef Hackl. He had given that name when he was arrested in 1945 until the Austrian police figured out who he really was. But he neglected to use that name again—or any other alias—when he obtained his bogus Italian passport from the Red Cross.[9]

Still Schwammberger's new documents did take him a long way from the prosecutors back in Innsbruck and in Poland. They had missed their chance during the many months he spent in prison. With his phony papers in hand, he could also thumb his nose at the country occupying the city where he had been raised as he boarded a French Liberty ship docked in the port of Genoa and bound for South America.

At the Red Cross office where he obtained his travel papers, Schwammberger had inquired about his travel op-tions. The Red Cross told Schwammberger he might con-sider the United States, Brazil, Bolivia, Paraguay, or Argentina. "Which one is most far away?" Schwammberger had asked the Red Cross worker.[10]

Josef Schwammberger's decision to flee to Argentina was an obvious choice for someone in his position. Buenos Aires,

---

*Of course, Eichmann's alias ultimately did not save him from capture and trial in Israel.

the city of "beautiful air," had already been the port of choice for hundreds of Nazis who had abandoned ruined Europe. The government of Argentine President Juan Perón had not been shy in welcoming such people. If Perón had erected a statue in the harbor of his country's capital, he might have had the inscription read, "Give me your tried, your prosecuted, your fearful." In the years after the war Argentina earned a reputation as the seat of the "Fourth Reich."

How had Argentina become so attractive a hiding place for so many runaway Nazis? One factor was the country's long-standing renown as an immigrant haven. Throughout the nineteenth century and during the first half of this century, Argentina was second only to the United States as the destination of choice in the Americas for Europe's emigrating throngs.

The country's population doubled between the years 1895 and 1914, to 7.8 million, one-third of whom, by the start of the First World War, were foreign-born. Some 80 percent of all Argentines were then immigrants or descendants of immigrants who had arrived after 1850. Argentines came predominantly from Spain and Italy, but there were large numbers of Germans, Russians, French, and Arabs, too.[11]

Argentina was also a popular destination for Jewish settlers. In fact, until the 1930s Argentina boasted one of the most liberal attitudes in the world toward Jewish immigration. By 1914 there were more than one hundred thousand Jews in the country, more than were then living in Palestine.[12] Between 1920 and 1930 more than seventy-five thousand Jews arrived, most fleeing the pogroms in Eastern Europe and Russia.[13]

Tremendous economic growth coincided with Argentina's population boom. The strong economy attracted more immigrants; more immigrants in turn fueled further economic expansion. The country's vast natural resources provided tremendous energy for both agricultural and industrial development. A largely European population also made the country an attractive investment for European capitalists, especially those from Britain and Germany.

The two decades preceding World War I brought an unprecedented economic boom to the country largely thanks to European immigrant labor and trade with Europe. Through the first several decades of this century Argentina was among the top five exporters in the world of corn, cotton, cattle, and wheat, to name just a few of its major commodities. By 1914 its per capita income equaled that in Germany.[14]

Cultural and political forces also paved the way for the large numbers of refugee Nazis who flooded into Buenos Aires after World War II. Argentina's political history had been dominated by leaders of powerful and rigid social institutions, notably the military and the Catholic Church. German immigrants were familiar with both, notwithstanding Hitler's rejection of organized religion.

Schwammberger's supposed reason for choosing Argentina also cannot be discounted as a main factor in drawing so many fleeing Nazis. The country was indeed far away from the clamoring prosecutors. It was also vast and under-populated. Obscurity was easily found. As one Argentine journalist noted, "In the 1950s we were 22 million people and we had 45 million cows."[15]

The rise of Perón in the 1940s was probably the most important reason why so many Nazis flocked to Argentina after the war. As unlikely as it seems, considering Argentina's national and ethnic diversity, a chauvinistic nationalist movement had gained considerable momentum during the 1930s. As with the German and Italian Fascist movements, the Argentine ultranationalists were fervently anti-Semitic, xenophobic, and anti-Communist.

Perón, who became the most influential leader in modern Argentine history, received his political education at the feet of Europe's leading Fascists. From 1939 to 1941 Perón was a military attaché in Rome, where he became a devoted student and admirer of Mussolini. When he returned to Buenos Aires during the middle of the war, he participated in a coup d'etat and was subsequently named minister of war and then vice president. He was elected president in 1946.

As the Argentine government moved sharply to the right, it clashed increasingly with the other major economic power in the hemisphere, the United States. The U.S. stranglehold on wartime markets in Europe further isolated Argentina from the Allied cause. In any case Argentina's military government was already inclined to side with the Axis powers. Its official policy of neutrality was widely interpreted as a vote of sympathy for Nazi Germany.

Tensions between the United States and Argentina continued to intensify with wartime passions. The United States denounced Argentina's government as Fascist largely because it refused to declare its allegiance to the Allies. Anti-Argentine rhetoric spewed from the State Department in Washington as Argentina continued to hold out during the final months of the war and, at least officially, remained neutral.

Finally, when there was no mystery left as to the outcome of the war in Europe, Argentina gave in to the wishes of the power that was clearly to dominate the continent in the coming years. On March 27, 1945, a little less than one month before Adolf Hitler committed suicide in his Berlin bunker, Argentina made the empty gesture of finally joining every other country in Latin America and declaring war on Germany.

Juan Perón, meanwhile, had been consolidating his power. For at least two years before he officially took control of the government, following his election in February 1946, Perón was the strong man behind a figurehead president. Perón bore all the trappings of a Latin dictator. He was authority incarnate. And he was charismatic. He enjoyed the support of the military and the church, and he courted the working class just as insincerely as Mussolini and Hitler had.

Not inconsistently Perón did nothing to discourage anti-Semitism among his followers. A gathering of Perón supporters—*Peronistas,* as they came to be called—often kindled anti-Jewish violence, as occurred during the night of November 25, 1945. Following a political rally in Buenos Aires, hundreds of *Peronistas* rampaged through Jewish neighborhoods in an evening of terror reminiscent of *Kristallnacht.*

"The police, who were present in great force, stood by passively while the Jews who had been knocked to the ground were savagely kicked," reported a *New York Times* correspondent on the scene. "The disturbances . . . have occurred with such regularity whenever large numbers of Peronistas have gathered, that it is hardly possible to doubt any longer that anti-Semitism forms a part of Colonel Perón's political stock in trade."[16]

All together, conditions in postwar Argentina could not have been more encouraging to Nazis looking for a safe and comfortable refuge from the dangers of life on the run in Europe. On May 4, 1945, just a few days before Germany's final defeat, one foreign correspondent noted that "among all the capitals of the countries at war with Germany, Buenos Aires has distinguished itself by being probably the only one where there were no public manifestations of joy over the fall of Berlin."[17] On the contrary, street demonstrators were more likely to shout support for Germany, admiration for Hitler, and hatred of the Jews.[18]

Not only did refugee Nazis find favorable conditions in Peronist Argentina, but Perón himself actually welcomed them into his country. Once Perón was elected president he did not turn his back on the soldiers of the Third Reich, even as he moved into line behind U.S. leadership in the Americas.

A newspaper profile of Perón several months after his February 1946 election made clear that the Argentine leader was determined to remain friendly with the survivors of the Nazi cause. After interviewing Perón, the correspondent wrote:

> Although Perón was one of the first [Latin American leaders] to realize that after the Allied victory Argentine rapprochement with the United States was the obvious course, and although he was prepared to give up lesser Nazi agents here and to smash what remained of German industry, he has stubbornly refused to yield the men Washington points to as the top Nazis. In fact, he has kept them close to his regime.[19]

In brazenly hypocritical fashion, while the U.S. government was excoriating the Argentines for sheltering Nazi fugitives, it was secretly recruiting top Nazi scientists for U.S. military research projects. In many cases these scientists had been involved in atrocities, including the use of slave labor from concentration camps and the use of camp inmates for inhumane and often murderous medical experiments.[20]

Further confusing the double-talk, the U.S. and Argentine governments actually cooperated in the recruiting of some of these scientists, with the Americans referring to the Argentines those German experts not needed in the States. The Americans were happy to deal with Perón on so sensitive and controversial a program. After all, making sure the former Nazi scientists enlisted with Perón's anti-Communist regime was far better than allowing them to sign up with the Soviets.

This was the world Josef Schwammberger and boatloads of other Nazi refugees entered during the first few years after the war. Perón promised to make Argentina a great nation, the leading power in South America. *El Líder*, as he liked to be called, vowed to make the country strong.* He

---

El Líder in Spanish means the same thing *der Führer* means in German: "the leader."

was not afraid to stand up to the imperialists, the Americans, the Communists, the Jews.

Schwammberger had traveled as far as he could from the smoldering remains of Hitler's Reich to resettle in the new world. Strangely, now that he was in Perón country, it was as if the world weren't so new after all. A power-hungry dictator was strutting among his generals, wagging his fist in front of masses of adoring citizens, foaming at the mouth over the Jews and the Communists. The only things missing from this Patagonian rehash of Germany-circa-1933 were a few concentration camps. The Argentine generals would correct that shortcoming before long.

From outward appearances and certainly from later statements, it does not seem that Schwammberger was much affected by his years as an SS commandant. He had been an SS man, so he could have found a sympathetic corner of the Argentine military where he could have worked and would have been welcomed, but he did not do so. Instead he returned to his pre-SS days, when he was a low-level clerk with a mediocre education struggling to find a dead-end job.

For a brief time Schwammberger had shown a flair for theatrical gestures of violence, whether he was storming through the Jewish ghetto on horseback or manipulating the cold terror of those minutes before an execution by drawing all eyes toward him as he donned his starched white gloves. Now, in a country known for its exuberance and grand romance, Schwammberger returned to his former status as a bland, faceless nobody.

This reversion, deliberate or not, was Schwammberger's key to survival. Even though the climate in Argentina was distinctly pro-Nazi, what mattered most was not being caught and sent back to face trial. And this was by no means assured, even half a world away from the scenes of his crimes.

As safe as the situation seemed in Perón's Argentina, Schwammberger could not have felt completely out of danger. He was, after all, a fugitive from justice. If he were discovered, the government might not consider him important enough to protect and might send him back to face possible execution.

Moreover, in spite of the rise of anti-Semitism under Perón, many Jews managed to break through the immigration barriers and enter the country during and following the war. Many ships filled with bedraggled survivors were turned away from the port in Buenos Aires during the war. But because Argentina was the only South American country to maintain political and economic ties with Nazi Germany, some courageous Argentine diplomats did arrange special visas for a handful of the Argentine Jews trapped in Europe.

After the war Perón promoted a renewed wave of immigration to help provide the labor for a massive reindustrialization drive. Tens of thousands of Italians and Spaniards came through Buenos Aires in the first few postwar years. Perón also specifically encouraged Ukrainians and Yugoslavs, among others. But immigration policy no longer favored Jewish settlers.

Even so, as many as fifteen hundred Jews, mostly refugees from displaced person camps in Europe, were granted legal entry between 1945 and 1949. More than ten thousand others entered illegally, smuggled in with the help of underground Jewish aid societies.[21]

The risk of recognition, therefore, was hardly nil, especially in the capital, where most of the country's Jews lived. A Nazi refugee's best hope for obscurity was to take advantage of the country's tremendous physical size. Outside Buenos Aires, there were distant mountain hamlets, vast grassy ranges—the pampas—and coastal villages so remote they were actually at the edge of the earth.

Upon arrival in the port of Buenos Aires, Schwammberger stayed a few nights in a fleabag hotel before landing a job as gardener on a farm owned by a German family outside town. The proprietor paid him no salary, only room and board. Several months later Schwammberger contacted Kathe back in Innsbruck, and she and their two boys prepared to join him.

After several months on the German farm, he left Buenos Aires for the Andean mountain town of San Carlos de Bariloche, an isolated outpost on the opposite end of the country near the Chilean border. The town enjoyed a reputation (and still does) for appealing to German émigrés. Germans were drawn to that mountainous region because the surroundings evoked memories of the Bavarian and Tyrolean Alps so beloved by southern Germans and Austrians.

In San Carlos Schwammberger lived among Germans, spoke German, drank German beer, talked about German politics, and enjoyed a life-style reminiscent of his youth. To support himself and his family, he got a job as a night porter in a hotel.

Finally, in the spring of 1953, Schwammberger ventured to the German consulate's office in San Carlos. He presented his old German passport, which he had rescued before setting sail, and requested a renewal. Not realizing whom it was dealing with, or perhaps not caring who he was, the consulate gave him a new German passport good for five years. No doubt the consulate outpost was accustomed to dealing with newly arrived Germans and simply winked throughout the renewal process.

Nearly forty years later German embassy officials in Buenos Aires insisted with appropriate vehemence that the German government would never have knowingly aided a fugitive Nazi, or any fugitive from justice for that matter. But at the time, these officials asserted, the German government simply did not know that Josef Schwammberger was a fugitive Nazi murderer.

Why would the German government, the German people consider themselves responsible for trying the Schwamm-

bergers of the world? The question points to what is argua-
bly the single most important force in postwar life in
Germany: the inescapable truth of the Nazi past and the
painful process of coming to terms with that past. Why not
Austria? Schwammberger was Austrian by birth after all.
What about Poland if that was where Schwammberger actually committed the crimes?

Austria had a very limited attention span when it came to
its connection to the Nazi past, even though it did try a
number of Nazi cases and had been prepared to try Schwammberger until his escape in 1948. At least in some part this
lack of interest in confronting Austrian complicity in the
Nazi Holocaust began with the Allies' coaching Austria into
thinking of itself as Hitler's first victim, not as a coconspira-
tor. The Allies had said as much in the Moscow Declaration
of 1943.

Poland was the country where the worst nightmares of
the Holocaust were realized, but the politics of the cold war
era were such that it would be many years yet before a
Western country would be comfortable delivering any criminal, even a Nazi criminal into the hands of a Communist
government. So Poland tried those Nazis it could get its
hands on, those who somehow had not managed to get out
of Poland before the Soviets overtook the country.

Schwammberger, and Nazis in general, came to be seen
as Germany's unique responsibility and special burden. Hundreds of Nazi criminals were brought to judgment, although
not necessarily to justice in German courtrooms in the decades following the constitution of the West German state
in 1949. These Nazis criminals, no matter that they had
been born in Austria, no matter that they had killed in
Poland, had served in the name of Germany. Only through
the effort of bringing fugitives like Schwammberger to justice might Germany move closer to clearing its name.

To many non-Germans the Nazi era remains both extremely familiar and completely alien. In our collective historical understanding we immediately identify nazism with evil incarnate. Photographs of concentration camp victims, newsreels of Hitler's furious orations, scenes showing the terrifying symmetry of columns of black boots goose-stepping—these images, products of our modern media age, over the years and after repeated reference have reinforced this idea. The Nazi evil has been burned into the world's consciousness.

But only for the Germans is the confrontation with that immediately familiar face with the queer black mustache a confrontation with themselves. No matter how sorely the German people might want to distance themselves from their Nazi past, no matter how many years pass, there can be no erasing that awful history in which every German, individually guilty or not, ultimately shares.

Günter Grass, one of Germany's most prized writers and long a staunch opponent of German reunification, speaks of "that permanent wound" and the "terrifying shame" of Germany's crimes.[22] In a speech commemorating the fiftieth anniversary of the German invasion of Poland, Grass acknowledged "the disgrace of the Germans," and argued that "there still remains, no matter how harshly we were punished, more than enough guilt, and time has not sweetened this sediment, a sediment that cannot be washed away with fine words."[23]

Not all Germans have confronted the Nazi past as aggressively and as frankly as Grass does. On the contrary, for many Germans the process of trying to forget the past began at "zero hour." For many Germans the past, too horrible to comprehend, too painful to accept, too remote (just as soon as it was over) to relate to, was better consigned to obscurity.

Josef Schwammberger managed to conceal himself in the far-off wilds among the expatriate Germans of the Argentine outback. His camouflage was adequate, if temporary, shelter from the world's memory. He was out of sight and forgotten. Germans back home could not have it nearly so easy.

In Germany the Allies were collapsing underneath the tremendous weight of their massive denazification program. Both elements of that program—the prosecution of Nazi criminals and the reeducation of the German people—were fast being undone by the political and economic realities of the day.

These realities, for example, demanded that many of those implicated in National Socialist activities had to be returned to positions of power and influence in their communities, like it or not. There simply were too many Germans who had been involved, in one way or another, in Nazi-related activities. There was no way Germany could be revived if they all were taken out of public life.

The weeding process had indeed created a feeling of bitterness among the German people as the numbers of Germans judged before ad hoc denazification tribunals reached into the millions. These tribunals, which were intended to prosecute only the lesser offenses, handed out modest punishments, ranging from a small fine to a few years in prison and the loss of civil service posts.

By the end of the decade, four years after Nazi Germany's surrender, it still was not clear how much longer the Allies intended to sustain the denazification program. Even following the so-called youth amnesty, which excluded from denazification those born after 1919, there were still backlogs of several million German citizens, many detained in massive temporary prisons.*

The scope of denazification was titanic. Reeducation, an-

---

*The modern-day version of the national shakedown might be the witch-hunt that followed the opening of the secret police files in the former East Germany. It was then revealed that a mind-boggling one in three East Germans had been a Stasi informant.

other important feature of the Allied effort, also proved unmanageable. A generation of German youth had grown up with Hitler's racial theories presented in school as if they were scientific gospel. Anti-Semitism and other mainstays of the National Socialist propagandist agenda had indoctrinated German children from the youngest ages.

But the Allies could not simply shut down the schools completely. And there were only so many qualified teachers. One historian who has assessed the Allied denazification effort in education concluded that ultimately it failed miserably. "As the Allies were helping the Germans to refashion their educational system, more and more of the old, questionable teachers were returning," this historian observed. "In Bavaria, by about 1947 at least 85 percent of the dismissed teachers had found their way back into the schools."[24]

Similarly, vacancies on the German courts quickly filled with judges who earlier had been found "unfit" because of their Nazi activities. As one British chronicler of postwar Germany found, "Within a year or two of the fall of the Third Reich it could be said that the judiciary in the Western zones had been well and truly re-nazified."[25] Many of these judges later were given responsibility for seeing justice done and, in a number of cases, for subverting justice when Nazi defendants came before their courts in criminal cases.

The problems that plagued these features of the denazification drive also bedeviled the Allies' program to prosecute those suspected of the gravest Nazi crimes. The scope of the effort was simply too enormous, and the German people exhibited a low tolerance for the occupation governments' idea of fair play.

Initially the Allies maintained a virtual monopoly on the prosecutions of suspected Nazi criminals. The legal authority the Allies claimed was a series of decrees, so-called laws drafted just before the end of the war. These "laws" were designed to cover actions never before covered by any law, such as "crimes against humanity," and generally to set the ground rules for prosecuting the Nazi offenses, both in the one international tribunal at Nuremberg and then in the subsequent independent Allied efforts.

According to these decrees, the Allies reserved for themselves jurisdiction over all crimes committed by Germans against Allied nationals. In a sense this meant that in the immediate postwar years, even if the Germans themselves had wanted to assume responsibility for prosecuting the major war crimes and Holocaust crimes, their hands were tied. As one expert on Nazi trials has observed, "This effectively removed most wartime offenses, including the mass murder of the Jews, from German judicial jurisdiction."[26]

The newly reconstituted and at least temporarily denazified German courts, however, were granted the right, with Allied permission, to hear cases involving crimes committed by one German national against another. This created a situation somewhat akin to trying to fit a circle neatly into a square. The German legal system is very different from the American and British systems, which are founded on common law traditions and rely on judges to interpret statutes. The German courts followed the more strictly defined German penal code. Unlawful activity under the code is defined explicitly. Judges do not interpret the law; they apply it.

In spite of the different judicial systems, the German courts were directed to apply the Allied war crimes decrees, which both helped and hindered German prosecutions of Nazi cases. On the one hand, Allied-manufactured law allowed German prosecutors great latitude in trying certain cases, such as individuals involved in *Kristallnacht* or the SS euthanasia killings of mentally retarded German children and adults. It also offered a shortcut through potentially thorny problems that would have arisen under the German system, not least of which was the fact that the law was retroactive. In addition, Control Council Law No. 10 "made no distinction between the perpetrator and his accomplice, rejected the defense of superior orders, and provided for penalties higher than the German penal code (which limited sentences other than death or life to a maximum of fifteen years.)"[27]

On the other hand, the use of the non-German law presented certain problems. One of the most fundamental principles of the German legal system—as in many legal systems—is the notion *nullum crimen sine lege*, a Latin expression that means "if it is not written, it is not a crime." Many German judges were annoyed at seeing individuals prosecuted for crimes that were not part of the German code. They chafed at the imposition of such a sweeping law as crimes against humanity and complained that the Allied law clearly violated the essence of the German legal tradition.*

From the German courts there came increasingly bold calls to be released from the burden of applying Control Council Law No. 10. In 1951 the Americans finally relented, and from that point on Germans were tried only for crimes defined in the German code. The broad-based crimes against humanity were certainly not among them. As a result, in the German courts Nazi criminals technically were not regarded at all differently from other criminals. Murder was to be treated as murder, whether or not the defendant wore the uniform of the SS.

Not for lacking suitable targets, the number of Nazis tried in German courts nonetheless dropped precipitously. In 1949 German judges convicted 1,523 defendants of National

*The Allies broadly defined crimes against humanity as including: "Atrocities and offenses, including but not limited to murder, extermination, enslavement, deportation, imprisonment, torture, rape, or other inhumane acts committed against any civilian population, or persecution on political, racial, or religious grounds whether or not in violation of the domestic laws of the country where perpetrated."

Socialist-related crimes. The following year the total dropped to 908. In 1954 the number plummeted to just 44. And the year after that there were a mere 21 Nazi convictions in German courts.[28]

Perhaps the most significant factor contributing to the steep decline in prosecutions was the change in attitude among the Allies themselves. The Germans saw the Americans and the British, too, struggling back home to maintain support for the denazification program. The examples set by the Allies did not inspire the Germans to be any more aggressive than necessary.

Why was American backing for the Nazi crimes program so vulnerable? One reason is that many prominent American lawyers and jurists, even some of those very much in favor of prosecuting Nazis, were uncomfortable with the absence of any appeal mechanism in the Allied Nazi trials. If one was going to hold up the American system of justice as representative of a morally superior social and political system generally, then it was disingenuous, these jurists argued, to hold up just part of that system. And an integral feature of the American judicial process was the right of appeal.

In some cases this argument was undoubtedly merely a foil, a legal rationalization for a more blatantly political posture. As the United States went to war in Korea in 1950, conservative sentiment in the United States increasingly came to see the Nazi perpetrators as the victims. The gruesome details of the Holocaust receded from memory the more relations with Moscow soured. Many Westerners began to recall that after all, the Nazis had been unbendingly anti-Communist.

The onset of the cold war further chilled American passions for trying Nazis in other ways. No sooner was Germany on the way to political and economic recovery than the Americans began applying pressure on the brand-new German government to rearm. The German authorities were more than happy to comply, under certain conditions, of course. In a word, the Germans wanted amnesty. And the Americans complied like a weak-willed parent giving in to a spoiled child.

On January 31, 1951, John J. McCloy, the American high commissioner for Germany, announced his plans for a massive and far-reaching commutation of sentences following a review of eighty-eight cases of major Nazi figures convicted during the twelve American-run Nuremberg trials. Many of those who had received life sentences, Nazis criminals responsible for tens of thousands of deaths, were free and walking the streets within a few years.

Indeed, in only ten of the eighty-eight cases McCloy reviewed was the original sentence left intact. Ten death sentences were reduced to life; fifteen inmates had their life sentences reduced to fifteen to twenty years; twenty-one Nazis saw their long-term sentences sharply cut; and thirty-one Nazis convicted at Nuremberg were released immediately, their sentences reduced to time served.

Clemency decisions continued at the persistent prodding of the German government. Private interests, such as German veterans groups and church officials, joined the call for amnesty. By October 1951 fully 50 percent of Nazi war criminals imprisoned in Germany had been released. As one historian concluded, "The United States had sold out its war crimes program—so had the British and the French."[29]

One of the first pieces of legislation to pass through the reconstituted Bundestag, the German parliament, was the First Law on Ending the Occupation, which formally repealed all Allied laws (including Control Council Law No. 10) and set December 31, 1956, as the date when the statute of limitations would expire on all crimes committed during the Third Reich with the exception of murder and manslaughter.

German attitudes clearly reflected a mounting dissatisfaction with the ongoing and probably, as far as many Germans were concerned, seemingly never-ending prosecution of former Nazis. That the Americans and the British and French, too, all were racing to release Nazis held in Allied prisons supported the impression that Germany's penance had gone far enough.

As the Allies lost their ability to concentrate on denazification, as well as their will to continue the Nazi prosecution program, the Germans lost their stomach for it, too. In an extensive survey of German opinion in the U.S. zone of occupation, American military pollsters found that in 1946 some 57 percent of Germans were satisfied with denazification. Two years later only 32 percent said they were satisfied. And in 1949 just 17 percent reported being satisfied. By 1953 a near majority of Germans, 40 percent of those polled, assessed denazification as having been detrimental overall.[30]

The longer the Allies remained in Germany, the more German attitudes toward Hitler and nazism softened. Partly this was due simply to the passing of time. But part of the revisionist romanticization of Hitler was definitely a reaction against the Allied denazification program.

Incredibly, in 1946, 40 percent of Germans said they believed that nazism had been "a good idea, just not well executed." Two years later an astonishing 55 percent of Germans held that view. By 1952 44 percent of Germans said they thought nazism had done "more good than bad."[31]

The backlash was hardly surprising. After all, as incomplete as the Allies' denazification program was, many Germans clearly believed that it had gone far enough. Many of the main perpetrators had been punished at Nuremberg and Dachau and at scores of other trial sites all across the territory of the former Reich. Hundreds of thousands of others had lost their jobs or worse following denazification proceedings.

By the early 1950s Germany was intent on the future, not

the past. Financial aid poured in to build again atop the ruins in both eastern and western Germany. There were even early signs of a coming prosperity.

The German people had been happy to stand up for the glory of the fatherland when Hitler was marching triumphantly across Europe. And German families had sacrificed for the boys at the front, as much as any other civilian population does during time of war. But by the end Hitler had brought the war home to Germany in devastating fashion. Now that it was over, there was farmland to be replanted, housing to be built, factories to be restored, sons and husbands to be mourned.

By 1955 the West German government had regained full sovereignty. And the German people increasingly began to consider the Nazi past neatly bundled and ready for disposal. The past was painful. But why dwell? The past could not be denied, but neither could it be changed. The present demanded everyone's full attention. And the future was on the way.

REDISCOVERING THE NAZI PAST

What are the roots that clutch, what branches grow
Out of this stony rubbish? . . .
—T. S. Eliot, *The Waste Land*

I n August 1992 a community improvement group in Milwaukee, Wisconsin, purchased an apartment complex for $325,000. In one of the units of the complex an ordinary-looking man named Jeffrey Dahmer had killed, dismembered, and in some cases cannibalized seventeen young men over a thirteen-year period. The discovery of the remains of some of the victims and Dahmer's subsequent arrest and trial shocked the entire country. Indeed, the Dahmer slayings became a sensation around the world.*

The Milwaukee community group decided to acquire the building in which Dahmer had committed these gruesome murders for one simple reason: The community members, including the distraught families of the victims, wanted the entire forty-nine-unit apartment complex torn down. One

---

*In February 1992 Dahmer began serving fifteen life sentences in state prison.

news account of the decision to buy the building noted that the "apartments had stood as a brutal reminder to the families of Dahmer's victims, who wanted it removed, as well as an unwanted attraction for gawkers visiting the neighborhood."[1]

The anguish in that community had been tremendous. Charges that the local police might have stopped Dahmer sooner only compounded the pain of the victims' families. Overwhelming shame over the way the victims had died made the grief over the deaths of loved ones that much more unbearable. The entire episode was just too painful to contemplate.

There is a common thread in the responses of those touched by the Dahmer killings and the Holocaust. The process of coming to terms with what happened in each case involves competing human instincts. On the one hand, it is natural to want to shelter oneself from pain, to try to eliminate or minimize or even lash out against the sources of pain. At the same time there is an implacable impulse to remember the past, however painful.

There are many vehicles for remembering the past: religious ritual, music and literature, physical monuments, informal reunions, and official commemorations. Those events honored through these means are not just joyful moments, birthdays and harvests and victories. In the United States, for example, November 22, the day of President Kennedy's assassination, is practically a day of national mourning. History itself is the study of not only the pleasant past but the entire past, painful and pleasant.

World War II was an all-consuming experience for most Americans, even though the physical ravages of the war were far from home. Not surprisingly, however, the moment from the war most widely commemorated in the United States, even after the passing of five decades, is the day of the Japanese surprise bombing of the U.S. military base at Pearl

Harbor. On that day the violence of the world war struck home most powerfully.

Germany's experience could not have been more different. Not only was the country physically destroyed, but the people were also emotionally defeated. Once again Germany emerged from several bitter years of fighting as the loser. Hitler had promised redemption for the humiliation of the November surrender that ended the First World War. Instead the country had been burned to the ground along with his maniacal visions.

On the surface Germany today appears healthy, strong, modern, successful. It is easy to forget that not so long ago Germany was a wasteland and that so recently the country, today one of the most important and most stable members of the Western alliance, was the most destructive power the world had ever battled. For Germans, however, the physical reminders of the ruin Germany suffered were and still are everywhere around them.

Visitors to the city of Frankfurt, for example, observe that the longtime capital of German banking and commerce today appears sterile, the skyline dominated by cold steel and glass structures, the feel of the place so un-European. Frankfurt lacks its former Old World charm and gives the impression that it was built from top to bottom with a postwar architectural sensibility, one that favored function over form, because that is precisely what was done.

In cities throughout postwar Germany the act of rebuilding was a cathartic experience. With each truckload of rubble carted off, with each new house that went up, with each new field replanted, the German people were rejuvenating their ravaged country. But in the process they were also attempting to bury the nightmares of their past just as surely as the victims of Jeffrey Dahmer's sordid killing spree tried to eliminate the reminders of their pain.

But clearly the past could not, cannot be erased completely. In Milwaukee the community association attempted to eradicate the physical reminder of a bestial serial killer. But there only one building had to be razed. Where would one begin in the land of the former Third Reich?

Complicating the question for many Germans was the irrepressible pride in German history, which, after all, had preceded the rise of Adolf Hitler by many centuries. Germany had given the world so many great thinkers, generals, scientists, and artists. Should the memory of all Germans, living and dead, average and glorious, be forever tainted?

Dachau, for example, had been the site of Hitler's first concentration camp. More than thirty thousand people had died there. It was a horrible place, where prisoners were starved and tortured, where cruel medical experiments were performed on living subjects, where SS men shot haggard inmates up to the final minutes of the war. Dachau had also been an internationally acclaimed artists' retreat during the nineteenth century and through the Weimar Republic.

How, then, should Dachau be remembered? Should the concentration camp be razed, like the apartment complex in Milwaukee? Could Dachau ever go back to being simply a quaint Bavarian artists' village? Or should the former concentration camp stand, a memorial to the cruelties of the Nazi past? Would the memory of the camp, because of the despicable crimes committed there during twelve years, overwhelm all previous and future memories of the place?[2]

In Berlin today the contrast between the ruined and the rebuilt is still visible and striking, as in few other German cities. Berlin holds many symbolic reminders of the changes that took place in Germany after the war and, just as interesting and important, the changes that did not take place. These symbols, some deliberate and some inadvertent, are sobering reminders of Germany's Nazi past.

One of western Berlin's most prominent landmarks, for example, is the bombed-out spire of the once-magnificent

Memorial Church to Kaiser Wilhelm. Allied planes reduced the building to a broken shell in the final campaign to take the German capital. In the 1950s Berliners debated whether to level what remained of the church. Berlin was rapidly being restored, and the looming husk of the church's tower stood out like a broken bottle on a smoothly swept beach. Ultimately it was decided to leave the eerie, hollow fragment as it stood.

But as one looks today at the battered church, surrounded by gleaming modern architecture, it is difficult to say if the memorial is intended as a reminder of what the Nazis did to Germany or of what the Allied bomber pilots did to Germany, or if, perhaps, the memorial is meant to recall both. Or perhaps the church shell remains as one of the few monuments to the Germany that existed before swastika banners draped the country.

For every German, those old enough to remember the church when it was whole and those too young to recall the sound of the whistling bombs that destroyed the structure, the ruin raises these questions. In Rome the ancient vestiges of Hadrian's Gate and of the grand Colosseum inspire pride in the history they recall. The Acropolis, on a hill high above Athens, also suggests a glorious past. Only time has eroded the structures that today make these cities historical wonders. This has not been the case with ruined Germany.

A few blocks away from the tattered Berlin church is the notorious Wilhelmstrasse area of the city. During the 1930s and 1940s the central offices of the most powerful Nazi organizations—the Gestapo, the Reich Security Main Office, and Hitler's headquarters and underground bunkers— were clustered along one small strip of this street. Inside the offices and conference rooms on Wilhelmstrasse, bureaucrats like Eichmann and Heydrich ironed out the details of the "Final Solution," generals orchestrated Hitler's military campaigns, and Josef Goebbels plotted his next propaganda blitz.

Wilhelmstrasse was buried under concrete rubble during the last days of the war. The area was sealed off in the following months until forty years later, when Berlin officials finally authorized excavations in the area. Underground torture cells that had been run by the Gestapo were discovered, along with the central offices of Heinrich Himmler and other SS officials. Amazingly, as part of a massive commemoration of Berlin's 750th birthday in 1987, city leaders organized the first documentation center and exhibit on the excavated grounds.*

As Reinhard Rürup, a German historian who prepared the exhibition catalog, noted, "A large segment of Berlin's population not only tried to forget the horrors of war as soon as possible, but also the crimes that had been committed while the Nazis were in power."[3] By the early 1980s, when Berlin officials agreed to allow excavation on the site, it was decided that "the area had been in oblivion much too long."[4]

After renewing his German passport at the German consulate in San Carlos de Bariloche, Josef Schwammberger waited another eleven years before becoming a full-fledged Argentine citizen on February 2, 1965. For all those years Schwammberger had been content to live as an illegal alien. Perhaps he figured there was a good chance of his returning home at some point. Perhaps he simply didn't see any point in risking another brush with the German government. The consulate might not be so accommodating the second time around.

Schwammberger's decision finally to obtain Argentine citizenship, just two weeks before his fifty-third birthday, was not spontaneous. There had been many changes in the world since he had come to South America, changes that had convinced him that he was not going anywhere near his

---

*The German government is converting the entire area into a museum.

former homeland and that if he did not soon acquire legalized status, his personal security might be in jeopardy.

Fortunately for Schwammberger, he had held on to the false Italian passport the Red Cross had given him after his escape from prison in Austria. That document had made possible his illicit overseas trip, and it allowed him to obtain citizenship a decade and a half later. As an Argentine citizen he would be safe, Schwammberger figured. And so he was, for a while.

Beginning in 1955, profound political changes had begun to eat away at the sense of security Schwammberger felt in the remoteness of his Argentine hideaway. In that year Juan Perón was toppled from power.

The Argentine dictator had inspired the extremes of love and hate among his people by the time of his ouster in a military coup. The regime he created had assumed a cult quality, an impression reinforced by the mass adoration of his blond princess, Evita. Perón styled himself as a classical Latin American liberator-hero, and millions of Argentines accepted him as a living myth.

But Perón had been unable to tame the Argentine economy, and that was his undoing. The United States, still smarting from Argentina's obstinate neutrality during the war, had not made the job any easier for Perón's economic ministers. In 1948 the United States had excluded Argentina from the rebuilding bonanza in war-torn Europe, which historically had been Argentina's largest market. The U.S. government's ban meant that Europeans could not use Marshall Plan funds to buy Argentine grains, meat, and other products. The restriction crippled Perón's efforts to spark a new industrial expansion.

The fall of Perón brought panic to the hundreds of Nazis who had grown comfortable in Argentina during the dictator's tenure. With Perón no longer in a position to assure protection, many Nazi fugitives left for other parts of South

America. Josef Mengele, for example, the infamous doctor from Auschwitz, left Argentina after Perón's downfall and sought refuge in a succession of remote villages in Bolivia and Paraguay.

Other major Nazi figures had already fanned out across the continent. Franz Stangl, the former commandant of the Treblinka death camp, had settled in Brazil after escaping from Europe. Martin Bormann, who had been among those hiding in Hitler's underground command center during the final days of the war, was rumored to be in various South American countries, including Venezuela. Klaus Barbie, the so-called Butcher of Lyons, had moved to Bolivia. Walter Rauff, the SS man who developed the mobile killing vans, had since made Chile his home.

Others, including Adolf Eichmann and Josef Schwamm-berger, decided to weather the political storms in Argentina. Schwammberger had his wife and two sons with him. After so many separations they were at last a family again.

The Schwammbergers had never known anything to-gether but a life of constant moving from one place to another, from one job to another, and, during the war, from one Nazi camp to another. The pattern of Schwammberger's life before and during the war followed him in his new life in Argentina.

Just as he had in Austria and Germany during the 1930s, Schwammberger switched around from one low-level job to another with great frequency. After a couple of years as a night porter in a hotel in San Carlos, Schwammberger took a job at a plantation about twenty miles from town. For three years he worked for the German proprietor there as a laborer raising pigs and chickens.

In 1956 Schwammberger returned to the coast, to the small city of La Plata, located about forty miles south of Buenos Aires. There he bought a modest house on the re-mote outskirts of the city.

La Plata was a very good spot for someone who wanted a life of obscurity. First, the city was far removed from the bustling capital, despite its geographic proximity. Named for the great inlet that cuts into the continent between Argentina and Uruguay, La Plata was a dusty rural town, like the sort found in Kansas or in California's Central Valley. Buenos Aires was self-conscious in its pretension to Europeanness. In its more elegant sections the capital seemed like Paris, with romantic architecture and grand boulevards and stylish shops and restaurants. La Plata had the feel of a cow town.

Not only was La Plata itself remote, but the part of the city in which Schwammberger lived could hardly have been called a legitimate part of the city. The barrio, or neighborhood in which he lived, was called *la cumbre*, which in Spanish means "the summit." But *la cumbre* was not atop anything. The barrio and its surroundings were flat as far as one could see. The house, which Schwammberger largely built himself, was little more than a shack, bounded by broad shade trees on a sparsely settled, unpaved road several miles from the center of town.*

La Plata was not an obvious choice, however. Many Nazis had congregated in other parts of the country, such as Buenos Aires, where they could lose themselves among the crowds. There were numerous Nazi communities in the mountainous province of Córdoba to the west and in the vast and sparsely populated region to the south, the rough country of Patagonia, made legendary by the Argentine cowboys, the gauchos.†

The town in which Schwammberger settled was thor-

---

*To this day the neighborhood remains undeveloped.

†It is strange that even today nearly every Argentine with whom one speaks takes as a matter of fact that these Nazi communities still exist. No one seems much disturbed by them or terribly surprised that nothing is done about them.

oughly indistinct. But the fact that La Plata was so humdrum a location may well have been precisely its chief attraction. "La Plata is a middle-class city with nothing special for him," noted Raúl Kraiselburd, the editor of the main daily newspaper in La Plata.

Dr. Raúl Ángel Nicolini, a veterinarian in La Plata, bought the house from Schwammberger in 1980. Nicolini, a solid, strong man whose three young sons run barefoot in the yard chasing after nervous hens, recalled that Schwammberger seemed like a decent person. "I was told when I moved in here that he was decent as a man, as a neighbor, and as a citizen," said Nicolini, adding that Schwammberger also had a reputation for keeping to himself.[5]

Schwammberger kept not only to himself but out of sight. For a time he worked as an orderly in a small hospital. He worked for several years on an assembly line in Buenos Aires for Siemens, the German electronics firm. He worked as an administrative aide at a petrochemical plant near his house in La Plata.

Schwammberger's life was obscure, but he had his wife and two sons. They had a home. He could always manage to find some job or another. All that was saying a lot for a former SS man who had narrowly escaped the gallows. The Schwammbergers did not have much in the way of material comforts, but at least they were free. The panic and chaos of the war and of the home they had left behind were indeed very far away.

In May 1960 panic returned to the quiet world of Schwammberger's remote refuge. Under the nose of the Argentine police, Israeli intelligence operatives captured his former comrade from the Austrian Legion Adolf Eichmann and spirited the so-called Architect of the Final Solution back to Jerusalem. The dramatic arrest of one of the most notorious Nazi figures touched off an international uproar.

The Eichmann trial—the first of its kind in Israel—raised

extraordinary and troubling questions.* Some among those
who supported the decision to undertake the daredevil mission to snatch Eichmann out of Argentina and to hold the
high-stakes trial worried about going too far in trying to be
fair to the man responsible for coordinating the transfer of
hundreds of thousands of Jews to the death camps. After all,
Jews had not received fair trials in Nazi Germany before
they were "sentenced."

Others, Jews especially, were anxious about the prospect
of so openly exploring the still-fresh memories of the still-
painful past. Israel had been born out of the Holocaust. The
will to rebuild the Jewish community, the need to look
forward, and the energy and determination of the survivors
had created an atmosphere of confidence and strength during the first years of the newborn country. Israel itself was
tangible proof that Jews had been heroes in addition to
martyrs. Millions of Jews had been killed during the Holocaust, but the Jewish people had survived. Now with the
world watching, Israel was going to delve into the dark
closet of the Nazi past and expose the pain and suffering of
millions of Jewish victims.

Critics of the plan to try Eichmann carped that Israel
could never be impartial, that he would not receive a fair
trial, and that one injustice did not justify another. Some
said Israel had no right to try Eichmann, even though the
law under which Israel claimed jurisdiction, passed ten years
earlier, had been modeled on the Allied decrees that had
formed the legal foundation for the Nuremberg trials.

Although many in the international community admired
Israeli ingenuity in tracking down Eichmann all the way to

---

*A surprising number of people today assume that Israel has tried
dozens upon dozens of Nazis criminals over the years. In fact, there have
been only two Nazi trials in Israeli history. That of Eichmann was the
first. John Demjanjuk's was the other; see page 224.

South America and supported Israel's right to try him, the Argentine government, for one, was irate. Arturo Frondizi, who had skillfully maneuvered himself into the presidency by attracting support from both the army and former Perón supporters, appealed to the United Nations Security Council to punish Israel for violating Argentina's sovereignty. Although most members of the Security Council were inclined to support Israel, the principle of national sovereignty threatened to persuade many, including the United States, to lean toward Argentina's position.

The UN diplomats finally achieved a compromise that was sufficient to assuage Argentina's wounded national pride. The Security Council debate had served to air Argentina's dispute, and with a qualified apology from Israeli Foreign Minister Golda Meir, the dispute was resolved.

The trial and Eichmann's conviction and his hanging in the early hours of June 1, 1962, had an enormous impact around the world. In a stirring passage at the end of his account of the trial, prosecutor Gideon Hausner described some of the thousands of letters he received from around the world.[6] One Jewish teenager wrote that she had never had uncles and aunts to visit on the Sabbath, and now she finally understood why that was so. A Jewish man wrote asking Hausner to make sure to charge Eichmann, on top of everything else, for the deaths of his three daughters who all had been killed at Treblinka.

The reactions from Germany were particularly moving. One angry German teenager wrote to Hausner to say, "We were not all Nazis. Now that people are beginning to forget must you remind them again?" Another letter came from a German couple that had just visited Dachau. No punishment, they wrote, was too severe for Adolf Eichmann.

Eichmann's capture and trial also resounded loudly for the many fugitive Nazis hiding out in South America, just as the fall of Perón had several years before. Shortly after

Eichmann's arrest, Schwammberger sent his wife and two sons back to Germany. They would not be bothered there. But if the Israelis or anyone else came looking for him, there was no telling what might happen. Schwammberger knew he would have to wait and see if the situation cooled off before figuring out when his family might be together again.

The political situation in Argentina became more and more unstable. And Schwammberger and the other wanted Nazis hiding out in Argentina never did receive a signal that the coast was clear. Instead, soon after the furor over Eichmann's trial, there was another booming signal indicating that they should continue to lie low.

In 1962 there was an upheaval in the Casa Rosada, the presidential palace in Buenos Aires.* A new government came in, and soon another Nazi in hiding went out, this time with the endorsement of the Argentine president.

The army had once again taken hold of power in March 1962 following President Frondizi's political demise. Many Argentines had grown frustrated with his inability to stimulate the economy and to curb inflation. Frondizi's secret meeting with Che Guevara, the Argentine-born hero of the Cuban Revolution, had provoked an outrage. The president's apparent catering to the interests of the left-wing Peronist elements in the labor movement, finally, was more than the right-wing forces in the military could stomach.

But the Argentine Army was not of one political mind. One faction, which came to be known as the Blues, included those who were sentimentally loyal to the exile Perón. Some actually favored the return of Perón himself as well as a regime founded on his style of authoritarian populism. These Peronists were decidedly more reactionary than the liberal

*Casa Rosada means "pink house," which is more or less the color of the grand colonial building that houses the executive offices of the Argentine president.

and socialist splinters that also claimed Peronist roots. The other faction in the military, known as the Reds, was staunchly anti-Perón and favored a strict military dictatorship as the surest formula for the country's political and economic revival.

The split in the dominant conservative forces in the country allowed a moderate, Arturo Illia, to win election the following spring. Illia, a country doctor before his entry into politics, certainly won the election, but he never became a popular leader. Still, as the economy rallied during his first months in office, he managed to hold together a fragile coalition.

Illia was leader of a faction of the anti-Peronist Radical party, which had been locked out of the president's palace since 1930. Immediately he began making overtures to Argentina's Jewish community, which numbered nearly five hundred thousand and was the world's third-largest Jewish community outside Israel. In meetings with Argentine Jewish leaders, Illia promised to ensure that anti-Semitic attacks, which had persisted throughout the Perón regime and the military juntas that followed, would cease. Historically opposed to the *Peronistas*, Illia's Radicals had long counted on Jewish political support. The new president's gestures were also part of an attempt to clean up Argentina's image, both at home and abroad.

But President Illia simply did not command enough support in the military to make good on his vows. Anti-Semitic outbursts continued during his term as both right-wing and leftist groups jostled for ways to damage his administration's credibility. Members of a right-wing nationalist organization, Tacuara, began attracting increasing attention in 1964, as they waged terrorist attacks against Jewish businesses and professionals.

On January 29, 1965, for example, Argentine police stumbled on the terrorist base camp of a group of neo-Nazi thugs in the wooded area near the Buenos Aires airport.[7] The commandos that very night had been plotting to bomb the homes of some two dozen prominent Argentine Jews. After an exchange of machine-gun fire, the terrorists dispersed. All the neo-Nazi hoods escaped.

The police did manage to confiscate swastika flags, maps showing which houses would be attacked, Nazi literature, and caches of small explosives. Eight months later police arrested some of the suspected participants, including a certain Horst Eichmann. Apparently one of the group's aims was to protest the trial and conviction of Horst's father, Adolf Eichmann. The son of the convicted Nazi was released the next day on the basis of insufficient evidence.[8]

Illia was not completely without means to retaliate against these reactionary elements. In August 1963 Gerhard Bohne, a sixty-one-year-old German lawyer, jumped bail in West Germany and fled to Buenos Aires. Bohne was fleeing charges of complicity in fifteen thousand murders during the Nazi euthanasia program, in which a total of some two hundred thousand mentally and physically disabled people were exterminated.

Bohne had first arrived in Argentina in 1949, the same year Schwammberger and dozens of other Nazis flooded the South American continent. When Perón was brought down in 1955, Bohne left South America and returned to Germany. Less than a decade later he was again seeking refuge in Argentina from postwar justice. After fifteen years the difference was that there was no Perón to protect him and Germany was prepared to come after him.

The West German government requested Bohne's extradition in February 1964. Just one month later Bohne was arrested in one of the Argentine capital's upscale neighborhoods. Denying direct involvement in the euthanasia killings, Bohne claimed that he had held a purely civil administrative post and therefore should not be prosecuted.

Although there was no formal extradition treaty between Argentina and Germany, President Illia, two weeks after Bohne's arrest, issued a special decree authorizing the fugitive's deportation.

In spite of Illia's decisive action, for a time Bohne's fate remained uncertain. The Argentine economy stalled, and with Illia's base of support already weak, he could not withstand the simultaneous pressures from the army factions on the right and the Peronist labor unions on the left. On June 28, 1966, Illia reached the limit of his political stamina. Yet another military junta assumed control of the government.

Illia's downfall marked the beginning of many years of terrible violence and unstable politics in Argentina. As far as Bohne was concerned, the president's military successors were not inclined to initiate a nationwide sweep of Nazis, but neither were they prepared to give the international community any more reasons than already existed for withholding support for the new regime. The army was already widely reputed to have affiliations with right-wing, anti-Semitic groups. Setting free a wanted Nazi would hardly improve that image. Argentina's economy depended too heavily on exports, principally to the United States and Europe. So the generals decided not to stand in the way of Bohne's deportation.

Nearly three years after his arrest Bohne was taken under heavy guard to the Buenos Aires airport and put on an airplane to Germany. Just six years after Adolf Eichmann had been stolen away from Argentina, Gerhard Bohne became the first Nazi officially expelled from the country.

Even as the Holocaust was taking place, many Germans were consumed with the desire to forget. "We had heard talk that the Jews were being killed," a former German army officer testified at the 1968 trial of eleven SS men charged with complicity in the murder of seventy thousand Jews in Russia and Ukraine more than 25 years earlier. The witness told the court that he and others had seen columns of Jews marching by, thousands of Jews being led to their deaths. Many of those were among the thirty thousand on their way to be machine-gunned at Babi Yar, the now-legendary ravine near Kiev. "We didn't discuss it much," the witness told the court. "The men wanted to forget about it."[9]

The will to forget began during the war and continued afterward. A German history textbook from the late 1950s written for junior high school students offered the following account of the Holocaust: "The Jews fared worst under Hitler. They were expelled from the German people. They were shipped by the thousands into concentration camps. Through hunger, disease and maltreatment, many died."[10]

Theoretically teachers were free to elaborate on that twenty-nine-word description. There was certainly plenty of room for further discussion. But few bothered. Many complained that there simply was not enough time in the semester, that the curriculum allowed them to bring their students only up through the First World War.

The real issue, however, was not that there was insufficient time. The problem was an unwillingness to face the Nazi past. Many Germans wanted to tear down the reminders of the past, just as the community improvement association in Milwaukee wanted to remove all reminders of Jeffrey Dahmer's heinous crimes. Many could not even speak of the past. "So they are silent," observed a highly regarded correspondent on European affairs on the scene in postwar Germany. "There is no tolerable answer, so the question is discouraged."[11]

The Nazi period was like a dirty family secret. This widespread attitude made even more difficult the process of bringing to justice thousands of major Nazi criminals still at large.

Nazi crimes cases were not a top priority of the Federal

Republic of Germany when it was created in 1949 out of the three Western zones of occupation. The three Western Allies, who still administered national affairs, turned over responsibility for any further Nazi prosecutions to the German authorities in 1950. The Allies had grown tired of that unpopular business. But by that point so had the West Germans.

Thousands of Nazi criminals had already been tried and sentenced. The Allies were rushing to grant amnesty and parole to those serving time, even those sentenced to lengthy or life prison terms. This wave of amnesty, as well as the distractions of other political and economic affairs, seemed to suggest that the Allies were tacitly endorsing closure and were offering a justification for forgetting.*

With no leader, no movement exhorting people to address the meaning of what had happened, the Nazi past was handled very quietly or else ignored completely. In the early 1950s Germany was busy getting on its feet again. In West Germany there was even the coming promise of the economic "miracle" just around the corner.

This unwritten policy of nonconfrontation with the past, this fear of breaking the silence about the past, explained, at least in part, why the 1950s were the most carefree years for the multitude of Nazi criminals on the run. How else could Josef Schwammberger walk into a German consulate in Argentina and renew his German passport without a hitch as he did in 1953? There were no checks on the system because there was no desire to have any checks.

The unfortunate truth is that in the 1950s many Nazi criminals, including Josef Schwammberger, did walk right into the German government's hands and nothing was done to hold them. Perhaps the name Schwammberger did not

---

*Interestingly the words "amnesty" and "amnesia" derive from the same word in Greek, *amnēstia*, which means "oblivion," the state of forgetting.

leap out at the consulate personnel in Argentina. After all, during the war Schwammberger had not exactly had a high profile outside Galicia, Poland. Or perhaps the personnel did know who Schwammberger was and cared more about protecting him.

In fairness, the Argentine authorities did not demonstrate much interest in rooting out the many Nazi fugitives living comfortably in their country. After all, not until the capture of Gerhard Bohne in 1964 was there even the slightest break from the government's decidedly pro-Nazi posture. Still, the fact remains that the postwar German government, a government with a great deal of moral authority to reclaim, neither tried very hard to track down fugitive Nazis nor protested very loudly when its efforts were challenged.

Schwammberger was not the only beneficiary of the lax German bureaucracy in the 1950s. In 1956 Josef Mengele, whose reputation certainly was widely known at this time, visited the German embassy in Buenos Aires, where he requested a copy of his birth certificate so he could obtain an Argentine identity card. Mengele gave his real name, which the embassy officials checked against records back in Germany. Once they had confirmed this information, the Germans handed it over to the Argentines. Inspired by the ease with which he was able to work with the German bureaucracy, between 1957 and 1959 Mengele traveled twice to Germany, where his family maintained a prominent manufacturing business.*

Nineteen fifty-five was a confusing turning point for Germany. In that year the country witnessed changes that simultaneously propelled it forward and dragged it back into the unresolved Nazi past. Just ten years after the fall of the Third Reich, Germany signed the so-called Transition Agreement,

---

*Karl Mengele and Sons still manufactures farm machinery in Günzburg, Germany.

under which the Western Allies finally returned full sovereignty to the West German government and welcomed Germans into the Western alliance, into NATO, into the future.

One week after the transition agreement went into effect, West Germans observed another milestone on the road leading away from the past. The German government had previously decided that May 8, 1945, would be the reference point for all Nazi-related crimes no matter at what point during the war they had been committed. This decision had allowed the West German state to prosecute crimes that were not even considered crimes during Hitler's regime and to prosecute long after the fact. The ruling also placed a limit on how long prosecutors would be authorized to go after such criminal suspects.

On May 8, 1955, the statute of limitations indeed ran out on all crimes connected with the Nazi period, with the important exception of acts involving manslaughter and murder. So the West German government, for example, from this date was barred from prosecuting Schwammberger for any wrongdoing connected with the sacks of gold and jewelry he had extorted from his Jewish victims in Poland.

These developments were like a costume change. The new outfit suggested a new set of values, a new outlook. But even though the old buildings on the set had been torn down and new structures had been put in their place, the past could not simply be wished into oblivion. Amnesty was no guarantee of amnesia.

As if history intended to underscore this point, 1955 was also the year when the country was made to realize how incompletely the German people had dealt with the Nazi past. The process of rediscovery happened quite by accident. When the former chief of police of the town of Memel filed suit in a routine labor dispute, it was revealed that he had been as SS officer and had participated in atrocities and mass shootings in Lithuania as part of an SS mobile killing unit.

The lawsuit inspired a complete reexamination of the need to prosecute Nazi criminals. The first major trial that followed was one involving members of the SS *Einsatzgruppen*. It was held in 1957 and 1958 in the university town of Ulm, near Stuttgart.

"In the course of the trial it was revealed that many of the gravest Nazi crimes, notably those committed in the East, had not yet been punished," German prosecutor Willi Dressen observed.[12] In the wake of this highly publicized trial, a handful of determined prosecutors began investigating other Nazi crimes cases until 1958, when the country's state justice ministers created a central office for coordinating archival information crucial to Nazi prosecutions.

With the exception of this office, in the town of Ludwigsburg near Stuttgart, there was little planning in what was mainly a haphazard program to seek out and prosecute the hundreds of Nazi criminals who had evaded justice. One observer in Germany noted at the time:

> The Nazi crime prosecutions did not begin on signal nor have they been carried forward systematically. There is no public policy to hunt down and punish the Third Reich's criminals. The cases arise because of a denunciation filed by a private person, because wanted men become available through their release from Allied prisons, because men with something to hide become careless with the passage of time, because of disclosures in trial testimony which point to yet another culpable individual.[13]

On one level this new attention to prosecuting Nazi crimes, concerted or not, was truly remarkable. No country, no people in human history had been subjected to anything like the Allies' war crimes trials program in the first years after the war. And now German prosecutors themselves were bringing dozens of indictments in cities large and small all across the country.

Between 1958 and 1968, in fact, German courts handled more than two hundred trials of former Nazis, many of them complex cases involving multiple defendants. In February 1968 alone there were some twenty Nazi trials in progress, including the above-mentioned Babi Yar trial.[14]

Many Germans had grown up with parents who were unable to explain what had happened under Hitler, who were unable even to pose the questions. Now, finally, these Germans had a chance to see and hear for themselves the facts. And these trials filled in many of the details of the Holocaust that had not been thoroughly covered in the earlier round of Allied-sponsored proceedings.

These trials created a wide-reaching, fully documented account, an indisputable historical record. In particular, through the trials of the commandants and SS personnel involved in the extermination missions in the eastern territories and in such places as Auschwitz, Treblinka, and Chelmno the cruelty and inhumanity of the Nazi regime were made vivid.

At the same time, however, the best efforts of the German prosecutors were often undermined as the courts proved stingy with convictions and lenient in the sentences imposed. Many Nazis were sent to prison, some even to serve life sentences, although these were frequently commuted to much shorter terms.*

On balance, however, the record of the German courts was dismal. The overwhelming favoritism shown to the Nazi defendants betrayed the conflict in German society over how to deal with the crimes of the Nazi past.

In all, from the end of the war German prosecutors initi-

---

*The West German constitution, adopted in 1949, had abolished the death penalty.

ated preliminary proceedings against more than 103,000 individuals.[15] This figure seems more impressive than it is. The bulk of these pretrial inquiries were conducted during the immediate postwar years, and the vast majority of them never made it to trial. In fact, more than 90,000 of these cases resulted in no punishment whatsoever, either because the case was never brought to trial or because the defendant was acquitted. Out of all the Nazis prosecuted by German courts since 1945, only about 6,500 people were convicted and sentenced.

German judges crafted plenty of rationales for excusing defendants in the cases that did make it to trial. The German penal code defined murder so precisely that judges had great latitude in applying the statute and therefore in excusing actions that could be construed as outside the narrow definition of the crime. Murder, most relevantly, was not just premeditated killing, plainly and simply. A murderer, according to the code, "kills a human being out of bloodthirst, for the satisfaction of sexual desires, for greed or any other base motives, in cunning or cruel manner."

A judge therefore might find that a defendant had killed a thousand people but that in each case he had done so swiftly (so that he could not be judged cruel) and under orders from a superior (so that he could not be judged to have killed for base motives). Courts frequently employed this sort of legal reasoning.

In numerous other instances judges stretched the meaning of the statute to accommodate an acquittal. On March 18, 1966, for example, Hermann Herz was acquitted of charges of complicity in the murder of fifteen men in eastern Prussia. Herz, a former Gestapo officer, told the court that he was merely carrying out a "legal" death sentence against the men, who had been part of a slave labor brigade assigned to remove all evidence of mass graves from the site of an earlier Nazi massacre.

On January 7, 1969, Daniel Nerling, a former SS sergeant, was acquitted of the murder of a Jewish laborer on a farm in wartime Poland. The prosecution had sought a life sentence, but the judge found that the defendant was in a state of "emotional disturbance" when he killed the Jewish man. What had upset the defendant so was the victim's undermining of his efforts to "keep order on the farm," the judge found. Apparently the Jewish man, no doubt being starved and worked to death, had hidden a handful of corn in his pockets.

Judges frequently dropped charges against defendants deemed "unfit" to stand trial. While the West German government was negotiating in 1964 with Argentina over the extradition of fugitive Gerhard Bohne, for example, prosecutors prepared for trial against the several other defendants involved in the notorious euthanasia killings. But in February 1964 two of the three defendants committed suicide. The case against the remaining defendant, Dr. Hans Hefelmann, who was charged with aiding in the murder of seventy-three thousand mentally disabled individuals, went ahead as scheduled. But the trial was stopped midway. Without regard for the irony of their decision, the judges cited mental infirmity as the reason for halting the proceedings against Hefelmann, who at the time was only fifty-seven years old.

When Bohne was finally returned to Germany, he was put on trial along with three others. Two defendants were convicted and were sentenced to eight and ten years in prison for their part in the systematic killing of about one hundred thousand people. Notwithstanding the effort spent tracking down Bohne and having him extradited, the charges against him were dropped midway through his trial, again because he was deemed unfit.

In many of the cases in which defendants were actually convicted, the sentences imposed were so lenient as to make "a mockery of the victims' suffering," in the words of one prominent former German prosecutor.[16] For example, eleven SS men were convicted in a Stuttgart court in an eighteen-month trial that found they had participated in the killing of some four hundred thousand Polish Jews. The lead defendant was sentenced to life in prison. But the other ten SS men received sentences ranging from just two and a half to ten years.

The West German legislature ensured that a cloud hung constantly over the Nazi prosecutions by repeatedly threatening to impose a statute of limitations on prosecutions for murder. The statute of limitations on manslaughter was allowed to expire in 1960. Only after extensive and contentious debates was the limit on murder prosecutions extended from 1965 to 1969 for former Nazis.* Then in 1968 the parliament amended the penal code so that murder without so-called base motives could not be prosecuted after fifteen years.

Although many individual prosecutors doggedly pressed their cases, there was still no leadership, no national support for the cause of bringing Nazi criminals to justice. Judges freely took advantage of the gaping loopholes in the German legal system. In one precedent-setting case Germany's Supreme Court in May 1969 overturned the conviction of a former SS officer found to have killed Jewish prisoners in Poland. The high court, citing the lower court's finding that the defendant had acted under orders, relied on the recently amended section of the criminal code to argue that the defendant had not killed out of "base motives" and therefore could not be found guilty of murder.

One of the justices offered that the German Justice Ministry must have "simply overlooked" the effect that the rewrit-

---

*In 1969 the limit on prosecutions of murder was again extended, this time until 1979, at which time, after yet another wrenching national debate, the limitation was lifted indefinitely.

ing of the code would have on Nazi cases.[17] But the effect was precisely the one many German legislators had been seeking for years. After all, the constant recounting of the Nazi past in these trials was for many Germans like incessant pounding on an open wound.

Dr. Richard Jäger, West Germany's justice minister in the mid-1960s and then a proponent of lifting the statute of limitations on Nazi-related crimes, acknowledged the importance of the trials but warned that the world must at some point consider the Germans as having paid their debt. "There can be no doubt that the people of Germany consider these trials necessary as atonement for the wrong that was done," Jäger noted. But there was frustration building among the German people, he argued, that such efforts were not appreciated.[18]

Now that Germany had rediscovered its Nazi past, would there ever be an end? Would there ever come a point when enough truly was enough?

CHAPTER 11

"WHAT TOOK
YOU SO
LONG?"

[For Germany] to join the civilized world, this was the
ticket.
—Simon Wiesenthal[1]

Thousands of Nazi criminals were tried in German
courts, with more and more investigated, indicted,
captured, and tried in each postwar year. Through
the 1950s and 1960s West Germany was fast rebuilding,
reestablishing itself as a major economic power, a trusted
military ally, and a stable democracy thrust up against an
increasingly hard-line Communist bloc to the east. Yet always, omnipresent, unshakable, there was the shadow of the
Nazi past.

To be sure, many Nazis with reprehensible crimes to their
names did worm their way out of convictions. And German
judges did not always hand out the stiffest sentences possible. Still, the German courts remained packed with Nazi-
related cases one year after another.

For Germans eager to get on with the future there seemed
to be no respite, no foreseeable release from the burden
of having to recall and be reminded of the Nazi past.

Always there was some other major Nazi just located who had evaded notice and whose crimes had gone unpunished. Or suddenly it was discovered that the leading perpetrators at one of the major death camps had never been prosecuted, and there would then follow a lengthy, complex public trial.

So it followed that in 1963 Germany held the so-called Auschwitz trial, which bared horrifying details of human cruelty and slaughter. In 1964 Germany witnessed the Treblinka trial, and in 1975 it began the lengthy Majdanek trial.* There were many other camps, many other individuals, many other trials.

Willy Brandt's election as West German chancellor in 1969 inaugurated a new era in German foreign relations. Brandt, a former mayor of West Berlin with impeccable anti-Nazi credentials—unlike some of his predecessors†— signaled the German government's interest in moving the country toward reconciliation with its past. By this Brandt meant more than merely settling accounts with the victims of nazism through monetary reparations.

Brandt understood the value of symbolic gestures, such as his pathbreaking visit to Warsaw in 1970, when he knelt in an emotional ceremony at the monument to the Jewish victims of the Warsaw ghetto. The German leader's act was a powerful statement of the German people's longing for relief from the burden of the Nazi memory, for reconciliation, even for some measure of collective forgiveness.

---

*In a separate action Franz Stangl, the notorious commandant at Treblinka, was successfully extradited from Brazil in 1967. In 1970 he was sentenced to life in prison, where he died the following year.

†Chancellor Kurt Georg Kiesinger had been a Nazi party member, and President Heinrich Lübke declined to run for a second term following accusations that he had been involved in the construction of Nazi concentration camps. See Mary Fulbrook, The Divided Nation (New York: Oxford, 1992), p. 208.

The continued trials of Nazi criminals, however, were ultimately the more tangible, the more substantive expression of Germany's commitment to its assumed obligation to the past. The country could not regain any moral authority as a democratic nation without gesturing meaningfully— and not merely symbolically—toward the crimes committed under Hitler. The German nation, in short, could not successfully move into the future without confronting its past.

Only through prosecution of Hitler's remaining deputies could Germany make any real progress in the effort to reckon with the Nazi past. A political speech, after all, might inspire, set the tone, outline a policy. But a speech was still, after all, just words. A trial, the product of a government's commitment to pursuing justice, however necessarily imperfect, at the very least represented a form of action.

Many other countries shouldered historical burdens from the time of the Holocaust. France had supplied the collaborationist Vichy regime. Poland and Ukraine had contributed thousands of avid executioners to work for the Nazi lords. Italy had given Mussolini. Croatia had unleashed the Fascist-nationalist and vehemently anti-Semitic Ustachi movement.

But Germany's burden was like no other country's. There was no way to ignore the connection, the pain, the national shame. There was no politically acceptable way to stop and say, "Enough is enough," although many tried to say just that, and many more thought that way. The constant reminding of Germany's Nazi past seemed to have become a fact one simply had to accept.

In practice, however, many Germans did ignore the reality of their country's and their countrymen's responsibility for the Holocaust. Although the Nazi trials continued, and the German parliament repeatedly endorsed their continuing, the process of bringing the perpetrators to justice was undertaken grudgingly. Some of the Nazi trials attracted more attention than others, but most stirred little interest among the general public.

History teachers might take their students on a field trip to the local courthouse if there was a good trial in town. But for the most part the process of bringing to justice the murderers of the bygone Nazi era was viewed as a distasteful but mandatory part of German life.

These ambivalent feelings account, in part, for Josef Schwammberger's ability to remain for so long undisturbed in the obscurity of his South American refuge. Germany had succeeded in winning the extradition of Gerhard Bohne not because of the fervency and persistence of its appeal but because political changes in Buenos Aires had allowed a fleeting opportunity for his expulsion. In tracking down Schwammberger, as was generally the case, Germany exerted only the minimally acceptable level of energy, a level low enough that he was able to enjoy many years of secluded freedom.

Numerous bureaucratic problems impaired what initiative there was among German prosecutors. For example, there was no uniform system for assigning prosecutorial jurisdiction over Nazi crimes, and this certainly accounted for some cases falling through the cracks.

The bounds of the Third Reich had extended far beyond the limits of what became the Federal Republic of Germany in 1949. After inheriting from the occupation authorities the burden of prosecuting all Nazi crimes cases, the justice ministers from the eleven West German provinces so divided the territory of the former Third Reich that each state prosecutor would be responsible for a certain geographic area.*

According to this arrangement, then, the city of Stuttgart

---

*One interesting legacy of nazism is modern Germany's peevish attitude toward centralized power. Germany is divided into *Länder*, which are roughly equivalent to states, except that they have more power than states in America. In a few cases a city, such as Bremen and Hamburg, is also a *Land*. So, for example, the state attorney for the *Land* of Baden-Württemberg, the capital of which is Stuttgart, functions like a cross between a U.S. federal prosecutor and a state attorney general.

was given jurisdiction over eastern Galicia, the part of Poland that included Przemysl. But a state prosecutor might also retain jurisdiction over a case if the defendant resided within that district at the time of arrest. Trials involving multiple defendants, of course, added yet another dimension to this jurisdiction problem.

Other factors further complicated the investigation of Nazi crimes. The Nazi hierarchy had been a convoluted web of overlapping chains of command that spanned an entire continent. Many documents were destroyed as the Nazis retreated, so not surprisingly, the job of piecing together the players and their places on the organizational charts was extremely difficult. Often one individual served many different assignments in many different locations over the course of a career—as was the case with Schwammberger, for example—and this added to the confusion.

If anything, however, the effect of these jurisdictional and investigatory complications only makes it more striking that nothing more was done sooner to bring Schwammberger to justice. For there was an abundance of information on him and his alleged crimes in Poland. The German government, for example, had access to the original investigative documents from Innsbruck, including all the material collected during Schwammberger's incarceration immediately after the war. If the German government did not know who he was when it issued the fugitive a German passport in 1953, then German government officials knew full well within just a few years of that time.

And by the early 1960s Schwammberger's name was circulating in the offices of not one but four state prosecutors. More than one German prosecutor knew of his crimes in detail and possessed substantive documentation supporting charges of murder under even the most stringent of definitions. By the early 1970s the German government even knew Schwammberger's precise whereabouts in La Plata, down to the street and house number.

In spite of all this overwhelming wealth of data, Josef Schwammberger remained a free man.

In 1959 the state prosecutor in the town of Kaiserslautern received a civil complaint brought against a Jewish survivor from Przemysl. Allegedly the accused had served as a kapo in the Przemysl ghetto, but the prosecutor quickly dropped the case for lack of evidence. In the course of a preliminary investigation into the matter, SS Commandant Schwammberger's name came up repeatedly.

When the Kaiserslautern prosecutor dropped the charges against the alleged Jewish kapo, the file on Schwammberger was forwarded to the Stuttgart state attorney's office, which had jurisdiction over Nazi-related crimes in Galicia. In Stuttgart the state prosecutor had already amassed a thick file on Schwammberger in the course of prosecuting Rudolf Bennewitz, the Gestapo chief in Przemysl who had overseen all three of the major deportation actions in 1942 and 1943. The trial against Bennewitz was discontinued two days before Christmas 1963 because of the defendant's ill health. Bennewitz died fully eight years later.

Schwammberger was also under investigation by the state attorney in the northern city of Braunschweig. During the mid-1960s that office began compiling information about him through its investigation of atrocities committed during the liquidation of the Krakow ghetto and at forced labor camps in the surrounding area. Among the camps under investigation by this prosecutor's office was the Heinkel aircraft factory near Mielec where Schwammberger had overseen the final liquidation of the Jewish work brigade in 1944.

Around the same time in Hamburg, Schwammberger's name was featured prominently in the trial of three former Nazi leaders in Przemysl. One of the three, Karl Reisner, had been the Gestapo officer who was stabbed nearly to death by Green, the Jewish man whom Schwammberger later executed. Reisner was fifty-five years old in 1969, when the Hamburg trial court sentenced him to life in prison after finding him guilty of eight counts of murder.* The other two defendants at that trial, Ludwig Schröder and Walter Stegemann, both former Nazi police officials in Przemysl, were acquitted and released.†

In 1963 the Stuttgart state attorney's office finally issued a warrant for Schwammberger's arrest, based on all the collected information, including witness statements taken in Innsbruck and Schwammberger's own written confession. Of course, the arrest warrant proved useless because Schwammberger was thousands of miles away, a fact that the German embassy staff in Argentina knew well by this point.

Three years later, in 1966, the German government also knew Schwammberger's rough whereabouts. In an internal memo dated November 30, 1966, the Braunschweig state attorney reported that Schwammberger was known to be living in Argentina and working as a clerk for the Buenos Aires office of Siemens, the German electronics giant. The same memo indicated that the Stuttgart state prosecutor's office so far had been unsuccessful in its attempt to have Schwammberger extradited. Perhaps the problem was the failure to generate a formal extradition request, the usual means by which governments express interest in gaining custody over criminal fugitives.

Two weeks before that internal memo was written, Argentina had put Gerhard Bohne on a plane bound for Frankfurt, making him the first Nazi extradited from that country. The moment certainly seemed opportune for the German

---

*Although the Stuttgart state prosecutor technically had jurisdiction over Nazi crimes committed in Przemysl, the Hamburg prosecutor handled the Reisner case because Reisner was living in the latter city at the time of his arrest.

†Stegemann was later reindicted and convicted on charges of "aiding and abetting" in the murder of four Jews. In 1981, at the age of seventy-five, he received a prison sentence of six years.

government to press the Argentine government to arrest and deport another known and wanted Nazi criminal. But that did not happen.

Six years later, in the spring of 1972, Schwammberger received the most serious direct threat to his security since his arrest in 1945. That April the world-renowned Nazi hunter Simon Wiesenthal telephoned Germany's central office for Nazi crimes investigations with dramatic new information about Schwammberger. Wiesenthal, relying on his sources in Argentina, reported Schwammberger's exact address on the dirt road in the run-down neighborhood in La Plata and supplied the name of a petrochemical company where Schwammberger was then working as an administrative assistant.

The German authorities had wanted Schwammberger—officially, that is—for nearly a decade. The former SS man had been in hiding for nearly a quarter of a century. Two months earlier he had celebrated his sixtieth birthday. Now officials in the German government knew exactly where Schwammberger was, and they had the number one Nazi hunter in the world, a man who was no stranger to the international media, watching to see how long it would take for them to respond. If Wiesenthal's information proved accurate, nabbing Schwammberger would be effortless.

The German authorities had no reason to regard Wiesenthal's sources as anything less than reliable. A survivor of numerous concentration camps, including Mauthausen, Austria's most notorious site, Wiesenthal had devoted his life's work after being liberated in 1945 to the search for fugitive Nazis. Having lost eighty-nine family members to the Holocaust, he had no shortage of personal motivation.

Especially in the years following the Eichmann trial in 1961, Wiesenthal became a tireless crusader, a compelling advocate of the notion that the countries of the world must commit themselves, better late than never, to bringing to justice the thousands of perpetrators of the Nazi Holocaust who had eluded punishment after the war. As long as a single Nazi criminal remained alive, Wiesenthal argued, then there was still time enough to take a stand, even if only a symbolic stand, for justice.

In the course of his work, combing archives, writing, prodding, lecturing, Wiesenthal had developed a worldwide network of sources and informants that fed him tidbits of information, from wild rumors to hard facts, about various Nazis in hiding. And he had found phenomenal success. Wiesenthal had been instrumental in the capture of some of Hitler's most infamous deputies, including Eichmann, Treblinka Commandant Franz Stangl, and Karl Silberbauer, the Gestapo agent responsible for arresting Anne Frank in Amsterdam.

Wiesenthal had grown up in Galicia and had set up an architectural studio in Lwow, the ancient Ukrainian city about fifty miles east of Przemysl. For a while he had shared an apartment there with a young man from Przemysl. So naturally he took great interest in Schwammberger's case.

In 1963, the year the Stuttgart state attorney's office issued a warrant for Schwammberger's arrest, Wiesenthal had paid a visit to the Tyrolean state courthouse in Innsbruck. The man by then known around the world as a Nazi hunter wanted to see what files, if any, the Austrian court still had on Schwammberger. Wiesenthal also wanted to know if there had been any progress in the government's investigation since the day the prosecution was interrupted in 1948 by Schwammberger's escape from prison.

Wiesenthal discovered that there had been absolutely no advance in the case itself. There was, however, one startling related development. "There was one thing new that I learned," he later recalled, his eyes watery with age. "The jewelry that was taken from him, the seven sacks, doesn't exist anymore. They had sold it all in auction in '56 for peanuts. [The lot brought about fourteen hundred dollars.]

I protested because the list [of the stolen property contained in the sacks] was evidence, because he was not only a murderer, but he raped these people of their money."*

Wiesenthal's information about Schwammberger's whereabouts, it turned out, was exact. And the German government, remarkably, actually did respond in good time. On December 1, 1972, just a few months after receiving the tip, the Stuttgart prosecutor's office issued a formal extradition request to the president of the Argentine Republic.

Now that Germany had finally acted and Schwammberger's recapture seemed near, a new glitch became apparent. In any extradition negotiation one country must request that an individual be extradited and a second country must then comply with the request. But Argentina, notwithstanding the expulsion of Gerhard Bohne several years earlier, was not quite ready to tango.

Argentine President Alejandro Lanusse did sign a decree on March 27 of the following spring granting West Germany's request. There was no need to pore over the dusty print of old extradition treaties, as might happen in some countries where agreements on the protocol for transfers of criminal suspects date from the nineteenth century. In Argentina's case no such treaty existed with Germany. Neither was there any need for the courts to decide the issue. Although Lanusse, the third general to lead the Argentine government since Arturo Illia's ouster in 1966, was more prone to concession and compromise than some of his hardline military colleagues, his was still government by decree. So on April 9, 1973, the order went out from the Casa Rosada, the presidential palace: Arrest Schwammberger.

Still, as willing as the president was to comply with Ger-

---

*Although the list would certainly have been evidence of a sort, Schwammberger could not have been tried on any charges related to the stolen property because the statute of limitations had long since expired on all Nazi crimes except murder. Still, the list could have provided a means of compensating surviving victims for their lost property.

many's request for Schwammberger—or as willing as he wanted to appear—other right-wing elements among the police and in the army were ardently opposed to turning over anyone connected with Nazi Germany. When the police went to enforce President Lanusse's order, those right-wing elements had their way.

A contingent of the La Plata police force, accompanied by a federal judge carrying an arrest warrant, arrived at Schwammberger's home a few days after President Lanusse gave the go-ahead. Schwammberger's elder son, Wolfgang, answered the door. An electronics technician, Wolf had returned to Argentina in 1970 with his German wife and had been living since then with his parents.

Wolf had been a young boy, just four years old, when his father was the camp commandant in Przemysl, but he had been old enough then for his proud father to show off to him on occasion. One day the father had ordered a Jewish man to strip off all his clothes right in the middle of the ghetto and had then chased the naked man through the streets, firing his pistol after him. The boy had laughed at his father's antics.

Three decades later the son told police that the man they wanted had left three weeks before. Wolf was taken to the police station for further questioning, but he had nothing more to tell. Clearly someone had warned Schwammberger in time.

The police suspected that Schwammberger had fled to Paraguay, where General Alfredo Stroessner was known to be more trustworthy than the Argentinians when it came to protecting former Nazis in his country.[2] Later Argentine police investigators discovered that a Canadian freighter had departed from the nearby port of Berisso on the very day Wolf Schwammberger claimed his father had left the country.

Back in Vienna, Simon Wiesenthal was exasperated when

he received the news of Schwammberger's escape. In a note sent to a friend in Buenos Aires, the Nazi hunter fretted, "Please explain how this could have happened because I really don't understand. We've worked for years on this case and now we have to start from the beginning again."[3]

In the fifteen years that followed Schwammberger's second escape from justice, two important historical forces gathered hurricane strength. Hard as they tried to forget, the German people continued to be haunted relentlessly by the crimes of the Nazi era. The Argentine people, meanwhile, became enmeshed in a ghastly civil war. When these two fronts collided, Josef Schwammberger found himself in the eye of the storm.

By the mid-1980s both countries were looking desperately for renewal. West Germany, by then one of the world's leading economic powers, began pleading more urgently with the world community for reconciliation. And Argentina turned toward a new era of civilian-led democracy with a frantic hopefulness after more than a decade of "disappearances" and terror.

Josef Schwammberger became a part of this cross-continental renaissance. Neither the SS man himself nor the crimes for which he was responsible were of any great significance to the people and governments of Germany and Argentina. After all, when he was arrested in 1945, Schwammberger had been very much a lesser figure compared with the leading Nazis being hauled before the Nuremberg tribunals. Schwammberger was certainly recognized as a "bestial killer," as the Polish authorities described him, but there were many Nazis in the dock who matched that description.

So when the Stuttgart prosecutors finally petitioned Argentina in 1972 for Schwammberger's extradition, it was not because anyone believed that the liquidation of Przemysl was the largest-scale crime of the Holocaust. Nor did Argentina open the back door for Schwammberger to escape a few months later because he mattered so terribly to anyone in that country's military elite.

In 1945 he was a suspected Nazi criminal whose actions were to be weighed and judged along with thousands of others. After more than forty years had passed, he was something more than just another Nazi murderer. Schwammberger's existence, the very fact of his unpunished deeds and his unrepentant life, made him a compelling symbolic figure.

The enduring weight of the Nazi burden, year after year, had been a defining force in postwar German society and politics. In a sense Germans themselves had joined the long list of Holocaust survivors. Not every German was a victim of nazism, and no German was a victim in the same way that Jews or Gypsies or Poles were victims of the Holocaust. But they were survivors. And the children of the generation that survived became children of survivors.

In the history of their survival, the years since the collapse of the Third Reich, the Germans proved very good at proclaiming themselves survivors but not very good at acknowledging or acting on the meaning of what they had survived. In the beginning the pain was too great, and there was an urgency about rebuilding the broken nation. One historian characterized postwar Germany as being under the spell of a "collective amnesia."[4]

The sense of duty to remember the past frequently collided with the desire to forget. Several generations of Germans, for example, had grown up with the story of Anne Frank, the teenage Jewish girl whose diary of life hiding from the Nazis in an attic in Amsterdam was discovered after she had been sent with her sister to their deaths at the Bergen-Belsen concentration camp. But for many Germans this moving story was a means to gloss over rather than firmly confront the past.

Both the translation of the young girl's published diary

and the popular stage dramatization omitted reference to the fact that the Frank family spoke German. Keeping the German people from this important detail, according to one historian, was a deliberate attempt to obscure the connection between the German victimizer and the Jewish victim.

"Out of both shame and sorrow, Germans have named streets, schools, and youth centers after Anne Frank," this historian has written, "but to this day most probably do not comprehend why, a generation ago, a significant number of their countrymen deemed it necessary to hunt down a fifteen-year old Jewish girl and send her off to suffer and die in places like Auschwitz and Bergen-Belsen."[5]

One outgrowth of these crosscurrents in German society during the 1960s and 1970s was a rising tide of support for the idea of *Schlusstrich*, a word in German that means, roughly, "enough is enough." As the years passed and the percentage of Germans born after 1945 increased, this point of view only seemed to gain legitimacy. Prosecutors increasingly were reduced to hauling white-haired men with walking canes before the criminal courts. Defendants not infrequently died in custody before their cases could be resolved. Some people even began to see the former Nazi as the victim rather than as the unpunished former victimizer.

But as the will to look ahead grew stronger, more and more reasons to look back forced themselves on the German conscience. In the late 1970s, in fact, there began another reawakening of interest in the Nazi past, and this time not only in Germany. The 1978 television miniseries *Holocaust* was seen by millions of people around the world and became for many an unforgettable introduction to the subject.*

A remarkable run of headline-grabbing incidents involving major Nazi figures and Nazi-related issues followed in the wake of the television series. Many factors contributed

*The show aired in Germany the following year.

to the reexamination of the Nazi period, including the curiosity of a new generation, the popularity of such writers as Elie Wiesel, a feeling of greater stability within Europe where ideas and history could be explored more openly, among others. All of a sudden, it seemed, the world was waking up to the Nazi past, as if someone had suddenly turned on the lights in a room long dark.

More than three decades after defeating the Nazis, the U.S. government authorized the creation of a special unit in the Justice Department that under an ambiguous name, the Office of Special Investigations (OSI), was assigned to investigate and prosecute Nazis who had entered the United States illegally. There had been a smattering of such prosecutions beginning in the 1950s, but nothing like the concerted effort then undertaken to strip Nazi criminals of the benefits of a free life in America.*

The "Nazi story" became big news in the 1980s as major international stories about Nazis and the Nazi past rained like confetti at a ticker tape parade. In 1981 the Justice Department's OSI successfully revoked the citizenship of John Demjanjuk, a Ukrainian-born auto worker from Cleveland whom numerous eyewitnesses had identified as Ivan the Terrible, one of the gas chamber operators in the Treblinka death camp.†

---

*Congress decided against prosecuting Nazis for actual war crimes. Nazis could be deported, or if they had obtained U.S. citizenship by concealing their Nazi records, they could be denaturalized and then deported.

†The case has since generated enormous controversy. Demjanjuk's defense had always rested on a claim of mistaken identity. After his 1988 conviction in Israel his lawyers obtained from the Soviet archives forty-year-old depositions of former Ukrainian guards at Treblinka that seemed to cast some doubt on whether Demjanjuk was ever at that particular camp. Finding the evidence inconclusive, the Israeli Supreme Court overturned his conviction in July 1993.

In February 1983 the government of Bolivia offered the German government custody of Klaus Barbie, who had been the ranking Gestapo officer in Vichy France and the man responsible for the deportation of thousands of French Jews, as well as the murder of scores of resistance leaders, Communists, and other political opponents. With national elections just one month away, German Chancellor Helmut Kohl refused to displease conservatives in his party, the Christian Democratic Union, by seeming too eager to dig up the Nazi past. It would be far better, Kohl calculated, to let someone else take Barbie.

France finally agreed to seek Barbie's extradition, which Bolivia granted after extracting a promise from the French government for a one-time foreign aid "grant." One correspondent who covered the Barbie trial described the bounty France paid in exchange for one of history's most wanted Nazi criminals as follows: Barbie's "airfare from La Paz to Lyon added up to a planeload of arms, three thousand tons of wheat, and fifty million dollars, which the Bolivian president came to Paris to collect two weeks later."[6]

Barbie's trial, as well as his conviction and life sentence, raised many difficult and painful issues for France, especially the matter of French complicity with the Nazis, a subject that had been even more repressed in France than nazism had been in Germany. (The Barbie story did not reflect well on the U.S. government either when it was revealed in 1983 that American military intelligence had paid Barbie as an informer after the war and had then helped him escape from the French police to South America.) Many in Germany were relieved to see that theirs was not the only country forced into emotionally charged confrontations with the Nazi past.*

Also in 1983, Arthur Rudolph, one of the leading pioneers of space travel in the United States, a man decorated as an

*Barbie died in a French prison in 1991.

American hero, agreed to give up his citizenship and leave the country rather than face charges that he had abused Jewish slave laborers at an underground missile factory in Nazi Germany. And in 1986 former United Nations Secretary-General Kurt Waldheim was elected president of Austria in spite of an international furor over charges that he had served in a Nazi unit that deported Jews from Yugoslavia and Greece.

One of the most sensational stories from this time unfolded in 1985, when the remains of Josef Mengele, the so-called Angel of Death, were discovered in a grave in São Paulo, Brazil. The discovery ended an intense multinational search for the missing doctor of Auschwitz, who was known for his role in selecting prisoners for death and for cruel medical experiments.

And then there was Bitburg, the controversy that began when Chancellor Kohl invited President Ronald Reagan to make a state visit at the conclusion of the economic summit of leading Western powers held in Bonn in June 1985. Kohl, the first West German chancellor too young to have served in the armed forces during World War II, made no secret of his interest in securing a gesture of reconciliation from the American president. Reagan was eager to comply.

The result was an uproar of protest when the two leaders selected a military cemetery at Bitburg, a small town near the Luxembourg border, as the site where they would meet for a wreath-laying ceremony. The reason for the outrage: The Bitburg cemetery contained the graves of forty-seven members of the Waffen-SS, Himmler's elite fighting force.*

In spite of the worldwide criticism, Reagan refused either to break his promise to the German leader or to buckle

---

*Some of the SS men buried at Bitburg had taken part in the massacre at Oradour-sur-Glane, the town that had lent its name to the Austrian prison where Schwammberger was first incarcerated after the war.

under pressure from a wide array of interest groups, including the U.S. Congress. Besides, the event promised to be vintage Reagan. The summer before, the American president and the leaders of the other former Western Allied powers had gathered on the Normandy coast, amid great pomp and photo opportunity, to commemorate the fortieth anniversary of D Day, the invasion that marked the beginning of the end of Hitler's tyranny over Europe. Few could lay a wreath as Reagan could.

Kohl and French President François Mitterrand had already stood, hand in hand, at a ceremony honoring the thousands of soldiers who had died at Verdun, one of the bloodiest battles of the First World War. The impact of the photograph of the two leaders recalled the image of Willy Brandt kneeling before the monument to the victims of the Warsaw ghetto. But Bitburg was neither Verdun nor the Warsaw ghetto. Bitburg involved the SS, and no wreath could cover that fact.

Still, Chancellor Kohl hoped to score some political points at home for the coup of Reagan's visit, and he did. Many older Germans in particular viewed Reagan's visit not only as an American invitation back into the circle of the leading Western powers but as an act of moral redemption for Germany. Younger Germans generally did not share the same sense of urgency for a demonstration of reconciliation. "I don't think much of gestures," one twenty-year-old German told an American reporter. "I think deeds would be better. They show something."[7]

Reagan's religious references gave a rhetorical boost to the call for *Schlusstrich*, for drawing the line. "All these men," Reagan declared at the Bitburg cemetery, "have now met their Supreme Judge, and they have been judged by Him, as we shall all be judged." Reagan's message was clear: The past cannot be undone. Look to the future.

On balance, however, Bitburg did not have the effect

Chancellor Kohl wanted. Once again Germany and nazism had been loudly and definitively linked in the world's consciousness. Those SS soldiers had been long buried in the Bitburg cemetery, but the reality of Germany's Nazi past, as the Bitburg affair clearly demonstrated, could not be so easily laid to rest.

President Reagan was willing to pronounce reconciliation with Germany's past, but much of the rest of the world was still hesitant. "Yes, Germans would love to forget," one prominent Holocaust historian told a conference at Northwestern University in 1989. "They do not have psychological independence, as we learned during the Bitburg crisis, when Chancellor Kohl thought that with one stroke he could end the forty years in the desert by having an American president visit a cemetery. And what happened? 'The past returns!' cried the German newspapers. 'The past is still here!' So they struggle with the past without letup."8

When attention focused once again on Josef Schwammberger in the months following Bitburg, the longtime fugitive from justice became a symbol of the past that had never gone away. Schwammberger was an impediment to Germany's absolution, to its unqualified reentry into the civilized world. The pressure in Germany to do something decisive about Schwammberger—to supplement words with deeds—became overwhelming.

Unfortunately for Schwammberger, change, change that was not going to allow him many more days of carefree living in the shadows of obscurity, had also come to Argentina. In October 1983 Raúl Alfonsín was elected president, ending more than seven years of military dictatorship and violent civil war. Alfonsín, the first member of the Radical Civic Union party to lead the government since Arturo Illia in the mid-1960s, was saddled with two major challenges: an economy in shambles and a country divided and demoralized after years of fighting between government military forces and leftist rebels.

Argentina's ruined economy, with a forty-billion-dollar foreign debt, the third largest in the world, would take years to restore. But Alfonsín was determined to take resolute action on the second issue: confronting his country's past. One week after he was sworn in as president, Alfonsín issued his first presidential decrees, the first official acts of his administration. The president called for swift prosecutions of the nine military leaders who had governed the country by junta since 1976. Alfonsín also announced that his government would prosecute leaders of the various leftist guerrilla groups that had waged more than a decade of terror.

Alfonsín's action was bold and risky. Argentina did not exactly have a solid democratic foundation. The generals had stepped down from power when the burden of governing became too unpleasant. The military's reputation had been deeply wounded by the so-called Dirty War, in which thousands of Argentine civilians "disappeared" and the country was torn apart by violence. The military leaders had been further hobbled by their inability to manage the economy and by the initially popular but ultimately humiliating mini-war with Britain over ownership of the Falkland Islands.*

Still, much as the military establishment had become weakened, no one considered the power of the generals and admirals completely destroyed. The new civilian regime would have to step carefully.

But Alfonsín was adamant about punishing those guilty of human rights abuses and other atrocities during the long civil war. The new president wanted to define the new government and, in a sense, redefine the political future of the country through these unprecedented trials. Without an honest reconciliation with the past, he argued, there could be no hope for democracy in the future.

---

*To this day the Argentines defiantly refer to the islands by their Spanish name, las Islas Malvinas.

"The past gravitates darkly over our future," the newly elected president declared in a nationally televised speech to announce his decrees. "The law's full weight should fall on those who put the death machine in action and those who took advantage of it to torture or satisfy personal desires."

Alfonsín could have been talking about Germany in 1945. The orders of magnitude, of course, differed vastly. But what postwar Argentina shared with post-Holocaust Germany was a longing for national healing. And the only effective means to that end was a blunt confrontation with the past.

Alfonsín had a related item on his agenda as he moved to restore democratic government to Argentina. The former human rights activist was determined to make a statement about the country's longtime reputation as a haven for Nazi criminals. Although it was certainly not the top priority on his agenda, an attack against this unsavory aspect of Argentine history was viewed within his administration as complementing the new government's efforts to bring to justice those responsible for the crimes of the Dirty War. Moving against Nazis in Argentina, officials in the Alfonsín government figured, would also be smart politically.

First, an aggressive move against Argentina's Nazi past would appeal to Argentine Jews, who had been longtime supporters of Alfonsín's political party. Although Jews constituted less than 1 percent of the country's total population, they had been hit particularly hard by the military's terror/antiterror campaign during the Dirty War. Of some nine thousand officially documented cases of "disappeareds," about fifteen hundred were Argentine Jews.

A bold assault on Argentina's reputation as a Nazi refuge would also be interpreted as a criticism of Perón, the man most identified with the efforts to shelter Nazi criminals and the leader whose spirit still inspired Alfonsín's main political opponents. Lastly, a commitment to root out Nazis in Argentina would send a positive signal to the international community, especially to the United States and Europe, where bankers and politicians, as always, held the power to help or hinder Argentina's economic recovery.

In November 1985 Argentine police arrested Walter Kutschmann, a former SS lieutenant who had participated in the killings of Jews and Polish civilians in eastern Galicia, not far from where Schwammberger had carried out his SS assignments. The West German government had requested Kutschmann's extradition as far back as 1970 but, as with Schwammberger's case, had not pursued the matter. In 1975 Simon Wiesenthal had publicly announced that he believed Kutschmann was living comfortably in Buenos Aires under the assumed name of Pedro Olmos. Sure enough, Argentine police found Kutschmann and took him into custody. But just as Schwammberger had been allowed to escape three years earlier, Kutschmann was released for no apparent reason.

Ten years later the Alfonsín government was not about to let Kutschmann slip away again. But by then the seventy-two-year-old former Nazi was in poor health. Nine months after his arrest, with his extradition pending in the Argentine federal court in Buenos Aires, Kutschmann succumbed to heart failure.

Kutschmann would have been the first Nazi extradited from Argentina since Gerhard Bohne twenty years earlier. His extradition would have heralded, in one small way, the arrival of a new beginning in Argentina. His trial in Germany then would have expressed a commitment to acting on—as well as speaking of—the importance of remembering the past.

Walter Kutschmann would have represented the coming together of the passionate desire in two countries for reconciliation with the Nazi past. Kutschmann's death denied him that place in history. Germany and Argentina would have to look to someone else on whom to confer those distinctions.

. . .

Josef Schwammberger had been given the gift of his life and
his freedom because the world, especially Germany, had
for so long lacked the total commitment to bringing Nazi
criminals to justice. He had lived at the edge of the earth,
protected by a government that had refused to confront the
elements in its society that had made it the continent's
greatest accomplice in the cover-up of Nazi crimes.

After forty years of freedom Schwammberger was hauled
back from the brink. In the fall of 1987, against his will and
in full view of the world, the ailing grandfather was pulled
from hiding and force-fed the details of his horrible deeds.

The beginning of the end for Schwammberger came the
week after Walter Kutschmann was arrested in Buenos Aires.
From his office in Vienna, Simon Wiesenthal was encouraged by the news that Argentina had collared one of the
most wanted Nazi criminals. But the tireless Nazi hunter was
not satisfied. Complaining to the press that there were still
many other Nazis living in Argentina, Wiesenthal singled
out Schwammberger. He decried the fact that the former SS
commandant, "who uses his own name and is a naturalized
Argentine citizen, lives in the city of La Plata."* What were
the Argentine authorities waiting for? Wiesenthal wanted to
know.

Once again Wiesenthal used his powers of persuasion to
nudge a government into action. Less than a week after his
tirade to the press the Argentine police went to Schwammberger's last-known address in La Plata and there met Dr.
Nicolini, the veterinarian who had bought Schwammberger's
house in 1980. Nicolini remembered Schwammberger and

*An interview with Wiesenthal on a Vienna radio station was appar-
ently the source for the coverage in Argentina of Wiesenthal's comments.
The newspaper *Diario Popular* picked up the story on November 20, 1985,
although it misspelled Schwammberger's name as "Schlaummberger."

told police he thought "Don José" had moved to one of the distant suburbs of Buenos Aires. Police investigators questioned the other former neighbors on the block, but no one had a forwarding address for the Schwammberger family.

Police also interrogated one of Schwammberger's former employers in La Plata, the manager of Petroquímica Sudamericana. The plant manager checked his files to confirm for the police investigators that Schwammberger had indeed worked there as a clerk and as a German translator but had left work abruptly and had never returned. The manager also recalled Schwammberger as a "partially bald, gray-haired, somewhat overweight" man who "seemed to be cultured, proper, friendly and timid."[9]

That was the extent of the police investigation. There was a flurry of coverage in the Buenos Aires press about the "other" fugitive Nazi, Schwammberger, but the Argentine authorities were unable to get the job done. Or perhaps the Alfonsín administration thought that Kutschmann, then still alive and sitting in jail, satisfied the new government's commitment to prosecute Nazis.

Two more years passed when, on October 11, 1987, Wiesenthal pressed the Schwammberger case once more. At a press conference in Jerusalem, the Nazi hunter announced that he had developed his own version of the FBI's most wanted list.[10] Placing fifth on this list of the ten most wanted Nazis still at large was Josef Schwammberger. The list, however, also included some individuals such as Heinrich Müller, former head of the Gestapo, who had not been seen since 1945 or whose whereabouts had been long unknown. But for their inclusion, Schwammberger would have been first or second on the list.

The point of Wiesenthal's ranking was to apply additional pressure to those governments widely known to be harboring Nazi fugitives. Syria, for example, was—and still is—widely believed to be harboring Alois Brunner, a former top aide to Adolf Eichmann. Brunner is the only Nazi believed still alive and ranked by Wiesenthal higher than Schwammberger.*

Wiesenthal's press conference had an immediate and decisive impact on Schwammberger's future. Two weeks after the Nazi hunter had reiterated his belief that Schwammberger was living in Argentina, the West German Ministry of Justice made its move. Through the office of the state prosecutor in Stuttgart, where the case against Schwammberger technically was pending, Germany delivered a second formal request for Schwammberger's extradition to stand trial for murder. From the West German embassy, located in a posh residential neighborhood in Buenos Aires, the extradition request was delivered directly to President Alfonsín at the Casa Rosada.

Within a few days of renewing its extradition request, the German government demonstrated that its commitment to seeing Schwammberger captured and returned for trial in Germany went beyond rhetoric. When word reached the German embassy in Buenos Aires that an informant was demanding payment for a tip that he promised would lead police to Schwammberger's hideout, the Germans rushed into action.†

Within days the German embassy in Buenos Aires received the go-ahead from government officials back in Stuttgart and Bonn, the West German capital. The state authorities agreed to pay a bounty of five hundred thousand deutsche marks (about three hundred thousand dollars at the

---

*Some unconfirmed news reports have indicated that Brunner died in Syria in the late 1980s.

†The German government has closely guarded the identity of the tipster, although it has been rumored that he was himself a former Nazi. One German government official in Argentina did acknowledge in an interview that the informant's first name was Andrés but refused any additional details. The German official himself asked not to be quoted by name.

time) for the tipster's information.* If the scheme worked, it would be the largest reward the German government ever paid for a wanted Nazi criminal.

Just three years earlier the German government had offered the same amount, three hundred thousand dollars, for information on the whereabouts of one of the most notorious figures in the annals of the Holocaust, Auschwitz Dr. Josef Mengele. (By 1985 the total purse for Mengele's capture was more than three million dollars, but the vast majority of that money was pledged by private sources and by the state of Israel.)

Suddenly, after so many years, after so many halfhearted attempts, the governments of West Germany and Argentina were acting as if they were serious. Germany was offering an extraordinary sum of money for Schwammberger's capture. And when the renewed extradition request was received in Buenos Aires, the Argentine authorities moved surely.

The German government's official version of the decision to resolve at last to bring Schwammberger to justice contradicted the obvious reality of the situation. German officials claimed that their interest in Schwammberger after forty years was simply a matter of wanting to follow the dictates of the law. The former Nazi was wanted for murder; he should therefore be prosecuted.

Kurt Schrimm, an assistant state attorney and the chief prosecutor on the Schwammberger case, made just this point in an interview.[11] A casual, unpretentious man, Schrimm seemed incapable of appreciating the irony of his offering such a matter-of-fact explanation for what was clearly a major prosecutorial breakthrough.

Schrimm worked out of a drab office decorated in the institutional style of an underfunded state agency: cheap,

*An etymological aside: The word in German for "bounty" is *Kopfgeld*, which is formed from the words *Kopf* for "head" and *Geld* for "money."

cluttered furniture, twenty-year-old travel posters from the state tourist authority, peeling paint and dim bulbs, over-stuffed files spilling out of broken cabinets. And he worked alone, for the most part. Of the 110 or so prosecutors in the Stuttgart state attorney's office, he was the only one responsible for handling cases involving Nazi crimes.

As far as Schrimm was willing to admit, the Schwamm-berger case, including the unprecedented bounty paid to bring the case, was just another day's work. "It is my duty" to prosecute Schwammberger, Schrimm explained. "It is not my decision. It is the decision of the law."

Argentina, too, according to the official rendition of the story, was acting strictly as if rounding up Schwammberger were the most natural course of action imaginable, as if it would be insulting to suggest otherwise. "It was part of the principles that the Radical party developed over one hundred years and which we were able to put in place when we came into government," said Antonio Trocoli, Alfonsín's minister of the interior from 1983 to 1987.[12]

But the reality was more complex than the simplistic explanations offered. Germany had not suddenly become serious about prosecuting all Nazi criminals, even about prosecuting Schwammberger in particular, not after four decades. And Argentina was hardly about to initiate a massive sweep of the country, a shakedown of the large and powerful German Argentine community. As Trocoli said, "We were conducting trials for the first time in our history of those responsible for these crimes here [during the Dirty War]. We had a national commission that worked for months to determine who was responsible. We couldn't be worrying about all these [Nazis] and what happened fifty years ago."

Both governments were looking for a symbol. And only one was really necessary. One Nazi would make the point. Kutschmann was dead. Someone needed to take his place. One Nazi, one elderly man, one more, one highly publicized trial, one more time.

For Germany it was not so much Schwammberger that mattered. It was not the law that mattered. It was the statement, the symbol, the gesture that counted. Germany was prepared to pay a large bounty for Schwammberger or Mengele or whomever. The particular Nazi was not as important as the fact that these individuals had evaded justice for so long.

President Reagan's administration—to draw an analogy— was grounded, among other things, in anti-Communist rhetoric. The Soviet Union, Reagan declared, was an evil empire. But as serious as the president was about his beliefs, he was not about to attack Russia. Reagan's invasion of tiny Grenada was more significant for its symbolic value than for its military importance. The degree to which the world was actually "safer for democracy" after the Caribbean island had been cleansed of communism was too minuscule to matter.

Similarly, President George Bush launched a large-scale military invasion of Panama in 1989, risking the lives of American soldiers and killing scores of Panamanian civilians in the process, all out of a commitment to arrest Manuel Noriega. But the military strong-arming involved more than simply dragging one lawbreaker back to Miami to stand trial for cocaine smuggling. The act was significant not because it satisfied any literal or legal purpose but because it had a political and symbolic value.

For their own reasons West Germany and Argentina wanted to make a statement against the Nazi past and for a future when the shadows of that past might finally be cleared away. But neither nation could launch a wholesale assault on the Nazi past any more easily than Reagan could have launched an invasion of the Soviet Union. The challenge was to confront the Nazi past as painlessly as possible, to find a symbol, to find a Grenada or a Noriega. Someone like Schwammberger, one of the most notorious Nazi criminals still on the loose.

The anonymous informant's tip, received just a couple of

weeks after Wiesenthal had held his Jerusalem press conference and after West Germany had reissued its extradition
request, proved conclusive in tracking down the longtime
fugitive. Schwammberger had averted capture many times
already. This time there were too many forces working
against him.

When he saw his name in every Buenos Aires newspaper
following the announcement of Wiesenthal's top ten list, the
seventy-five-year-old Schwammberger fled the modest home
on the outskirts of Buenos Aires where he had lived since
selling his La Plata shack in 1980. An acquaintance, a German rancher, invited him to spend some time at an estate in
the mountain village of Huerta Grande, near the city of
Córdoba, some five hundred miles west of the Argentine
capital. Maybe the excitement would pass, just as it had
several times before. Maybe in a few weeks people would
stop asking questions, stop wondering, and Schwammberger
could return to his retired life.

For two weeks Schwammberger stayed in a cabin on the
grounds of the mountain ranch. Then, on Friday, November
13, 1987, at about one o'clock in the afternoon there was a
rap on the door. Outside stood a contingent from the Córdoba Police Department and a federal judge holding a warrant for his arrest.

The gray-haired former SS man smiled because he knew
who these men were and why they had come. The police
asked if he was Josef Schwammberger, and the cornered
Nazi confirmed his identity. He did not bother trying to
give a false name as he had the first time he was arrested,
forty-two years before. This time the elderly Nazi had only
one question. "What took you so long?" he asked mockingly.

Several hours after his arrest a bomb exploded at a synagogue in Buenos Aires. The blast ripped apart the front doors
and shattered several windows. Police reported no injuries.
No suspects were ever found.

CHAPTER 12

EXTRADITION

The Argentines are a people who like to close the
chapter and be done.
—Guillermo López, Argentine prosecutor[1]

Kurt Schrimm, the prosecutor in the Stuttgart state
attorney's office assigned to the Schwammberger
case, arranged to fly to Buenos Aires as soon as
he heard the news. One of the most wanted Nazi criminals
in the world was again in the hands of the police almost
exactly forty years after his escape from the French prison in
Austria. Now the man who had found quiet in his Argentine
oblivion would be forced to confront the barbarities he
committed in his earlier life.

Before there could be any movement on Germany's fifteen-year-old request for Schwammberger's extradition,
however, Schrimm would have to make absolutely sure that
the man Argentine police had captured in the Córdoba
mountains was the same man Germany wanted for murder.
Even though Schwammberger admitted his identity when
he was arrested, the German government would not release
the three-hundred-thousand-dollar bounty until his identity
was certified.

Another reason for making sure the elderly man arrested in the Argentine mountains was indeed Schwammberger was that there had been false reports and even false arrests in other Nazi cases, which had proved extremely embarrassing to the governments involved. In 1967, for example, Guatemalan federal police arrested an elderly rancher they believed to be Martin Bormann, the long-sought former deputy to Hitler. They were mistaken. Five years later a German-born man was arrested in Columbia and accused of being Bormann.*

With every reason to be cautious, therefore, Schrimm located copies of Schwammberger's fingerprints in the Innsbruck police files dating back to his 1945 arrest. Accompanied by a fingerprint specialist from the state Ministry of Justice in Stuttgart, the German prosecutor traveled to Buenos Aires. He arrived just ten days after news of the aged Nazi's arrest had triggered the bells of wire service machines around the world.

In that time Schwammberger had been taken from the police headquarters in Córdoba to Buenos Aires and then on to La Plata. A federal judge there, Vicente Luis Bretal, assumed jurisdiction over the extradition case on the basis of the fact that Schwammberger was still identified in Germany's extradition request as a resident of La Plata, even though he had not lived there for seven years.

In La Plata Schrimm met with Judge Bretal, a portly and formal but friendly man. Schrimm compared Schwammberger's fingerprints with those of the seventy-five-year-old man sitting in the La Plata jail. The prints matched. "He

---

*Bormann was the only one of the major Nazi war criminals tried in absentia by the International Military Tribunal at Nuremberg. He was convicted and sentenced to death. In April 1973 the West German government ended most of the speculation about Bormann's mysterious fate with an announcement that Bormann's remains had been unearthed at a Berlin construction site.

always said he was Schwammberger," Schrimm noted un-
emotionally.

Schrimm did not meet Schwammberger on that trip. The
German prosecutor would have to wait until Schwammberger was delivered to the hands of German authorities—
if indeed that was to happen. In addition to his meeting with
Judge Bretal, Schrimm introduced himself to his counterparts
in the Buenos Aires federal prosecutor's office and to officials
in President Alfonsín's Justice Ministry. Schrimm wanted a
read on just how committed the Argentine government was
to following through with Schwammberger's extradition. "I
discussed with the judge and the prosecutors bringing
[Schwammberger] here to Germany for trial," Schrimm recalled of the meetings. "The judge had said, 'I don't know,
we'll see,' and the prosecutor said, 'We will hope.' "

At last there was good reason to hope for those who
believed that forty years of justice delayed in the case of
Josef Schwammberger had meant justice denied. But before
the aged Nazi could fulfill his symbolic function in Germany,
he would have to play his part in Argentina's dramatic confrontation with its past. Through the process of his extradition Schwammberger proved Argentina's determination to
wash its hands of its dirty past. As Judge Bretal observed,
the case against Schwammberger "signified an interest in
changing the image of the country."[2]

President Alfonsín had already demonstrated his commitment to confront Argentina's fascist past through his government's efforts to prosecute hundreds of military officers and
leftist rebel leaders, those most responsible for the atrocities
committed during the Dirty War. After trying the generals
who had commanded the most violent regime in Argentine
history and had driven the country to economic ruin as
well, the Alfonsín administration began prosecuting scores of
lesser officers.

Many countries throughout history have held isolated

military trials, even war crimes trials. In the United States, for example, during the Vietnam War numerous military officers were tried for atrocities committed against Vietnamese civilians, most notably during the massacre at My Lai. But the real precedent for the far-reaching trials in Argentina had been set four decades earlier in Nuremberg.

Much as the Allies had sought through the Nazi crimes trials to contrast the virtues of democracy with the perils of Hitler's fascism, Alfonsín sought through the military trials to mark Argentina's passing from the fascist past into a democratic future. But the Argentine people, especially the legions of lower-level soldiers and officers, had only so much tolerance for a prolonged national soul-searching. In this, too, there had been a precedent set in Germany.

One expression of the anxiety caused by the military trials in Argentina came seven months before Schwammberger was arrested. A group of mid-level army officers revolted in protest over the continued prosecutions and took control of a small army base near the Argentine capital. In a dramatic display of political courage, Alfonsín personally intervened and met with the mutinous captains, finally convincing them to free the base they were occupying.

Alfonsín returned to cheering throngs in Buenos Aires. He was at the acme of his political career. In a speech to supporters, the president observed that the multipartisan support given him in his efforts to quell the uprising had demonstrated to the world Argentina's "definitive decision to live in democracy."[3]

But the Argentine president's moment of triumph also signaled the unraveling of the government's commitment to continue the military prosecutions. Alfonsín learned from the experience that he could not continue the trials indefinitely. There were calls from many quarters for amnesty, for saying "Enough is enough," for leaving the unalterable past alone already. The point had been made. Of course, to the families of the "disappeareds" and the other victims of the civil war, to all those who believed that the country had not achieved a complete accounting for the past, the point was lost.

The prosecution of Josef Schwammberger in Argentina also communicated to the world the new democratic government's commitment to change. A decisive action against a Nazi who had lived so openly and against whom there appeared to be such overwhelming evidence, would go a long way to demarcating the present democracy from the Nazi-sympathizing past. Indirectly, prosecuting Schwammberger was also a way to attack Argentina's Peronist past.

There was another reason for responding decisively to Germany's renewed request for Schwammberger's extradition. Just as Germany's leaders were anxious to prosecute Schwammberger as a means of reconciling Germany with the rest of the world, so did Argentina need to reconcile itself with the rest of the world, particularly with the West. Argentina's fragile democracy, as always, would live or die on the viability of the nation's economy. A new Argentina, one where repressive generals were no longer tolerated, one where Nazi criminals were no longer welcome, was an Argentina that could be accepted again in the family of respectable nations.

For the new generation of political leaders, the message and the refurbished image were what mattered. It was not necessary to prosecute every army captain for human rights abuses during the Dirty War, although many would have preferred to continue the trials. Likewise, government officials figured it was not necessary to track down all the aged Nazis living off government pensions. One case was enough to make the point that Argentina was determined to begin afresh and to turn away from the ugliness of its past.

If Germany and Argentina had prosecuted Josef Schwammberger because it was the right thing to do, because it was the law, because of sterling intentions, good faith, and a commitment to right and justice, then the two governments would have acted much sooner and the elderly Nazi would have grown old in a German prison cell.

But the prosecution of Schwammberger had little to do with a commitment to justice and everything to do with politics. The prosecution of Schwammberger, an act of remembering, was at the same time a step in the direction of forgetting.

Schwammberger's arrest in the mountains outside Córdoba was still no guarantee that he would stand trial in Germany for the thousands of lives he had taken in Poland so many years before. The Alfonsín administration was committed to extraditing Schwammberger and to making a symbolic statement through the ex-Nazi's extradition, but the path from the Argentine police station to the German courtroom was by no means clear.

One concern for the Alfonsín government was the potential reaction among the influential Argentine Germans. Not surprisingly they were not pleased about Schwammberger's arrest for the same reasons that many Germans in Germany were unhappy that the government was continuing Nazi trials involving elderly defendants so many years after the fact.

Germans had made important contributions to Argentina throughout the country's history through capital investment, immigrant labor, and military training and equipment. Some believed the focus on Schwammberger and the renewed attention given to Argentina's past association with Nazi Germany might reflect badly on the many Argentine Germans who had nothing to do with Hitler.

Émigré groups frequently raised similar complaints in the United States when prosecutors sought to deport someone from their ranks who had concealed involvement in Nazi atrocities in order to gain American citizenship. Ukrainian American groups, for example, protested strenuously when the Justice Department moved against John Demjanjuk beginning in the late 1970s. These groups criticized the U.S. government's prosecution as somehow being an attack on their community.

During the Holocaust many concentration camp guards had been recruited from countries occupied by Nazi Germany, not only from Ukraine. After the war émigrés from these countries, many of which fell under Soviet domination, were outspokenly, even rabidly anti-Communist. Any efforts to prosecute one of their numbers for "Fascist" crimes, therefore, were perceived as part of some Soviet-sponsored campaign.

Anxieties within Argentina's German community were unfounded. The Schwammberger case did not signify the beginning of an all-out attack against Nazi fugitives in the country, much less against the entire German community, any more than the government was prepared to proceed indefinitely and at all levels against its military. Schwammberger would be the first Nazi extradited in twenty-five years, only the second in the country's history. In all probability the laws of nature would ensure that he would also be the last.

In addition to the political considerations that surrounded the case, two important and overlapping legal issues needed to be resolved before Schwammberger could be sent to Germany for trial. First, an Argentine court had to decide to grant Germany's extradition request even though no formal extradition treaty existed between the two nations. Second, Schwammberger had to be stripped of the Argentine citizenship he had acquired more than twenty years earlier because, under Argentine law, the government may not extradite a lawful citizen.

Judge Bretal in La Plata was assigned the extradition case.

His task was to decide whether Schwammberger's Argentine citizenship indeed was a barrier to his extradition and whether Argentina would recognize Germany's right to prosecute Schwammberger. A separate and simultaneous proceeding before a federal judge in Buenos Aires examined whether Schwammberger had obtained his Argentine citizenship fraudulently by concealing his involvement in Nazi-related crimes.

Schwammberger's devoted protector and guide through the maze of the Argentine judicial system was his gritty, chain-smoking defense lawyer, Dr. Miguel Ángel Siri.* A brash, slick-haired, criminal defense lawyer, Siri worked out of a small office that reeked of stale cigarette smoke at the end of a dark hallway in a run-down office building near the federal courthouse in Buenos Aires. A handsome, charming man, Siri had a rapid-fire speaking style. Frequently he darted quickly from one thought to the next in no particular order, all the while fidgeting, shifting in his seat as if he were on a caffeine and nicotine buzz, as clearly he was.

During Schwammberger's three-year-long legal battle Siri was more than the former SS man's legal adviser, more than merely his courtroom advocate. Siri was—and remains—Schwammberger's defender in the fullest sense of the word. "Schwammberger told me, 'I never killed anybody,' " Siri said in an interview, "and I believed him."[4]

Siri became involved in the case through a friend of Schwammberger's elder son, who lived with his wife and children outside Buenos Aires. "The [Schwammberger] family didn't have any money," Siri recalled, "and they wanted to know who they could trust."

A few days before his arrest in Huerta Grande, Schwammberger had burned his hand on some loose electrical cable.

*"Doctor" is an honorific many Argentine lawyers and other professionals use.

When he arrived in La Plata, therefore, he was taken immediately to a hospital for treatment. "It was totally deformed," Siri said. "So he had it operated on so he could open his hand again. He stayed in the hospital while he was sick."

When Schwammberger was transferred back to a prison cell in La Plata, the defense lawyer finally met with his client. "He was, how can I say, very much at peace, a grandfather, like those grandfathers who know everything," Siri recalled, describing his first impressions of Schwammberger. "He told me it wasn't worth defending [him], that it just wasn't worth it, because they were going to extradite him anyway. He was aware of the political considerations of his case."

After several meetings Siri became fond of his client. The lawyer saw in the old man qualities that those who remembered Schwammberger wearing an SS uniform would have found impossible to believe. "He's very sensitive, very emotional. I'd bring him chocolate, and he would smile like a child. And cheese. He loved Roquefort."

In the La Plata extradition case Siri's defense was limited to arguing that if Schwammberger, an Argentine citizen, were to be tried anywhere, it ought to be in Argentina. The country requesting Schwammberger's extradition in 1987, Siri asserted, was not the same country in whose service he had allegedly committed murder. The place where the crimes were supposedly committed, Galicia, was not even part of Germany any longer.

Moreover, Siri argued, it was neither legal nor fair to try Schwammberger for crimes that allegedly occurred so long ago. "I don't understand why they would prosecute someone after so long," he exclaimed. "He's a man of seventy-some years; he has lived within the law, led a peaceful life."

In the other proceeding, the denaturalization case in Buenos Aires, Siri's chief point of defense was that Schwammberger had been an upstanding citizen for more than two decades and that there was no hard evidence to prove that he had committed any of the crimes he was accused of having committed. "The primary cause for taking away citizenship is fighting for the enemy," Siri argued during an interview. "But to revoke citizenship for crimes that have not been proven, that occurred forty, fifty years ago, for which there is no evidence, that is crazy."

Schwammberger's defender rejected the viability of testimony from survivors so many years removed from the source of their memories. Listening to the survivors leaves the impression that Schwammberger was some sort of monster, Siri complained. "But they never say which Jew. They say, 'One day, in 1943 or 1942, in a cemetery, some people were made to dig a grave and then they were killed and put in it.' They never say which Jews."

Beyond these core defense arguments, some of which were barely legitimate as legal arguments, some of which were more sound, Siri went one step further in both Schwammberger's extradition and denaturalization proceedings. Not only was there no proof that his client was guilty, Siri maintained, but his client was innocent.

Any lawyer attempting to wage a defense of Schwammberger's case might raise questions of jurisdiction and evidence similar to those Siri offered. But Siri's defense became personal as well as legal. He was determined to present Schwammberger as a victim of injustice, as a harmless, gentle old man. The characterization indeed seemed to fit the physical image of the seventy-five-year-old former Nazi. But it bore no resemblance to the impression created by those who remembered him as a thirty-year-old whip-cracking SS man.

Relying on pseudocriminal psychology and his own impressions, Siri's defense of Schwammberger devolved into an exercise in the absurd. "Look at any book on the criminal mind," the lawyer ranted, lighting a new cigarette with the butt of another. "They all say that someone who commits such brutal, horrible crimes would be horrible all the time. He never killed one single Jew in all the years he was in

EXTRADITION

Buenos Aires, and he had plenty of opportunities because Buenos Aires is full of Jews. If he did all the things he is supposed to have done, how could he come here and be such a peace-loving person?"

Guillermo López, one of the lead prosecutors in Schwammberger's citizenship case, shared few personal qualities with the man who was his principal adversary in the case. Both men were in their early forties and were tall and handsome. The Schwammberger case was for López, a ten-year veteran in the federal Justice Department, one of the highest-profile matters in his career, just as it was for Siri. "The case was an extraordinary opportunity for me, one that comes only once in a lifetime," said López, who also worked on a federal prosecution team that handled several of the military trials.[5]

Like Siri, Lopez was surprised by his first impressions of the elderly former SS man. Describing his first visit to Schwammberger in jail, Lopez said he was astonished at the sight of a frail, sad-eyed grandfather. He was amazed that this man was accused of the most heinous crimes he had ever heard described. "I expected to see someone like the SS in the movies," López recalled of that jail cell meeting. "Instead I saw a man, peaceful, polite, a grandfather, very clean. If you put this man in the plaza with grandchildren, he'd fit perfectly. I expected to see a [Charles] Manson."

There ended the similarities between López and Siri. Siri was rough, while López was refined. Siri was slick, while López was smooth. Siri tended to rave, while López took his time, cogitated, waxed philosophical. Siri viewed Schwammberger as nothing more than an elderly man unjustly torn from the deserved comfort of his old age, while López considered him a major criminal whose prosecution stood as a symbol of the changes that had taken place in Argentina.

"Before Schwammberger the attitude in Argentina was to close one's eyes," López later reflected. "In 1983 [the year Alfonsín came to power] the society changed its way of thinking completely. And Schwammberger was a manifestation, the externalization of that change in attitude. This change in attitude toward the Nazis is part of a greater change in attitude, toward the concept of liberty, of justice, of rights. There's no going back to the old ways. There's no turning the clock back."

Working on the Schwammberger case opened López's eyes to the meaning of Argentina's move from authoritarian rule to democracy. On a more personal level the experience also forced him to see things he had never noticed before, to realize that he had been blind to certain social realities.

Jews had always been an influential group in Argentine society, López remarked, but "always there was an anti-Semitic attitude." Through his involvement in the case López began to appreciate this fact as he gained insight into the Jewish people's experience during the Holocaust. "For a long time we didn't have Jewish judges. Maybe we had one or two so we could say we had them. But really there were none."

The four survivors who traveled to Buenos Aires to testify at Schwammberger's denaturalization trial also had a profound effect on Lopez. "I was very impressed with the witnesses," he recalled later. "An Argentine would have wanted to kill Schwammberger—and kill him quite well! But these witnesses came because they wanted to see justice."

López remembered one witness in particular, Morris Reiter, a survivor from Przemysl who lived in Toronto, Canada. Reiter told stories that everyone in the courtroom found disturbing. However, López recalled, he and the presiding judge were not moved to tears by Reiter's testimony. "The judge and I didn't cry only because as Argentines we think men shouldn't cry," Lopez said, smiling.

When Abraham Secemsky heard the news that Josef Schwammberger had been arrested in Argentina, the first

thing he did was pray. "I immediately went to the synagogue
to thank God," recalled Secemsky, a retired clothing de-
signer then living in Chicago.[6] The second thing he did was
call Nazi hunter Simon Wiesenthal's Los Angeles headquarters to find out whom he could speak to about testifying
against Schwammberger.*

Secemsky had survived nine forced labor camps in Poland
and had encountered many men wearing Nazi uniforms. "I
forgot the others," Secemsky said. "But Mr. Schwammberger
I never forgot."

News reports of Schwammberger's capture had reached
scores of survivors from Przemysl and Rozwadow and Mielec
all over the world. Many, like Secemsky, were eager to come
out of more than forty years of obscurity and announce that
they were still alive and still remembered the murderous
deeds Schwammberger had committed fifty years before.

Nazi hunter Wiesenthal, who had followed the Schwammberger case for forty years, worked through his Los Angeles-
based research center to provide the Argentine prosecutors
with the names of witnesses willing to go to Buenos Aires
to testify. Secemsky and two other survivors leaped at the
opportunity when the Argentine government called. Wiesenthal even covered the travel costs for the witnesses when
officials of the nearly bankrupt Argentine government hesi-
tated over the expense.[†]

So in July 1988, in the middle of the Argentine winter,
Secemsky, along with Edward Blonder and Morris Reiter,
went to Buenos Aires anxious with anticipation over a meeting for which they had waited more than half their lives: a

---

*The Simon Wiesenthal Center was established in 1977 to promote
the study of the Holocaust.

[†]Other individuals and organizations, notably Nazi hunter Elliot
Welles of the New York-based Anti-Defamation League of B'nai B'rith,
also actively supported the effort to locate witnesses and facilitate the
Argentine and, later, the German prosecutions.

face-to-face confrontation with the man who had haunted their nights for forty-five years.*

Reiter, who had settled in Toronto after the war, considered the Argentina trip the fulfillment of a lifelong obligation. Blonder, a retired cabinetmaker from Miami, was driven by the desire to satisfy a vow he had made after his liberation from Auschwitz when he realized he had survived the Holocaust. If he were ever given the chance, Blonder had promised himself, he would meet Schwammberger again and show him how he had survived.

When the three men arrived in the Argentine capital, they learned that they would have to settle for a confrontation with Schwammberger's defense lawyer. The defendant himself had decided to remain in his prison cell in La Plata. After having come so far and having waited so long, the witnesses were still gratified to know that with their testimony Schwammberger might never again live as a free man.

While Judge Bretal in La Plata reviewed the legal issues surrounding Germany's extradition request, Judge Marcelo Eugenio Whatelet welcomed the three North American Jews to his hearing on the Argentine government's challenge of Schwammberger's citizenship.† If the prosecution could show that Schwammberger had obtained Argentine citizenship through falsifying or concealing material information—that is, his involvement in Nazi crimes—then he could lose his citizenship and with it any protection against extradition.

Many Nazi fugitives in South America, like Schwammberger, obtained citizenship in their host countries as an added measure of security against being handed over to prosecutors back in Germany or elsewhere in Europe. The

*Argentina is south of the equator, so its seasons are the opposite of those in the United States.

†A fourth witness, Cesia Miller, testified several weeks after the three men.

capture of Gerhard Bohne in Buenos Aires and his subsequent extradition to Germany for trial in 1966 had been all the warning many Nazis had needed to seek citizenship. It was no coincidence that Schwammberger had acquired naturalized status just one year after Bohne's arrest.

Many Nazi fugitives in the United States had followed the same path in trying to avoid detection and prosecution. Most Nazis hiding in the United States, however, had not waited as long as Schwammberger had before obtaining citizenship. On the other hand, Nazis in the United States had not had such avid champions in the White House as those hiding in Argentina had had in the Casa Rosada in Buenos Aires.

Ultimately, however, no protection was absolute. During the 1950s and 1960s the U.S. Immigration and Naturalization Service prosecuted a handful of Nazis for concealing their Nazi affiliations to obtain U.S. citizenship. In 1979 the Justice Department's OSI began expanding the effort to ferret out Nazi criminals who had illegally entered the country. After thirty years of tacit tolerance of Nazi criminals living in the United States, OSI prosecutors had tremendous success in denaturalizing and expelling such individuals.*

Guillermo López and the rest of the Argentine prosecution team hoped for similarly favorable results when Judge Whatelet opened Schwammberger's denaturalization trial on the morning of July 5, 1988. In a dingy courtroom in the Argentine federal building in downtown Buenos Aires, López led the interrogation of Morris Reiter, the first of the survivor witnesses to testify. After identifying his witness, López asked Reiter to describe his contacts with Schwammberger in the Przemysl ghetto.[7]

---

*As of March 31, 1993, the OSI has had a nearly perfect track record. In eighty-five cases the government has lost only three times. Numerous other cases are still pending.

Reiter told the court that he made wooden bookcases for Schwammberger and that their first encounter was a discussion about the project. Reiter lived and worked in the half of the ghetto reserved for the SS workshops, the so-called *Arbeitghetto*, or working ghetto. Reiter also made wooden suitcases for Schwammberger, which, he later learned, the Nazi commandant used for storing all the valuables he took from the Jews in the ghetto.

What were the conditions under which the Jews were transferred from Przemysl to the other camps? López asked. "The same conditions under which cattle are transferred," Reiter responded.

Did Schwammberger employ any special measures against the Jews during the evacuation or to prevent escapes? López probed. "Being surrounded by the SS, that was enough," Reiter answered shakily. "The SS members had rifles and bayonets with which they whipped the people and told them to go faster all the time. Before the evacuation everything of value was taken from them, rings, watches, gold teeth, and also they took their coats and shoes so that they could not escape and they put them in wagons that were open, that were not for transporting people, but cattle."

Schwammberger's defense lawyer, Siri, conducted a cross-examination that was as scattered as his conversational style. In one series of questions, for example, he asked if Reiter was Jewish. Reiter confirmed that he was. Siri then asked if Reiter knew the organization Beate Klarsfeld, apparently referring to the noted French Nazi hunter. Reiter said he did not know the group. Without pursuing the matter, Siri next asked whether Reiter had ever brought a civil action against Schwammberger. Reiter testified that he had not.

Siri next wanted to know if Reiter was receiving any compensation from the German government or any other government. Reiter confirmed that he did indeed receive a pension from the German government, a payment afforded to all Holocaust survivors who can document a certain measure of physical disability. Reiter told the court he had been receiving the modest pension for more than thirty years.

Strangely, Siri inquired if Reiter was a practicing Jew. Reiter answered that he considered himself a Conservative Jew—that is, not as strict in observing religious regulations as Orthodox Jews. In a bizarre follow-up Siri then inquired if Reiter knew what a *goy* was. The witness said that he did not use the term but that he knew it referred to those who are not Jewish, such as Catholics and Protestants.

What were his feelings toward Schwammberger? Siri then asked. "I have no reason to hate him or to hold any rancor toward him because that is not going to help him," Reiter answered. "Everyone has to respect and be respected. During the war it was not so. Everyone has his religion, Catholic or Jewish, and it has to be respected or else the result will be negative."

Siri clearly had no coherent defense to offer his client. The defense lawyer asked a number of other questions of Reiter, but they managed only to elicit additional details of Schwammberger's brutal treatment of the Jewish prisoners in his charge.

In the afternoon Edward Blonder took the stand. Again López first led the witness through his testimony. Blonder recalled Schwammberger and his German shepherd, Prinz, and the forced labor workshops of the Przemysl ghetto. Once a week or so, Blonder recounted, the workers were made to line up for a roll call. At one of these assemblies a teenage boy standing in line happened to bend down to pick up something. "Schwammberger's aide saw the young man and went to draw his weapon, but Schwammberger stopped him and told the young man to kneel down," Blonder testified. "The young man on his knees stayed looking at Schwammberger face-to-face, and then very rapidly he fired and killed him."

Blonder was chosen to cart away the body in a wooden wagon. The witness told the court that he remembered touching the body and feeling that it was still warm.

Some of Siri's cross-examination, again, was simply bizarre. The only success Siri seemed to have was in getting the witness to admit that he had never personally witnessed Schwammberger taking valuables from anyone in the ghetto. At another point, however, Siri began to ask how Blonder could be certain who was responsible for killing people but then withdrew the question, perhaps remembering that Blonder had already testified to incidents that made him an eyewitness to murder.

At the next day's session Schwammberger's defense lawyer left the courtroom in the middle of Abraham Secemsky's testimony and did not bother to return.

Five years after Raúl Alfonsín's election as president, the Argentine government was finally poised to extradite its first Nazi in more than a quarter century. On November 28, 1988, Judge Bretal of La Plata delivered his decision. After reviewing the history of extraditions in Argentina, background on the Nazi trials at Nuremberg, the history of the SS, and written statements from some of the survivors of Przemysl and Rozwadow, Bretal granted Germany's extradition request.

Judge Bretal rejected every one of Schwammberger's defense arguments. The Federal Republic of Germany, he decided, was indeed the legitimate heir to the Third Reich as far as prosecuting Nazi criminals was concerned. One could not allow crimes, not least of all the crimes of the Nazi Holocaust, to go unpunished simply because the map of Europe had been redrawn.

Bretal also rebuffed Siri's argument that Schwammberger was an Argentine citizen and therefore ought to be tried in Argentina, not Germany. As the judge pointed out, Schwammberger allegedly committed the crimes for which Germany was seeking his extradition nearly twenty-five years before he obtained Argentine citizenship. Clearly, the judge decided, Schwammberger had sought naturalization as a shield from prosecution, an act that should not be condoned.

Schwammberger's fate would be doubly sealed if Judge Whatelet in Buenos Aires found that Schwammberger had obtained his Argentine citizenship through deceit and that it should therefore be revoked. While waiting for a decision in that case, Siri appealed Judge Bretal's finding.

In spite of the progress made so far in Schwammberger's extradition, the seventy-six-year-old Nazi's fate was hardly sealed. In addition to the uncertainty surrounding the final outcome of the two legal proceedings, two other important developments suggested that there was still a chance that Schwammberger might never be extradited, that he might never actually stand trial for murder.

The Argentine political landscape changed dramatically after Schwammberger's arrest, and this raised some doubts about the government's continued commitment to returning the elderly Nazi to Germany. In the last year of his administration President Alfonsín began to lose his grip on power. The man who had shown such fortitude and charisma began to project malaise as he saw his public support eroding. The opposition Peronists had won sweeping victories in provincial elections in 1987. Alfonsín's inability to spur the economy and control inflation bedeviled his government and raised Peronist hopes for recapturing the presidential palace in the 1989 national elections.

Sure enough, on May 14, 1989, a dashing lawyer named Carlos Saúl Menem, the fifty-eight-year-old son of Syrian immigrants, was swept into power. It was a historic moment in Argentine political history. For the first time in sixty years one democratically elected president handed power peacefully to a democratically elected successor.

Menem was vibrant in victory, a refreshing change for a people who had grown accustomed to Alfonsín's dour, bulldog jowls. Recognizing that national self-confidence was critical to rebuilding the country's economy, Menem projected a youthful, can-do image. His instinct for photo opportunities, such as one in which he posed in a bathing suit, and the playboy image he cultivated, were just what the Argentine voters ordered.

But Menem's election was initially a cause of great concern for those anxiously awaiting Schwammberger's extradition to Germany. Many worried that Menem might not share Alfonsín's commitment to supporting the prosecution against Schwammberger and to cleansing Argentina's longstanding reputation as a sanctuary for Nazi criminals.

One cause of concern was Menem's Arab heritage. Some, especially those in the Argentine Jewish community, wondered if he would be as sympathetic as Alfonsín to Jewish concerns. Alfonsín had enjoyed strong support in the Jewish community, even going so far as to include several Jews in his cabinet. Some critics, reflecting the anti-Semitic strains not so deeply buried in the Argentine consciousness, nicknamed the Alfonsín administration the Radical Synagogue, playing on the name of Alfonsín's political party.

Menem's Peronist pedigree gave little comfort to those fretting over the new president's attitude toward the Schwammberger case or to the Jewish community in general. After all, Juan Perón had introduced Mussolini-style fascism to Argentina, cut off Jewish immigration to the country during the Holocaust, and endorsed anti-Jewish violence. Moreover, Perón was the very reason that Schwammberger and dozens of other Nazis had come to Argentina in the first place.

Menem also sparked concern about Schwammberger's fate because of the clear message of his presidential campaign. Menem appealed to the Argentine people to close the book on the past and look toward a brighter future. Alfonsín had never suggested that the military trials should continue indefinitely. But Menem went so far as to begin granting amnesty to those already serving time. Pleading the need for national reconciliation, he went on a pardoning binge. Many worried that as president Menem would adopt a similar forgive-and-forget attitude toward Schwammberger.

But politics is rarely predictable. Menem quickly began to deal effectively with the sputtering economy where Alfonsín had failed so awfully. Menem allied himself politically with the United States and with Europe, where Alfonsín had tried to assert himself as the leader of the so-called unaligned nations, a term that lost its relevance in the post-cold war era.

And in spite of initial skepticism, Menem condemned the authoritarian roots of his own party and refused to turn his back on the Argentine Jewish community. Alfonsín had traveled to dozens of countries during his presidency, including many Arab countries, but he had never visited Israel. Some criticized Alfonsín for deliberately avoiding Israel so as not to offend his unaligned allies, many of whom tended to be pro-Palestinian and anti-Israeli. Early in his administration, by contrast, Menem vowed to go Israel.

The new president also committed Argentine support to the allies during the Gulf War in 1991, setting himself in stark contrast with Argentina's neutrality during the Second World War and with Alfonsín's entire approach to foreign policy.

Finally, Menem also affirmed the Argentine government's commitment to seeing Josef Schwammberger extradited to Germany to stand trial. Schwammberger had lost his appeal of the La Plata extradition case in August 1989, just two months after Menem assumed the presidency. One month later Buenos Aires Federal Judge Whatelet revoked Schwammberger's Argentine citizenship. And in November

1989 Menem's attorney general, Oscar Roger, submitted to the Argentine Supreme Court the government's brief arguing for the upholding of the lower court decisions in both cases.

Only one court's opinion now remained between Schwammberger and a criminal trial in Germany. More than ever, time was a critical factor. Schwammberger, by this point, was nearly seventy-eight years old. Just two days after the Argentine government had filed its appeal to the Supreme Court, the significance of this fact came into sharp focus.

On November 23, 1989, Schwammberger was found collapsed in his La Plata jail cell. He was taken immediately to the prison hospital, where it was announced that he was in a coma resulting from a drug overdose. Forty-one years earlier, the onetime druggist's apprentice had been clever enough to use prescription drugs to sneak his way past his Austrian prison guards. Now, as he was so close to being returned to Germany to face judgment as a Nazi murderer, it seemed he might just have pulled off the ultimate escape.

Suicide had been a favored tactic by Nazi officials facing capture or trial. Hitler and Goebbels had taken their own lives in the Berlin bunker rather than fall into enemy hands as Mussolini had. In his Nuremberg jail cell Göring had crunched a cyanide capsule between his teeth minutes before he was to have gone to the hangman.

Other Nazi figures had died under more mysterious circumstances. Walter Rauff, the inventor of the mobile killing vans that were used with such devastating efficiency in the Nazi-occupied eastern territories, died in a Chilean jail in 1984 before he could be extradited. And Walter Kutschmann, of course, died in his Buenos Aires jail cell in 1986, conveniently, just before his extradition to Germany could be finalized.

Schwammberger's medical emergency also smelled of scandal. At first doctors reported that Schwammberger had overdosed on a sleeping pill that prison authorities had pre-scribed for him. Subsequent tests revealed that Schwamm-berger had also ingested a second sedative, one that the prison officials had not prescribed and that, in combination with the other drug, probably triggered the coma.

Doctors were able to resuscitate the elderly Nazi twenty-four hours later. Extra security was added to monitor his cell. But the question of where Schwammberger obtained the second drug remained unanswered.

Four months later Schwammberger was well enough to receive news that his appeals had finally been exhausted. On March 20, 1990, the Argentine Supreme Court issued its rulings in both the extradition and denaturalization cases. The high court ruled that Germany's extradition request ought to be granted because Germany indeed had a legiti-mate claim to try Nazi crimes, and it found that Schwamm-berger was not entitled to the protection of Argentine citizenship because he had procured that status fraudulently.

The court's opinion in the denaturalization case paid spe-cial attention to the defense advanced by Schwammberger's lawyer. Siri had attempted to reduce to the absurd the prose-cution's claims, but instead the court found his approach absurd. "He says, in effect, that if the deeds attributed to his client are true, then Schwammberger was a compulsive, maniacal killer of Jews," wrote Supreme Court Justice Eu-genio Bulygin. "But because he lived in Argentina for forty years without killing even one Jews [Siri further argues], it follows that he never killed anyone. The same 'argument' could be used to demonstrate that Eichmann for all his life was a philanthropist dedicated to helping Jews in need."[8]

The Supreme Court's sometimes sarcastic opinion cleared the last obstacle to Schwammberger's extradition. As the final details for his transfer were negotiated by Argentine and German officials, the elderly former SS man said his good-byes to his wife and son.

On the afternoon of May 3, 1990, Josef Schwammberger was taken to the Buenos Aires international airport. Christoph Hölscher, an assistant prosecutor from Stuttgart, had come to accompany him on the flight to Germany. A West German doctor and a number of Argentine and German security police officers were also ready to make the trip.

The next morning Schwammberger landed in Frankfurt. He looked weary and frightened as he stepped carefully down the airplane stairs and onto the tarmac. A police van was waiting to take him on the three-hour drive to Stuttgart. Josef Schwammberger was home again.

CHAPTER 13

THE MEANING
OF SURVIVAL

A man's dying is more the survivor's affair than
his own.
—Thomas Mann

During the forty years Josef Schwammberger
spent in his Argentine refuge, Sally and Arnold
Susskind struggled to rebuild their lives. For
them life had to go on even after the guns had fired the last
shots of the war, after the last victim of the Holocaust had
died of starvation or disease. All around them there had been
death on a biblical scale. Through some mad combination of
fortune and misfortune they had outlasted the conflagration.
Something inside each of them had proven resistant, resilient.

In 1947, while they gathered their strength and awaited
immigration papers in a camp for displaced persons at Bergen-Belsen, they had a baby girl. Eagerly, desperately, they
had begun the process of living again, of reliving, of refilling
as best they could the empty spaces. Nothing could replace
the lives lost, but a new life, a new beginning, a new child
at least represented a step toward the future and out of the
mire of the painful past.

The Susskinds had wanted to move to Israel, to fulfill their lifelong ambitions and join in the national dream finally being realized in the Jewish settlements of Palestine. In the cities being built, on the arid land being irrigated, in the armies being trained, a battered people was forging the foundations of a new nation. "I had bought furniture, a gas range, refrigerator, all German-made," Arnold recalled. Sally had a sister who had managed to emigrate before the war. They planned to join her in the port city of Haifa.

But while they were still living in the displaced persons camp in Germany, Arnold was forced to undergo surgery on a ruptured disk in his back. He realized that he would have to put off the move to Israel. "This was now 1950, and it was tough in Israel. How you going to do physical work?" Arnold wondered.

So in July 1950 Arnold and Sally moved to New York where—hard as it may be to believe for those who know the New York of the 1990s—they felt their lives would be less physically strenuous. Arnold got a job in the shipping department of a factory that made engraving machines. They had a house in a residential part of Queens, and at night Arnold went to school to learn English. "I progressed and became a junior manager. And I was successful, and I bought a stationery store, just like I used to have before the war."

In 1970 Arnold sold the business and went to work part-time for an advertising agency in Manhattan. There he had a disturbing encounter with the past. "I met over there, how you call it, a receptionist. I saw she has an accent. So I said, 'Can you tell me where you from?' She said, 'I am originally from Holland.' And I said, 'From Holland? I have a sister there.'"

The truth was that Arnold had neither seen nor heard from his sister, Annie, since she had moved to Amsterdam before the start of the war. They had completely lost contact. While he was still living in a displaced persons camp in

Germany, Arnold had tried in vain through the Red Cross to locate her. He didn't know whether to assume she had survived, perhaps taking a new identity to save herself, or to figure she had been killed. He did not know what to think.

Now, after more than thirty years, this Dutch secretary not only said she knew the family of Annie's husband but promised to see what she could find out the next time she went home for a visit. "That's how I found out my sister died," Arnold related, letting out a deep breath he seemed to have been holding through this story.

When she returned from Holland, the receptionist gave Arnold the name of his lost sister's best friend, a woman who had since moved to Chicago. When Arnold contacted the friend, he learned that she had managed somehow to save something that had belonged to Annie: a tattered album containing photographs of Arnold's family. "That's the way I have pictures of my parents, because I didn't have any before," Arnold explained, adding thoughtfully, "It's a lot of things happen in life."

To the Susskinds, Josef Schwammberger was more than a symbol, more than some abstraction of the Nazi evil. For them he was—and remains—very real, very specific, very memorable. Schwammberger stood out as the most important "thing" that happened to their lives. The SS commandant took their four-year-old son. He sent their friends and families to the gas chambers. He erased their traces from the villages and cities of their youth.

To most people the Holocaust is a generalized concept, a term simultaneously remote and familiar.* The label, meant

*Ironically the term "Holocaust" was not even widely recognized until the late 1950s because the killing of Jews in concentration camps was not widely viewed until then as a historical event distinct from the Second World War. See James Young, *Writing and Rewriting the Holocaust* (Bloomington: Indiana University Press, 1988), p. 87, who argues that non-Jewish historians especially were hesitant until this time to differentiate between Jewish and non-Jewish victims.

to encompass and suggest everything, ultimately reduces a complex historical period to the most simplistic interpretation and only more so over time. But the essence is not the whole. As far as Arnold and Sally are concerned, they are Holocaust survivors, but more to the point, they are Schwammberger survivors. Those who survived were not only victims of dark and destructive forces—violent anti-Semitism, rabid nationalism, and nazism—but also people, the Schwammbergers of the Holocaust, individual men with haunting faces and unforgettable voices.

Surviving the Holocaust, in short, was only the beginning. Having survived Schwammberger and the Holocaust, Arnold and Sally had to struggle to survive the survival. "We had a hard time," explained Sally. "When we were liberated, we had nothing. It was a fight for surviving, for raising some children, for getting some education."

Even if they had found the mental strength to put away all thoughts of what they had lived through—an impossibility—there were still the countless physical reminders that could never be eliminated. There was the time, for example, several months before his liberation, when an SS man shot Arnold in the leg as he and a column of haggard Jewish prisoners were led along an icy road on a "death march" toward Buchenwald.

"We already had bleeding sores, shoes were falling apart, snow and cold," Arnold remembered. "This guy was holding on to me, and the SS man saw him falling down. I couldn't hold him, he was only maybe eighty pounds. So [the SS man] aimed at him and shot my leg. I felt the blood coming out, only I couldn't say nothing. Then it was stiff. I suffer even today on that when it's bad weather."

The most enduring hardship of survival, however, was the unending burden of the memories. Survivors do not exist as survivors for only a moment in time. Just as an addict can recover but never be cured, so a survivor is liberated but can never be completely freed from the thing survived. The drug that courses always through the bloodstream of a survivor is memory. It may be repressed, it may grow faint, but it is never erased.

Fifty years after their miraculous reunion at Bergen-Belsen, Arnold and Sally Susskind appeared in the kitchen of their modest home as an average elderly couple. They did not wear neon signs around their necks identifying them as Holocaust survivors, although the numbered tattoos on their forearms marked them indelibly as the once-doomed. Yet they did witness such horrors as one imagines possible only in the hellfires of an inhuman other world. They witnessed, they survived, and uncontrollably they remembered.

This inescapable fusion with the past was for the Susskinds like a life sentence without parole. The millions who died took their pain and suffering with them to their graves. To the survivors fell the burden of remembering that past for the rest of their days. Every day and every night offered another chance to endure the excruciating memories.

The nightmares continued long after they had settled into their new lives in America. At least once a week Arnold awoke in a sweat. Sally's bad dreams came even more frequently. As she explained, waving her swollen, arthritic hands, "You can write books, you can make movies, but you can never know what it was really like."

To the Susskinds there is nothing at all unusual about their ability and desire to remember. For them there is no other choice. "You remember what you cannot forget," explained Arnold. "Some things I do forget. But you get together [with other survivors]. This one remembers this; another remembers that. That's how you remember. I don't really have such a great memory. I wouldn't say so. Only these are things in you. Sometimes it comes to my mind something is fifty years dead. And all of a sudden comes to me something like a light. You live in a place so many years, you are born there, you are raised there. There is a lot of history."

Arnold and Sally have been open about their experiences. "You know, when my grandson was in fifth grade," Arnold said, "and his teacher was a Jewish person, and I became very friendly with her, and she invited me I should come once in a while and explain the Holocaust story to the kids. And I was teaching them a little Hebrew."

Arnold was always surprised to find how little the children knew about history and about the Holocaust. That was not the case with their own child. Arnold and Sally taught their daughter and their grandson so they would understand. "Our grandson used to say, 'I'm going to bury them [the Nazis] here and here and here,'" Sally related. "At two years old! Because I told him. My daughter, she knows. But a lot of people said, 'What am I going to tell them? They're going to cry.' The children, they didn't want them to have this."

Many survivors, it is true, hid themselves away after the war, bottled up the past, refused to confront it, expose it, tried as hard as possible to forget or at least to keep it to themselves. Many did not want to impose on their children the pain of their past. Some felt guilty for surviving when so many did not.

Opinion polls suggesting that large segments of the population would rather have the Holocaust simply forgiven and forgotten have underscored the significance of those Holocaust survivors, like the Susskinds, who were determined to remember. A 1986 Harris poll found that 42 percent of Americans thought Jews should "stop complaining about what happened to them in Nazi Germany." A Roper poll from around the same time found that 40 percent of Americans believed Jews "should stop focussing on the Holocaust."

Similar results have been found in Europe. In a poll of German attitudes toward Jews taken less than one year after the fall of the Berlin Wall in 1989, 39 percent said they believed "Jews exploit the National-Socialist Holocaust for their own purposes." Nearly 40 percent of those polled said Jews today, as in the past, exerted too much influence over world events. And perhaps most disturbing, 58 percent said they believed it was time to put the memory of the Holocaust behind them.[1] In a similar study of Austrian attitudes 53 percent said they thought "it is time to put the memory of the Holocaust behind us."[2]

Even while the Holocaust was still raging, there were those who sought to guarantee that the crimes of Nazi Germany would not be forgotten. The world owes a great debt to those who did not survive but who kept some record of what was happening during the last days of their tortured lives. Anne Frank could never have imagined how many people would one day read her diary and through it gain some insight into what it was like to live in that time. Others, those who stashed and buried notes and messages and documents and journals, were well aware that they were ensuring that the world would believe and remember what happened and how it happened.

Many Holocaust survivors, even some from Przemysl, wrote memoirs about their experiences.[3] In addition to the multitude of personal accounts, there have been numerous semiofficial histories written of various towns and villages in Poland. These "memory" books were actually collections of essays and remembrances written by survivors. Articles in Hebrew and Yiddish gave the history of the town and the Jewish community, biographies of well-known rabbis and community leaders, and the story of the liquidation of the town's Jewish population.[4]

Some survivors pursued more private means of ensuring memory. One woman from Przemysl sat herself down shortly after she had been liberated by British troops at Bergen-Belsen and wrote a chronology of her experiences so she would never forget what she had been through. Then she put her chronology in a safe-deposit box. Decades later, when she felt her memory growing more and more fuzzy, she could consult her scraps of yellowed paper to help her fill in the gaps.

For the Susskinds, talking about the past seemed to bring an odd sense of comfort. Most of their friends were Holocaust survivors. They settled in a neighborhood in Queens, across the East River from Manhattan, which was heavily Jewish and housed a large number of survivors. They both became active in Jewish community organizations. Far from trying to escape the past, the Susskinds surrounded themselves with constant reminders of their past.

Some Jewish scholars and writers have worried that if Jews dwell on the Holocaust, they will only further impair their own self-esteem, that they will perpetuate the image of the Jew as victim. However, remembering can also be a means to "conquer the shame," as one historian has observed. "Put otherwise, Jewish memory is a way of keeping faith with the dead and those who have survived, making sure that their terrible suffering is not forgotten."[5]

Following closely the developments in Josef Schwammberger's case was also a way for the Susskinds to keep faith with the dead and keep in touch with their past. The day he learned Schwammberger had been arrested in Argentina was a memorable one for Arnold. "I was glad he was caught. At that time we still didn't believe he would be sent to Germany."

When Schwammberger was indeed extradited from Argentina in May 1990, Kurt Schrimm, the Stuttgart prosecutor, began assembling testimony from potential witnesses all over the world. In the months leading up to the trial, Schrimm, along with Schwammberger's German defense lawyer, Dieter König, and the judge in charge of the case, Herbert Luippold, traveled to New York, Miami, Tel Aviv, and other cities where survivors could more easily come to give their statements.

Both Arnold and Sally testified at the German consulate in New York when the traveling German court came to town. Sally was unable to pick out the defendant from a group of wartime photographs. But Arnold managed. "I recognized right away," he said with a boast.

Only a few witnesses had traveled to Buenos Aires to testify at Schwammberger's extradition proceedings. Now, with the German prosecutor gathering witness statements— the Germans call them protocols—many more survivors had a chance to tell their stories. For some, testifying against Schwammberger was like unburdening their souls. For others, the opportunity represented a chance to unlock the pent-up sorrow and fear, or to vent deeply rooted rage, or to fulfill a sense of duty to the dead.

The quasi-courtroom atmosphere of the pretrial hearing also proved an emotional shock to many survivors. Those who had found audiences for their stories in the past were accustomed to sympathetic responses. But it was not the German lawyers' job to be sympathetic. They could be polite as possible, but their mission was to listen to the testimony and assess the credibility of the witness.

In order to test for accuracy, the lawyers needed to challenge the survivors for specific details. Both prosecution and defense had to be extremely sensitive to this point. Schrimm was fortunate because he had a list of more than one hundred potential witnesses, many of them eyewitnesses to killings committed by Schwammberger. Often in Nazi crimes cases prosecutors had only a couple of witnesses with whom to work. With Schwammberger, Schrimm could concentrate on putting forward only his most credible testimony.

From the defense point of view, the clarity of the witness's memory was also crucial. The prosecution had no documentary evidence, aside from Schwammberger's 1945 written confession. The entire case then would turn on the quality of testimony from those who claimed to have witnessed firsthand Schwammberger's alleged crimes. As the former

Nazi's defense lawyers saw it, their only hope for success was to assail, but delicately, each witness's credibility.

For many of those who came before the court—and who later came before the trial court in Stuttgart—these depositions were excruciating. They could not understand why there should be any question about their truthfulness. Any challenge to the reliability of their memory was seen as a challenge to their integrity and a personal insult. They had been there, and they had seen with their own eyes. Who could make up such stories?

Sally's visit to the German consulate in New York was traumatizing. She had already indicated to the lawyers that her memory was not so finely tuned when she had been unable to pick out Schwammberger's face from a group of photographs. Then, when she told the German judges that she had seen Schwammberger in the act of shooting a Jew in the ghetto, Schwammberger's defense lawyer asked her if she could recall what kind of gloves the SS man was wearing.

"So I said, 'Do you remember fifty years ago what you were wearing?'" Sally screeched, re-creating her indignation. "And he said, 'A black-colored uniform.' And I got so, you know, how could he ask a question like that? So I told him I was so upset, and he said, 'I'm sorry, Mrs. Susskind, don't get upset, but I get paid to do this. I have to defend him.' And I said, 'I don't care, don't ask me such questions. I am not now in Germany under Hitler's commander.'"

Arnold's day before the German lawyers went more smoothly. For six hours he recounted his experiences in Przemysl during Schwammberger's reign. The prosecutor was pleased with his testimony and asked if he would be willing to testify in person when the trial itself got under way the following spring. "They begged me to go," Arnold bragged.

Many survivors were eager to testify against Schwammberger in court. Others, such as Dr. Marcel Tuchman, were nervous about confronting Schwammberger in person but ultimately considered themselves bound to go no matter how painful the encounter. Some felt the trip would be too strenuous, physically and emotionally. One woman who had survived Schwammberger and the Przemysl ghetto worried about her heart condition and wondered whether a face-to-face meeting with Schwammberger would kill her. (She ended up overcoming her fears and testifying.)

Others simply could not be persuaded to go back to Germany for Schwammberger's trial or for any other reason. The German government offered to cover all expenses— and did so—for any witnesses who traveled to Stuttgart to testify at the trial. But money was not the issue. Arnold Susskind, for one, just could not bring himself even to set foot again in Germany. The associations, no matter how old, were still vivid. Fifty years had not erased the fear and the distrust.

"To some Germans, [Schwammberger] is a hero," Arnold explained with uncharacteristic excitement. "To some, he didn't kill enough Jews. I'm sure of that. I don't trust the Germans no matter how democratic they are, especially when they come together with the east. Is a bunch of Gestapo over there, Nazis plenty. Who can trust them?"

Arnold could no more easily imagine facing Schwammberger again, actually sitting in the same room with the man who had sent his parents to their deaths. "I can't face him. I wouldn't be responsible for myself. How would you, God forbid, someone murdered your family, how could you sit across from the murderer? I can't. Maybe if I were younger, yes. But I am not in a position to do it."

There was another reason for Susskind's refusal. As pleased as he was over Schwammberger's arrest, he believed that the crimes the SS man had committed were so great that they could never be compensated for or otherwise rectified in any courtroom. Especially after so many years had passed, after

Schwammberger had enjoyed the life of a free man for so long, Susskind wondered what would be the point in going to such effort to see him locked in jail.

"In Germany is no death penalty," Arnold noted. "So let's say he'll get life. He's seventy-eight years old. Believe me he will have better in jail over there than some people not in jail. So what's the use? Just the aggravation and things like that?"

The Susskinds simply believed they had taken the process as far as they could go. They felt a sense of obligation to their past and to Jewish history, and that was why they were willing, even eager to testify in New York. Yet they had grown old. And they had been survivors for some fifty years. They could bring themselves to come only so close to the man they had survived.

As many times as they had talked about it, as much as the Holocaust had haunted their nights, as much as they had sought comfort in those who shared the experience and gladness in the purely innocent ones, their daughter and grandson, there still were moments, even for them, when the whole thing seemed impossible. "It really was a miracle how we survived," Sally concluded. "Maybe it was a dream. Maybe it's not really true."

Sam Nussbaum had good reason to be so pleased with himself. After all, he enjoyed a comfortable retirement. He had a spacious home in Overland Park, a pleasant suburb of Kansas City. He had a close-knit family, four children and six grandchildren, all grinning in the wall-to-wall photograph that hung over the sitting room sofa. One son had followed his path into the plumbing business. One son was a rabbi. Nussbaum and his wife of nearly fifty years had their health and financial security, too.

In conversation Nussbaum showed himself to be, like many elderly men and women, a great storyteller. He also delighted in a certain arrogance. He was not the least bit shy about boasting of how ingenious he had been through the many years of his life. When he started in the plumbing business in Kansas City in 1948, for example, he was broke. "I didn't have a nickel in my pocket."

If he was going to earn the best wage, he knew he had to join the union. But there were no Jews in the plumbers' union in Kansas City at that time. So he determined to beat the system. He was fast, and the quality of his work was high— he would be so bold as to say—and he managed always to finish just minutes before the union inspector came around to try to throw him off the job. Finally, the union officials collapsed like panting dogs that give up trying to catch their own tails. They asked him to join.

Ingenuity, that was the theme of Sam Nussbaum's life, as he told it. That, too, was the theme of his survival. Being clever saved him from the fate that his parents and five brothers and sisters all met during the Holocaust.

In his own eyes Nussbaum viewed himself during the years in Poland as an innocent, as a young man who was buffeted from the edge of one precipice to the brink of another. "What happened to me, you wouldn't believe it," he reflected during an interview nearly half a century later. Nussbaum marveled at the dangers he faced, the times he managed to escape just a step ahead of certain death. He acknowledged a measure of luck, too, even serendipity. But mainly, looking back on that time, Nussbaum credited his wits, his ability to recognize an opportunity and to take advantage of it.

As he highlighted his experiences during the Holocaust years with dramatic stories of near catastrophe, the secret of his success became clear. Ingenuity alone did not save his life again and again. Luck was not his only blessing. Sam Nussbaum survived because he ingratiated himself with his persecutors, including the man who sent his family to their deaths, Josef Schwammberger. These relationships were usually founded on his abilities as a handyman. In each case his reward for a job well done was a reprieve from execution.

That was how Nussbaum avoided being selected for deportation and death during the first major *Aktion* in the Przemysl ghetto. Likewise, he avoided the wrath of Schwammberger by fixing the SS man's sink and building him a vodka distillery. He bought off the camp kapo at the Polish mine where he was taken from the ranks of the condemned at Auschwitz to work as a slave laborer. Time after time Nussbaum found a way out of trouble, even death.

In his view, Nussbaum could not have behaved any differently. He stood close to Schwammberger, true. He repaired the man's toilet. He ran odd job errands for him, saw him nearly every day. But what harm was done? "I didn't do nothing," Nussbaum insisted. "I just fixed the plumbing and made vodka for him. I didn't cooperate with him. I just normal. He didn't give me any food. I was starving. But I fixed all the leaks they had in the camp."

Schwammberger did grant Nussbaum one favor, however, and it was the ultimate form of gratitude, considering the circumstances. "He didn't do nothing special for me except that he did not kill me," Nussbaum said.

Nussbaum's conduct during the Holocaust remains difficult, if not impossible, to assess. Some may find it easy enough to say uncategorically that it would have been better to face death before knowingly helping the Nazis to kill Jews—or anyone for that matter—especially if helping meant serving on the Jewish police or acting as a kapo. Others might argue that even more innocent people would have suffered, more would have died, if only the most heartless, the most remorseless individuals had filled those positions.

But what about the plumber? Who can really say what one

would have done in Sam Nussbaum's place? As he himself pointed out, he was hardly the only one given a way of avoiding the gas chambers. Everyone who worked for a crust of bread sewing uniforms, sorting the clothing left behind by those who had just passed through the gas chambers, burying the dead, acting as a medic in a concentration camp barrack, all the people who worked to stay alive also at the same time in some small way lent a hand to the Nazis' extermination effort.

Duldig, the first head of Przemysl's Jewish council, was a martyr for refusing to turn over Jewish children to the Gestapo. Teich, Schwammberger's aide-de-camp, was a criminal for assisting the Nazis directly in the extortion of valuables and the rounding up of innocent Jews for deportation to the death camps. Everyone whose conduct fell between these two extremes was a Sam Nussbaum.

Nussbaum survived. He made his choices, and he lived nearly fifty more years to testify to his experiences and tell the world what he saw. He survived, but he also suffered. After his liberation the suffering continued, just as it did for the Susskinds, although in different ways.

The woman he married was also a Holocaust survivor, but they rarely discussed what they had been through. Instead the Nussbaums dealt with their feelings of loss and pain in quiet, indirect ways. Pointing to the family portrait hanging over the sofa, Elizabeth Nussbaum proudly pointed out each child and grandchild. The wall-size portrait showed a healthy brood. "We lost all of our family during the war," she offered, as if passing a secret. "So it's nice for us to have such a large family."

Nussbaum's four children never heard much about their father's ordeals. He meant to shelter them from the emotional burden. Perhaps he hid the truth from them. He tried on occasion to offer some insight. Once he went to his daughter's high school to talk about his experiences, but after a few minutes he broke down in tears in front of the class.

When Sam Nussbaum heard the news of Schwamm-berger's capture in Argentina, after so many years of nearly absolute silence about his past, he finally "woke up" and started talking. "I was not asleep," he said, laughing. "I was like any other Jew. What could we do? We lost a family. I lost a family, and I thought I got to take it. But Schwamm-berger was really the cause. And when I saw the little picture that Schwammberger was caught in Argentina, it really woke me up."

Nussbaum called the Wiesenthal Center's Los Angeles headquarters. "Right away, the next day," Nussbaum recalled. Rabbi Marvin Hier, the center's executive director, spoke with Nussbaum directly. "And as soon as I called him, Rabbi Hier said, 'You know Schwammberger?' And I said, 'Yeah, I know him real well. He knows me, too.' So he said, 'I'll call you right back.' Just like that."

CHAPTER 14

TRYING

MEMORIES

You put me into the world, You spared me in time of
danger and death, that I might testify. What sort of
witness would I be without my memory?
—Elie Wiesel[1]

Affter Josef Schwammberger stepped off the plane
from Buenos Aires, German police helped him
into a car to take him to Stammheim, Stuttgart's
maximum security prison. Three months later the former SS
commandant was officially indicted and charged with the
murder of at least 50 individuals and with accessory to murder of at least 3,377 others.

A German court prepared to hear the case. A German
prosecutor was determined to see him locked up for the rest
of his life. And Schwammberger had one simple response:
He could not remember.

From the moment of his capture up to the day of his
successful extradition, there still had been something fantas-
tic, unreal about the story of this long-ago Nazi commandant. The names of the villages where he had supposedly
participated in thousands of murders and other Nazi barbarities had meant little to the average Argentine observer.

Strange-sounding villages were too far away, in physical distance, in time, in relevance. The same few mug shots had appeared in the Argentine press over and over again, showing Schwammberger either smiling in his SS uniform or as a puffy-faced old man. Reconciling the two images was all the more difficult because Schwammberger never appeared in court during his extradition proceedings.

Even after finally being tracked down and captured, Schwammberger had managed during the three years he spent hidden away in an Argentine jail to postpone a direct confrontation with his past. His Argentine defense lawyer had pleaded all sorts of arguments to try to keep him from being extradited to Germany. Nothing had worked. Schwammberger could delay, but ultimately nothing could keep him from being forced to make the long journey back to Germany and the even longer trip back in time to face his Nazi past.

From the moment he arrived in Germany, that past and the significance of Schwammberger's trial came much more clearly into focus. More than forty years since his escape from the Allied prison known as Oradour, Schwammberger was going to stand trial in a German courtroom as a Nazi murderer.

Schwammberger was no longer an obscure elderly Nazi who had committed atrocities in some unfamiliar corner of Poland. He was no longer a prisoner in a dusty cell in some remote part of the world. He was in Germany. He was one of the most wanted Nazi criminals still alive. And the charges outlined in his indictment were real, specific, concrete. Josef Schwammberger killed Jews "in a cruel fashion out of a feeling of self-superiority and racist hate," the state prosecutor said in a statement announcing the indictment.

Schwammberger's arrival in Germany generated immediate notoriety. Survivors were lined up all over the world to come to Stuttgart to testify. Officials at Wiesenthal's

Los Angeles office announced that in the three years since Schwammberger's 1987 arrest, they had made contact with more than seventy Jewish survivors willing to testify. Schwammberger's Nazi past was still very much alive nearly half a century later, and it was eager to meet him.

Unlike his experience in Argentina, this time he would not be allowed to sit out the proceedings in the prison hospital. He would have to face his accusers, look them in the eye, hear their cries, stand near enough to smell their breath, just as he had looked in the eyes of the men and women he killed fifty years earlier.

There was, however, still one way Schwammberger could escape, and he found it and made it the heart of his new legal defense. The sight of Schwammberger descending from the airplane upon his arrival in Germany, looking like a fragile and frightened old man, had been a powerful one. Schwammberger exploited that image when the Stuttgart prosecutor's office announced the murder charges against him. His response was a plea of not guilty by reason of loss of memory.

Schwammberger simply could not remember, his new defense lawyers claimed. He was a seventy-nine-year old man after all, and the prosecution was trying to hold him accountable for events that supposedly happened fifty years ago. Who could remember that far back?

As Schwammberger acknowledged, his memory was not completely blank when it came to this period of his life. Through his lawyers he did admit to killing one Polish Jew in Przemysl because of what he termed, cryptically, "special circumstances." As for the other counts in the indictment, he would say only that he could not remember details but was sure he was innocent.

Memory was the key to the Schwammberger case on another important level, too. Schwammberger's return to Germany coincided with revolutionary political developments in the country. Just six months earlier the Berlin Wall had come crashing down. That autumn East and West Germany were finally remarried after a long separation. Josef Schwammberger would be the first major Nazi tried in the newly reconstituted Germany, and he would be a painful reminder of darker days in the country's history. At the most jubilant moment in fifty years of German history, Josef Schwammberger arrived to remind Germany and the rest of the world that the Nazi past was not forgotten.

At the same time his trial, even before it began, served a seemingly contradictory purpose. From the moment Schwammberger arrived in Germany he was designated the "last Nazi." The international media seized on the label, building up the trial as probably the last time a major Nazi figure would ever stand trial.

In Ludwigsburg, the small town north of Stuttgart where the central office for the investigation of Nazi crimes is located, German officials confirmed that indeed, Schwammberger in all likelihood would be the last. As he was being readied for trial, the office was still investigating several dozen cases, prosecutors there admitted, but no one matched Schwammberger in stature.[2]

Besides, even if other major Nazi figures could be tracked down and arrested, Nazi crimes cases had become extremely difficult to prosecute. Witnesses had to be found and evidence had to be gathered, and these tasks were not so easily accomplished when the crimes were so many years old.

Schwammberger's case was a rarity. There was already a large body of material, including statements from numerous witnesses that had been collected over the years in Poland, Austria, and Germany. And there was Schwammberger's own written confession as well. Finally, and most important, there was a exceptionally large number of living eyewitnesses willing and able to testify.

Schwammberger's designation as the "last Nazi" meant

that his trial would serve as another rallying point for the proponents of reconciliation, for those calling out to the world to release Germany from the burden of its Nazi past.

The simple fact that Josef Schwammberger was brought to trial for murders committed fifty years before was an extraordinary act. "It must be the first time in a modern trial that someone is being charged with events that took place half a century ago," observed Dieter König, Schwammberger's lead court-appointed defense lawyer and an experienced defender of accused Nazis.[3]

But the Schwammberger trial meant far more than the bringing to justice of one man, the reconciling of one Nazi's crimes. No matter how many or how few people even noticed Schwammberger in the excitement of so many other dramatic events unfolding in Germany, the belated trial of this elderly former Nazi killer was still, in essence, the trial of all the years of Germany's unresolved Nazi past.

Most Germans today are too young to remember what Stuttgart looked like in May 1945. At that time Allied planes had flattened the city where Daimler and Benz pioneered automobile manufacturing in the 1880s. By the end of the war more than one-third of Stuttgart's dwellings had been reduced to rubble.

In the decades since the end of the war Stuttgart had been rebuilt magnificently. The capital of Germany's third-largest *Land*, Baden-Württemberg, prospered as important German concerns such as Mercedes and the electronics giant Bosch helped engineer not only the local but the entire country's economic rebirth. German businesses in Stuttgart were so successful, in fact, that Stuttgarters came to enjoy one of the highest per capita incomes in all Europe.

In spite of the importance of industry to its economy, Stuttgart retained in certain parts the air of a charming village. The city that is home to so many car makers—

Mercedes, Porsche, and Volkswagen—converted its center, which is several blocks wide and about a mile in length, into a pedestrian zone. There one finds the top hotels, restaurants, and museums, all along a promenade that leads past the elegantly restored eighteenth-century palace that was once the home of the duke of Württemberg.

The state courthouse in Stuttgart, by contrast, is a modern structure on a hill overlooking the bustle of activity in the city center. Wedged inconspicuously between apartment buildings in an unremarkable residential neighborhood, the courthouse stands as evidence of Germany rebuilt.

Inside this cold government building a fight over the memory of Germany was waged. It was a struggle between Germany's past and its future, a showdown between remembering and forgetting. On Wednesday, June 26, 1991, the murder trial of former SS Commandant Josef Schwammberger began at long last.

The first day of the trial was a circus. Reporters from around the world converged on provincial Stuttgart and the usually quiet courthouse to witness the opening of the "last" major Nazi war crimes trial. Curious residents and representatives of Stuttgart's tiny Jewish community also packed the benches at the back of Courtroom Number 1.

Outside the building a dozen or so neo-Nazi youths protested Schwammberger's trial. The youths were well dressed, not like the tattooed skinhead stereotype. These cleaner-cut extremists in steel-toed black boots waved a German flag and carried signs that read ARE GERMANS ALWAYS WAR CRIMINALS? They shouted for Schwammberger's immediate release.

The protesters also besieged Simon Wiesenthal, the eighty-four-year-old Nazi hunter who had come from Vienna to observe the start of the trial. Wiesenthal was used to verbal attacks in public. He had even had numerous threats on his life over the many years he had spent pressing his agenda.

"I was surrounded by neo-Nazi protesters," Wiesenthal later recalled. With a veteran's unflappability, he scolded the boys as if he had just caught them rolling dice. "I just smiled at them and said, 'One day your children will not be proud of what you're doing.'"

At the front of the courtroom the lawyers began to arrive and to take their places. To anyone accustomed to the way criminal trials are conducted in the United States, the German system would seem strange and confusing. German courts follow an inquisitorial approach rather than the adversarial system used in American and British courts. In practical terms this means that in German trials there is no prosecution or defense case per se. Each side, prosecution and defense, has its own strategy and arguments, but the "case" is essentially a cooperative rather than competitive process. The lawyers recommend and interrogate witnesses, but the judges, not the lawyers, actually conduct the trial.

In most criminal trials in Germany there are five judges, three professional jurists and two citizen jurors, plus two alternates. Each judge has an equal vote. German proceedings do not use a jury as American trials do. The presiding judge leads the interrogation of witnesses, establishes the major points of each witness's testimony. Then the other judges question the witness, and finally the prosecutor and defense counsel add their questions. The defendant himself may even ask or be asked questions at any time.

Waiting for the proceeding to get under way on the morning of Schwammberger's first day in court, the prosecutor and defense lawyers greeted one another amiably and shook hands. Then they stepped into black robes just like those the judges wear. Lead defense lawyer König conferred with his junior partner at the defense table.

A bear of a man, König at the same time possessed a professorial dignity. In the privacy of his own office he favored a pipe, and he spoke with the measured precision of a learned man. The sixty-six-year-old lawyer had plenty of experience with controversial clients. He completed his legal studies after his release from an American prisoner of war camp.[4] König had seen action against both the Russians in the east—"I came to the eastern front, or better to say the eastern front came to me," he quipped—and the Americans in northwestern Germany.

One of König's first high-profile cases occurred in 1963, when he defended an East German border guard who had skipped off to Stuttgart (where his sister lived) after he had shot a man trying to flee to the west across the Berlin Wall. At his trial the guard was found guilty of attempted manslaughter and sentenced to more than a year in prison. But since the defendant had already served nearly a year during the pretrial phase, König's client was released two weeks after the trial.

König also represented high-profile white-collar criminal defendants during his career. And he had even defended one of the members of the Red Army Faction, the so-called Baader-Meinhof gang, whose anarchic campaign of kidnapping and violence terrorized Germany in the late 1960s and 1970s. In fact, Stammheim, the prison where Schwammberger was being held, had been specially constructed to house the notorious young terrorists.

Through the years of his trial practice König also represented a number of accused Nazi criminals, always as a court-appointed defense lawyer. "There were many more cases at that time, in the 1960s," he reflected, "so it was not so extraordinary."

Like many criminal defense lawyers, König defended the importance of due process, even when that meant according rights to accused murderers like Schwammberger. The defense lawyer noted that during the pretrial process of gathering witness statements some survivors berated him for defending an admitted Nazi murderer like Schwammberger. But König insisted that he was just doing his job, that all he was providing was legal representation, something to which everyone, even an accused Nazi, was entitled.

König's law partner and Schwammberger's codefender, Achim Bächle, echoed these sentiments. Bächle, who is twenty years younger than König, observed that if they refused to represent Schwammberger, there was no telling who might take their places. "A man in my situation cannot say no," Bächle explained in an interview. "Otherwise you only get lawyers who are National Socialists or are on that side. And I think it is terrible for countries on the outside, like USA, to hear these lawyers say things."[5]

But as much as König and Bächle claimed allegiance to the defense lawyer's time-honored credo—that everyone is entitled to a legal defense—both clearly reserved some special sympathy for Josef Schwammberger and for the other Nazis they have defended. Neither man was ever a Nazi or a Nazi sympathizer as such. In fact, König was married to a woman who was half Jewish, and Bächle, a member of the liberal-centrist Free Democratic party, had political aspirations and even ran once, unsuccessfully, for a seat in the German parliament. But König especially expressed feelings for those of his past Nazi clients who he believed were "just following orders."

He told, for example, of one former Nazi he defended, a soldier who had been assigned during the war to a unit that repaired military transport equipment behind the lines. The unit commander had grander visions. Detailed to Ukraine in August 1941, just weeks after the German invasion of the Soviet Union, the commander ordered his men to sweep through a village and "ordered all the Jews killed." König's client, "an unhappy poor guy" named Hermann, "was sentenced for having shot in two actions by order of his company commander," the lawyer said. "He would never have killed a Jew or anybody. But he had a very narrow-minded way of thinking and believed he had to follow the order."

As for Schwammberger, Bächle clearly held more than a

defense lawyer's detached professional interest in his client's future, just as Miguel Ángel Siri had when he defended Schwammberger in Argentina. "The stress coming over him at times is something nobody can feel," Bächle said. "He's an old man. He's alone. Yes, he has two lawyers, but that's all. His family is far away. Everyone is against him."

As he prepared to face trial for murder, Schwammberger indeed was alone. His wife and one son had remained in Buenos Aires in total seclusion. They refused to speak to anyone and, at Schwammberger's urging, did not come to Stuttgart. His younger son had settled in Munich with his wife and, in spite of the short distance, refused to visit.

But Schwammberger had been treated well since his arrival in Germany. He had received top-rate medical care, including a prostate operation he needed soon after his transfer from Argentina. As he acknowledged in a meeting with prosecutor Schrimm, his conditions were much improved over those during his last years on the run in Argentina and the three years in the La Plata prison. "I should really be grateful to you," Schwammberger told Schrimm, "because it is so much nicer here than in Argentina."[6]

Prosecutor Schrimm's courtroom demeanor was similar to König's. A tousle-haired man in his early forties, Schrimm was soft-spoken, deferential, and proper. But outside the courtroom he was casual and modest, a stark contrast with König, who clearly enjoyed talking at length about himself.

The Schwammberger case was a major breakthrough for Schrimm, a ten-year veteran of the state attorney's office. He had handled only two other Nazi crimes trials in those years. Both involved far less significant defendants, and both had ended without convictions. "In the first case we had some witnesses who could identify [the defendant] and some who could not," Schrimm explained. "He was acquitted in the end because it could not be definite. In the second trial we had just one witness who I could not speak to beforehand because he came all the way from Poland. And then he came and said, 'This isn't the one I meant.' "

The availability of witnesses was not a problem in the Schwammberger case. "When he was arrested, I had the names of about thirty witnesses," Schrimm recalled. Mostly these were names of witnesses who had testified against other Nazis who had been at one of the Poland labor camps with Schwammberger. "Then I saw when they were born, and I thought maybe half of them would still be alive. But they led me to others. And I heard one hundred thirty or one hundred fifty witnesses by the end."

Many of those survivors anxiously waited their turn to tell their stories in court, in front of Schwammberger himself. When two security guards escorted the elderly defendant to his seat at a small wooden table, the trial that would give them that opportunity was finally under way.

König and then Bächle stepped up to give Schwammberger perfunctory handshakes. Once seated, Schwammberger reached for the glass of water that had been placed before him. He was dressed simply, in plain slacks and a simple beige cardigan. His face betrayed no emotion. He looked as if it were his business to sit just where he was.

The judges and alternate judges filed in, at last. The lawyers and spectators rose from their seats. The large room, the largest courtroom in the building, was spare and clean. A wrought-iron sculpture of the Baden-Württemberg state insignia hung over the judges' bench. Long metal microphones peeked up from the tables in front of the lawyers and judges like slender plants growing out of the seafloor.

Judge Herbert Luippold, a distinguished-looking man in his fifties and the chief judge of the Baden-Württemberg state court, served as the presiding judge. Slowly and firmly he called the court to order and began to read the charges against the defendant.

Born February 14, 1912, in Brixen, South Tyrol, son of

Florian and Helene Schuler Schwammberger, the accused stood charged with murder and with aiding and abetting murder, the judge read. He outlined briefly Schwammberger's SS background, noting that before killing many of his victims, the defendant had "inflicted on them pain and torment of the physical or mental kind out of callousness and meanness."

Reading from the indictment, the judge recited the list of Schwammberger's deeds: He had shot a rabbi on Yom Kippur while commandant of the Jewish forced labor brigade at Rozwadow in 1942. He had personally selected those unfit for work and therefore for death, just as surely as Josef Mengele had made his selections on the platform at Auschwitz.

As the commandant of the ghetto in Przemysl, Judge Luippold further told the court, Schwammberger had shot Jews who attempted to escape, Jews caught attempting to barter for food at the ghetto fence, and still others for no apparent reason at all. Other counts against Schwammberger referred to his penchant for having his German shepherd attack prisoners, to his ordering Ukrainian guards to execute Jews who hid from the Gestapo, and to his brutal beating of prisoners during the ghetto's final resettlement operation.

Schwammberger sat impassively through the entire recitation. Given an opportunity to make a statement to the court, Schwammberger spoke in halting fragments of sentences. He muttered that he had indeed escaped from a French prison but wanted to correct the court's assertion that he had been a technical sergeant, claiming that he had only been a staff sergeant.* He repeatedly lost his train of thought. In the snatches of his mumbled speech he did

---

*Schwammberger's rank has never been definitively resolved, largely because the SS destroyed so many documents during Germany's retreat from the advancing Russian troops in Poland. But Schwammberger did tell Austrian police in 1945 that his last rank was *Oberscharführer*, or technical sergeant, not *Unterscharführer*, or sergeant.

manage to assert that he had never even heard of a place called Rozwadow and that he had done nothing wrong during his command of the ghetto at Przemysl.

Schwammberger was not charged and therefore not subject to be tried for any actions during the time he was commander of the forced labor camp in Mielec in 1944. The reason was that the Stuttgart prosecutor had not mentioned Mielec in its extradition request to the Argentine government. Under the extradition agreement, the German government was permitted to try Schwammberger only for crimes committed in the two places mentioned in the extradition request.

Before the trial could proceed any further, Schwammberger's lawyer asked the court to allow the defendant to undergo further medical tests to determine if he was fit, physically and mentally, to stand trial. König argued that his client was not only physically debilitated because of a heart condition but also mentally incapable of following the testimony. Under the circumstances, the defense counsel argued, the case against Schwammberger should be suspended indefinitely.

Had Germany waited too long? Survivors from around the world were waiting to testify, waiting to bare their souls and the pain of their memories, to memorialize their experiences and the names of the towns where they had been born. But now there appeared to be, once again, serious doubt whether they would have that opportunity. The trial might be over before it could even begin.

The same fate had greeted many Nazi defendants over the years of Nazi crimes trials in Germany. There was some validity, however, to the claim that Schwammberger's defense lawyers were trying to make. If they could demonstrate that he was incapable of understanding the charges against him, if he was, in effect, unable to confront his accuser, then it could be argued that he would not receive a fair trial. The right to confront one's accuser had been one of the founding principles of the American system of justice for more than two hundred years,* and the idea has long been a part of German law as well.

The conflict between the fervent interest in punishing the perpetrators of the Nazi Holocaust and the interest in doing so without sacrificing the spirit and traditions of democracy had plagued the prosecution of Nazi criminals since Nuremberg. It was more than a matter of pride in Western democracy that led the three Western Allies to be so scrupulous in the conduct of the early war crimes trials. Suspected Nazi criminals were afforded legal counsel, given access to documents that might even help their case, and in some cases even granted acquittals. The same could hardly be said of the Nazi regime's idea of justice in and out of the courtroom.

The contrast between Western democracy and Nazi fascism was precisely the point. Victory in World War II would have been meaningless if the victors had imposed Nazi-style justice on the Nazi criminals. The Allies—and their democratic German heirs—determined to be fair even if to a fault. As former Supreme Court Justice Robert Jackson remarked just after agreeing to lead the prosecution before the International Military Tribunal at Nuremberg, "Courts try cases, but cases also try courts."[7]

In a totalitarian state the dictator determines what is "fair." In a democratic society competing interests must be balanced, compromises must be struck. And that was the challenge in resolving Schwammberger's plea for mercy on the basis of his advanced age and his claim that he was unfit for trial because he could not remember anything about the relevant period of his Nazi past.

Schwammberger had been plenty competent at the time the alleged crimes were committed. He had been a powerful

---

*See the Sixth Amendment to the U.S. Constitution.

man. As one witness later testified, to the Jews of the Przemysl ghetto, Schwammberger was their God, their Satan. And
of course, he had not shown any leniency toward the elderly
or the very young. Would it therefore be fair to halt his trial
simply because he had managed to remain a fugitive from
justice for forty-five years? Would stopping the trial be
fair to the many people who not only remembered what
Schwammberger had done fifty years before but could not
for the life of them ever forget?

Judge Luippold clearly favored going forward with the
trial. But he was also determined that the trial should be fair,
so he allowed the defense's request for a second medical
review.

Schwammberger had already undergone a thorough physical and psychological examination thirteen months before,
shortly after arriving at the Stammheim prison. The most
serious psychological deficiency the experts had uncovered
was the defendant's facility for selective recognition. In other
words, the doctors concluded that Schwammberger could
remember much more than he was willing to admit and that
he could be just as alert mentally as he wanted to be.

However, Schwammberger was not in the finest physical
form. He required a hearing aid in each ear. He had an
irregular heartbeat and was recovering from prostate surgery.
Recognizing that the trial would be stressful for a man of
Schwammberger's age, the court had agreed to limit the
proceeding to just two sessions per week. The court would
hear testimony only on Wednesdays and Fridays for two
hours in the morning and two hours in the afternoon.

Schwammberger's reexamination revealed no new information. Doctors found that his mental condition had not
deteriorated, as his defense lawyers claimed. The conflict
between the need to be fair to Schwammberger and the
need to see the judicial process continue was averted. The
trial would proceed.

When the trial recommenced in the second week of July,

the first of more than forty survivors arrived to begin the process of retrieving from the deepest recesses of human memory and from the darkest days of human history the story of Josef Schwammberger's three long years as an SS commandant.

Although the trial went forward, Schwammberger clung stubbornly to his position. He had never been in Rozwadow, he insisted through his defense lawyers. And he was not responsible for any of the atrocities he was accused of committing in Przemysl. His 1945 signed confession to the Austrian police, he argued, had been given under duress and should not be considered.

His lawyers readily admitted outside the courtroom that they did not have much of a case. Unlike American trial lawyers who might speak to the press, even play to the press, but would never concede glaring weaknesses, Schwammberger's lawyers were astonishingly open. They acknowledged that loss of memory was not exactly a compelling defense. Schwammberger "says it was 50 years ago and he doesn't remember anything," defense lawyer Bächle told a reporter at one point during the trial. "He cooperates with us but we have no real case of our own."[8]

The trial, and therefore the fate of Josef Schwammberger, ultimately came down to a test of those who claimed they could remember. One after another they came to Stuttgart to confront Schwammberger. Abraham Secemsky and Edward Blonder, both of whom had gone to Buenos Aires during Schwammberger's extradition proceedings, repeated their stories for the Stuttgart court. And there were many others.

Julian Zielinski came from Frankfurt to tell how he had seen Schwammberger push two dozen Jews into a burning barn. Leon Gottank came from Los Angeles to tell how Schwammberger had shot his friend Leib Pater. Sarah Ehrenhald came from Tel Aviv to corroborate the story; Pater had been her husband. Helena Caspi, a seventy-five-year-old piano teacher, also came from Israel to tell how she had seen Schwammberger shoot three Jews trading clothes for scraps of food at the ghetto fence in Przemysl. Max Millner, who survived the Holocaust that claimed eighty-two of his family members, came from Israel to tell how he had witnessed Schwammberger shoot Rabbi Frankel in Rozwadow on the Jewish holy day of Yom Kippur.

For each witness the daylong testimony was grueling. Some broke down in tears before they were through. Others maintained their composures until they finished. One woman who traveled to Stuttgart from New York to testify said afterward that she had felt so drained from the experience and so upset from seeing Schwammberger again that rather than return home right away, she treated herself to a visit to Israel, to be "cleansed."

There was very little that Schwammberger's defense lawyers could do to counter the steady flow of eyewitnesses. "It's a very difficult position for a defense lawyer," Bächle explained in an interview. "He cannot help us. He can't say, 'No, that's not true, and I have two witnesses to support me.' We can only read all the witness statements and then compare. The defense position must be that there are seven, eight, nine stories about the same event. We don't want to say that one witness or another lied. But it has been a long time, and people don't remember correctly. It's a normal thing. We can only say, 'Perhaps something happened, but we don't know.' "*

Bächle's senior law partner, König, felt more comfortable attacking the character as well as the credibility of some of

---

*Again, it is remarkable that the lawyers were as frank as they were. Bächle made these comments in an interview with the author in October 1991, not even halfway through the trial.

the witnesses. "With these witnesses who have suffered very greatly, you must handle them with care," he said. "And yet in most cases you know that they cannot be telling the truth."

The confrontation over memory and the high level of emotion behind the testimony frequently created explosive moments in the courtroom. During one witness's testimony König provoked a shouting match. In a gravelly voice eighty-one-year-old Julian Zielinski was recalling a terrible incident in which he claimed Schwammberger had participated. From a hiding place in the Przemysl ghetto, Zielinski had witnessed the SS man using his German shepherd to herd twenty to thirty Jews into a burning barn. Then Schwammberger joined other Nazi officers in shooting the prisoners who tried to escape from the flames.

First Judge Luippold led Zielinski through the main points of his testimony. The witness described the ghetto, recalled names of streets, explained the difference between the working ghetto and the nonworking ghetto. The court had heard the same introductory material many times already. But Zielinski was asked to cover the same ground again. If his memory was faulty, it would be easy to detect discrepancies with testimony already given.

Throughout the first part of the testimony Schwammberger, wearing a light-colored windbreaker and pale green slacks that fell above his ankles, had sat impassively, as usual. Late in the morning König asked for the session to be postponed because Schwammberger was claiming not to feel well. The judge agreed to recess the proceeding until the afternoon but refused to delay it any further.

As the judge announced the recess, Schwammberger's expression changed completely. As if he had been given a shot of caffeine, he animatedly leaped to his feet and walked over to chat with his lawyers for a few minutes before being led away.

In the afternoon Zielinski was called to the judges' bench to consult a map of the Przemysl ghetto which he himself had prepared. The prosecutor, the two defense lawyers, and Schwammberger himself joined the witness in a huddle in front of the judges to watch as Zielinski pointed to the place on the map where the burning barn had been located.

König protested that the map Zielinski had prepared was not precisely accurate in its scale. Perhaps, he suggested pompously, Mr. Zielinski would prepare another map, an accurate map, one that could be of some real use.

Zielinski looked at König in disbelief. But the judge resolved the dispute by pulling out an official map of Przemysl, one that raised no objections from Schwammberger's defenders.

While the group was still gathered before the bench, Judge Luippold asked Zielinski if he recognized Schwammberger. Zielinski nodded energetically. Then the judge asked Schwammberger if he recognized Zielinski. Schwammberger shrugged his shoulders. One of the other judges joked that after all, it had been a few years. Everyone laughed. Everyone, that is, except Zielinski.

When the lawyers and Schwammberger and the witness all sat down again, König began his cross-examination. Picking up on the point he had been trying to make in challenging Zielinski's map, the defense counsel again took issue with the witnesses's ability to recollect the incident accurately. König noted that in an earlier statement the witness had claimed he heard about the burning barn incident, and now he was claiming to be an eyewitness. Zielinski insisted he had seen everything—Schwammberger, the snarling dog, the guards shooting, the Jews trying to escape from the burning barn—all with his own eyes.

König then asked the witness whether he meant to testify that Schwammberger was three meters (about ten feet) from the barn when he fired the shots or thirty meters (about one hundred feet), as he had claimed in an earlier statement. Zielinski's face went red. He jumped to his feet, knocking back his chair. Frantically he started gathering up his papers to leave the courtroom, all the while screaming at a dismayed König, "Three meters, thirty meters, what difference does it make? He killed them! I saw him killing them!"

Other witnesses understood better that the defense's only hope was to poke holes in the credibility of the survivor's testimony. Sam Nussbaum, for example, made a point of trying to prove the clarity of his memory to the judges. He looked upon the experience as he would a mechanical problem to be solved, as another test of his ingenuity.

Nussbaum's testimony, actually, was extremely important to the case for two reasons. First, he was an eyewitness to several incidents that were the basis for charges in the indictment. Second, as Schwammberger's personal handyman in the Przemysl ghetto, Nussbaum came into the proceeding with the court and the lawyers expecting from him a higher-than-average level of credibility.

Among other details Nussbaum testified about one summer afternoon in 1943 when Schwammberger called him over to perform some chore in the ghetto. Schwammberger was out strolling with his wife and his German shepherd. Anxiously Nussbaum joined the couple.

"There was a Jew shot, lying on Czarnieckiego Street," Nussbaum testified. "He was shot on the lower part of his body, and he was bleeding. I thought we was going to miss him, but Schwammberger walked straight to him and stopped. So we did, too."

The wounded Jewish man looked up and pleaded for some water. "I remember as if I were looking at him now," said Nussbaum. "He says, 'Wasser,' means he wants some water. And Schwammberger went, looked at him, and took his right foot and flipped him over on his stomach. And he took out his pistol. And I'm looking. And I made a special point to look on the missus. What she's going to do when he shoots. And she turned around, she looked backward. I looked to him and I looked at her. I looked both ways. And he shot him in the back of his head. And the judge asked me, 'Todt?' Did he shot him dead? And I said, 'Yes, he shot him dead.' Back on his head."[8]

Nussbaum's recollections clearly were vivid. He remembered details, street names, fragments of dialogue. But he also remained calm through the sometimes picayune tests that the judge and defense lawyers used to test his recall. After he had testified about Schwammberger's alleged murder of the injured Jew, for example, the judges asked Nussbaum to identify Schwammberger's wife from a collection of photographs. Nussbaum picked her out immediately. But he also pointed out to the court that the photograph did little justice to how attractive Kathe Schwammberger was in those days.

"You know how a picture is when it comes out dark?" Nussbaum said several weeks after his appearance in court. "She looked like she had black hair. I told the judge she had blond hair. He knew I knew her. See? He laughed when I told him that."

One after another the witnesses came in to identify Schwammberger, but he could not—or else refused to—identify them. Sometimes he would flash a smile that to some may have appeared as a smirk. Once in a while he scribbled a note on the pad in front of him, for no apparent reason and to no apparent purpose. Occasionally he actually spoke.

During Nussbaum's testimony, for example, Judge Luippold asked the defendant if he recognized the witness. Schwammberger said he did not. Did he remember anything about the distillery Nussbaum had claimed to have made for him. "I don't recognize that," Schwammberger replied.

Nussbaum interjected, "He says he does not remember,

but he had me lock the cars, and that was my family inside. He remembers me."

Judge Luippold pressed Schwammberger. "Here is yet another witness who says, 'Mr. Schwammberger, I knew you well,' " the judge noted.

Finally Schwammberger managed to put more than a few words together at once. In a voice suddenly firm he said, "There were 10,000 or 15,000 of them. The 15,000 can know one, but that doesn't mean the one knew 15,000."[10]

Now Schwammberger was remembering a bit too much. His defense lawyer jumped to his feet to suggest that his client was fatigued and that perhaps Schwammberger had gone far enough for that day's session. And so he had.

Media interest in the Schwammberger trial trailed off after the novelty of the first day. There were periodic articles in all the major Western press, but there were too many other important stories to cover in Germany: the economic and political difficulties brought on by the merging of the affluent western and downtrodden eastern halves of the country; the constant bickering among European economic and foreign ministers over the shape and substance of the European economic union; the outbreaks of neo-Nazi violence against refugees from Eastern Europe; the national furor over the opening of the archives of the former East German secret police.

The German press followed the trial dutifully, but the snail's pace of the proceeding robbed the story of the sustained drama inherent in most important criminal trials. The testimony continued month after month without television cameras lined up outside the courthouse, without neo-Nazi demonstrations, without the celebrity presence of Simon Wiesenthal.

Members of the Stuttgart Jewish community maintained a regular vigil to keep track of the trial's progress. And area high school teachers occasionally brought in a class for a living history lesson. "It's hard for a young German to convince himself that this all happened," noted one teacher, who brought her students in to prove to them that "it all" really did happen.[11]

But numerous pauses and delays caused the proceeding to stutter along, and this certainly contributed to the lack of sustained popular interest. In November 1991, right in the middle of the trial, the entire court, judges and lawyers, traveled to Poland—leaving the defendant behind at the Stammheim prison—to see first hand the remnants of the ghetto in Przemysl.

The goal was admirable, even though there was not all that much for the court to see there. The building that housed the Judenrat today is a school for intellectually disadvantaged Polish students. Not much else remains of the former Jewish quarter. The court's junket meant that the trial in Stuttgart shut down for more than one week.

Before the trip to Poland the court had taken a one-month recess for no apparent reason other than that it was the end of the summer. The following spring the court again traveled to New York to accommodate several witnesses who could not make the trip to testify in Stuttgart.* The witnesses certainly appreciated the effort, but meanwhile, the trial dropped from the public's consciousness during that intermission. And of course, all the while the trial was in active public session, the court was meeting just two days per week.

Another reason for the lack of popular interest in the trial clearly was the ambivalent attitude among Germans. The very fact that an eighty-year-old Nazi was standing trial for crimes that supposedly were committed nearly fifty years

---

*The members of the panel of judges took turns reading to the court the depositions of those witnesses who were unwilling or unable to travel to testify.

earlier was a source of tremendous discomfort and mixed feelings.*

Schwammberger's defense lawyer Bächle characterized the two positions this way: "One [group says] it's not necessary to make the trial. It costs a lot of money. He's a very old man, and it happened a long time ago. Perhaps he will die soon because he is so old. So let him go back to Argentina. The people who died in '42, '43, they won't come back alive if we make this trial. The second [group says] that it is our duty to make a fair trial and give punishment for people who committed these crimes. Those people died in Poland, and so we must do this. I think opinion is about fifty-fifty."

Bächle himself walked the line between the two points of view. While there was clearly an obligation to punish the guilty, he said the continuation of the Nazi trials was for Germany nothing more than a bald political decision. "We want to show our friends and neighbors that this [nazism] will never happen again."

No one better expressed or indeed embodied the mixed emotions of the German people toward the continued confrontation with the Nazi past than the popular mayor of Stuttgart, Manfred Rommel. Rommel occupied a unique position as mayor of the city that hosted the Schwammberger trial. As the son of Field Marshal Erwin Rommel, the famed Desert Fox, the mayor also had a unique historical perspective.

Erwin Rommel earned a reputation as a professional on the battlefield and a gentleman when he was off duty. One historian described him as "a throwback to the medieval knight in his personal traits, a master of modern warfare in his professional attainments."[12] And although he was much admired by Hitler, Rommel in his life and through his death avoided the taint of nazism.

---

*Schwammberger celebrated his eightieth birthday during the eighth month of the trial.

Rommel had become disgusted with Hitler's determination to continue the war long after it was clear that Germany was defeated. After the failed coup against Hitler in July 1944, one of the plotters revealed that Rommel had agreed to assume the leadership of Germany after Hitler's death and to sue for peace with the Allies. Three months later two generals dispatched by Hitler presented Rommel with his choice: trial for treason or suicide. The field marshal chose the poison tablet and spared his wife and fifteen-year-old son the embarrassment of a public humiliation.

The son grew up to be mayor of Stuttgart, a post to which he won three consecutive eight-year terms. Mayor Rommel came to be admired nationally as a pragmatic and independent politician. In recent years, as Germany has been racked by neo-Nazi and right-wing violence against the tens of thousands of refugees pouring in from Romania and Yugoslavia and other depressed countries to the east, he became a voice for tolerance. At a 1991 rally in Stuttgart in support of rights for foreigners in Germany, he exhorted people to "confront bigotry and violence with the deepest resolve."[13] (Stuttgart's percentage of foreign-born workers—nearly one in five—is among the highest in the country.)

A tall, well-built man with spectacles and a pleasant face, Rommel also pleaded tolerance toward the German people, whose sensitivity about their Nazi past has for so many years gnawed at the national soul. "We should learn from the past, but we shouldn't become the victim of the past," Rommel said, sitting at the end of a long table in his office in Stuttgart's *Rathaus*, or city hall. "We cannot change what is over. The past exists forever, but the future is still possible. You can influence the future, so we should learn from the past and improve the future."

Many of those in Germany who utter similar sentiments usually follow such comments by suggesting that Germany should therefore be released from its burden, that enough is enough already, that Germany should be allowed to leave its past behind.

But Rommel expressed a different view of the situation. He accepted that aggressive study of the crimes of the Holocaust, even the trial of an old man like Josef Schwammberger, was politically and socially necessary for Germany. And he was willing to endure the hardship of confronting the past, as a matter of necessity, for as long as might be necessary.

The trial of Schwammberger or of any Nazi criminal, Rommel admitted, forced Germans to confront this difficult converging of past and present. "If you see the problem with some common sense and some feeling for reality," Rommel said, referring to the question of whether or not someone like Schwammberger should be tried, "then it is almost impossible to stop this."

The field marshal's son gritted his teeth to express any support for the criminal proceeding. "I can understand the Jewish side," Rommel offered. "There were whole families killed, old people, children. And this is not to be forgiven. I can understand."

A moderate politician, Rommel also knew well what it meant to grow up German, and he was not incapable of finding some room for empathizing with the German experience during Hitler's rule. "In a dictatorship it is possible to seduce people," he said forgivingly. Most Germans, after all, did not vote for Hitler because of his views on Jews, the mayor lectured. As for the concentration camps, he admitted, many Germans just looked the other way. "The human mind is capable of forgetting things that are uncomfortable."

But Germany has come to understand democracy and openness and a free press, the mayor asserted. Part of that openness is a confrontation with the past. It must be understood. "The extraordinary period of the Third Reich should be studied and analyzed and not forgotten," he proclaimed.

Rommel also seemed to be saying that time is ultimately

on the side of those who believe that the constant reminders of the Nazi past, however necessary, are still a hindrance to Germany entering a more positive, or perhaps, one might say, a more "guilt-free" age. As the field marshal's son noted, at least as far as the continued trials of Nazi criminals are concerned, there is not much time left, if any at all, once the trial of the "last Nazi" is done.

"Personally, I don't think too much for this [Schwammberger] trial," Rommel concluded. "The witnesses are old, Schwammberger is old, and there is a lot of confusion. I am glad when it is over, with the help of nature."

Nature could not rescue Josef Schwammberger. In the eleven months of his trial only a couple of witnesses proved marginally sympathetic to his cause and character. One Jewish survivor from Przemysl, Louis Berger, surprised everyone in the courtroom by testifying that Schwammberger had not been cruel to him. This was the most ringing endorsement Schwammberger received from any witness, backhanded as it may have been.

The seventy-one-year-old witness recalled his days as a shoemaker in the forced labor camp in Rozwadow under Schwammberger's command. "Nobody bothered us, everything was all right." The testimony was considered a vote of confidence in Schwammberger, even though he had always denied even being in Rozwadow and had testily rebuked the witness for claiming to have made shoes for him. "No, that must be a mistake," Schwammberger spoke out during Berger's testimony, "nobody made boots for me."[14]

The other witness called to appear on Schwammberger's behalf was Erich Scharf, a former SS man who claimed to have worked with Schwammberger in the SS regional headquarters in Krakow during the period just before Schwammberger received his first independent command, the forced labor camp at Rozwadow. Scharf's testimony was a powerful tribute to the difficulty of trying any crime fifty years after the fact. It was also, perhaps, an omen for the defendant.

Moments after taking the stand, the seventy-nine-year-old Scharf collapsed in a heap. A doctor in the courtroom rushed to the ex-Nazi's side but was unable to resuscitate him. Scharf lost his life, and Schwammberger lost a rare character witness.

By the spring of 1992 dozens of other witnesses had spent a day in the Stuttgart courtroom remembering the character of the man who had left an indelible impression, whose crimes they would never forget. "His actions are imprinted on my brain until the day I die," Abraham Secemsky told the court. Together the witnesses painted an incontestable portrait of Schwammberger.

Nearly fifty years had passed since the days when he had worn the black uniform of the SS, and Schwammberger had become a pathetic creature. Still, although he was a shriveled shell of his former self, that was no defense. He could not remember—or so he claimed—but that was no defense. Almost fifty years had passed, and that was a shame; but it certainly was no defense. The witnesses remembered some details and not others, and some witnesses did not tell exactly the same story in every detail as other witnesses; but enough witnesses provided corroborating testimony and proved credible enough that Schwammberger's one defensive tactic was rendered ineffective.

In an act of some desperation in the final days of the proceeding Schwammberger brought in a third defense lawyer to make his closing argument to the court. König and Bächle would have argued that time had taken its inevitable toll on the ability of the witnesses to recollect their experiences with precision. They would have pointed to inconsistencies in individual testimony and to contradictory statements among witnesses. The lawyer Schwammberger drafted to make his final appeal to the court was willing to go even further.

Manfred Blessinger, a trial lawyer from a small town in the foothills of the Bavarian Alps south of Munich, told the court not only that the evidence against Schwammberger was weak and contradictory but that he believed that much of what had been said about the Nazi period had been contrived.

Echoing the sorts of claims popularized by right-wing extremists and neo-Nazis, Blessinger disputed the fact that Schwammberger had ever supervised a Jewish forced labor camp at Rozwadow. The lawyer said the Nazis would have considered it preposterous to use Jewish labor, even slave labor, in German industries, especially security-sensitive, war-related industries, for fear of sabotage.

There were no documents saying Schwammberger was an SS commandant at Rozwadow and Przemysl, Blessinger pointed out. They all had been destroyed. Millions of pages of documents did survive to verify the Nazi campaign to exterminate the Jews. There were death camp registers, correspondence, mobile killing squad registers, transport logs, and so on. But the only document the prosecution had to prove Schwammberger's wartime crimes was his own confession. Otherwise, the prosecution relied on the testimony of those still alive to recall their experiences firsthand.

Attacking the credibility of the survivor witnesses barely veiled Blessinger's radical Holocaust-denying claims. Preying on the natural susceptibility to disbelieve something as extravagant in its violence and inhumanity as the Holocaust, Blessinger simply asserted his doubts and hoped for the best.

The German press responded with outrage. A major newspaper in Frankfurt, for example, editorialized that Schwammberger's defense "tried to use extreme right-wing ideological biases to substantiate its case."[15] Blessinger insisted that he was not a neo-Nazi.

The last-minute fireworks amounted to nothing more than a diversion. The case against Schwammberger had already been made. Schwammberger offered no substantive defense.

And so on May 18, 1992, Judge Luippold convened the court for one final session.

Once again the foreign press showed up in force. Once again neo-Nazi protesters lined up outside the courtroom, waving signs and handing out leaflets protesting the "lie that only one country was guilty." Once again Josef Schwammberger faced a moment of decision.

"With this decision, the court has shown that Nazi criminals can be prosecuted even today," Judge Luippold said as he prepared to announce the court's verdict.

A young man wearing heavy black boots and a belt bearing the SS insignia jumped up from his seat in the packed spectator's section and yelled, "Freedom for Schwammberger." Security police rushed to the protester and hauled him outside to join the other chanting neo-Nazis.

Schwammberger smiled vaguely as Judge Luippold pronounced him guilty of killing 25 Jews, including Rabbi Frankel in Rozwadow. The court also found him guilty of accessory to murder in the deaths of at least 641 people, including those Jews Schwammberger had helped round up for a mass execution in Przemysl. Although Schwammberger had originally been charged with many more killings, the reach of the guilty verdict was nonetheless impressive considering how much time had passed.

Judge Luippold declared that it was incredible that Schwammberger remembered nothing of his tenure in Poland. In light of the extraordinary terror Schwammberger had imposed on the Jews in his charge, the judge said, it was a miracle any had survived. "Schwammberger was a committed Nazi who took part in cold-blooded, planned mass murder and must pay for his crimes," the judge said. "Why did these people meet with such a terrible fate? Only because they were Jewish."

Judge Luippold asked Schwammberger if he had any statement to make.

Schwammberger looked up and said plainly, "I regret everything that happened during that cruel time."

That was all. And it was over. Nearly fifty years had passed since Schwammberger had fired his last pistol shot in the Przemysl ghetto. Fifty years later the elderly Nazi was escorted from the court to begin the rest of his life sentence.

CHAPTER 15

THE SHADOW

I'm familiar with the history of my country, and I will never forget it. But I have to take decisions which will affect the future.
—Helmut Kohl[1]

J osef Schwammberger's life spanned the rise and fall and aftermath of Hitler's Nazi regime. But more than simply follow alongside, as a line parallel to the thread of Nazi history, Schwammberger's life represented and reflected the struggle to understand, to make sense of this awful chapter in human history.

When Schwammberger escaped from the Oradour prison in 1948, he was not just attempting to avoid punishment. By denying the system, the process, the survivors, and history itself the right to prosecute him for his deeds, he was in effect denying what he had done. As he vanished from view and into the forgettable corner of his Argentine exile, he removed himself completely from consideration, from consciousness. His countrymen, the ones left behind, arose from the darkness of their defeat, rubbed their eyes as if they had awakened abruptly from a fitful sleep, and went on about their business.

The moment of his belated confrontation with justice presented another rude awakening. Josef Schwammberger was retrieved from the hills looking like Father Time himself, a hunched old man with bushy eyebrows and blotchy skin. Once again a people rubbed their eyes, this time in disbelief.

In the final minutes before Arnold Susskind's liberation from Buchenwald, an SS man had smashed him in the face with the butt of his rifle and demanded to know how the Jew had managed to survive. "Are you still alive?" the SS man had barked as he knocked Susskind to the ground. Nearly fifty years later, Josef Schwammberger, who very easily could have been that SS man, was escorted to the defendant's table in a German courtroom to stand trial. And it seemed as if the same question were still on so many minds: "Are you still alive?"

That is the story of Josef Schwammberger, the story of a quintessential Nazi. His is the real story of the life and afterlife of the Third Reich. This one SS man, this SS everyman, illuminates the meaning of surviving the Holocaust, the lifelong struggle over the Nazi memory.

Many perpetrators did escape punishment. But some were pursued and were caught, and the stories of their deeds were told. Many Jewish survivors did insulate themselves within their new lives and their new families and refused to face the pain of their past lives and deaths. But many spoke and wrote and cultivated the memory. Many Germans did turn away and repress the bad feelings, but some stared the beast squarely in the eye.

Perhaps the fact that the Holocaust seems so incomprehensible draws us inexorably to its memory, as the curious are compelled toward the Sphinx. For the last fifty-odd years historians have documented, scholars have studied, philosophers have pondered, theologians have inquired. There were movements, we have learned, that must account for what happened, at least in part. And there were historical and socioeconomic forces. And Hitler's charismatic leadership, his extraordinary abilities as an orator, and the evil genius of his propaganda all played a part.

Still, all the collected theories and studies and partial answers do not add up to a satisfactory explanation. Why? Why did this happen? That will be forever the puzzle of the Nazi Holocaust.

A thresher catches a farm boy's arm in its mechanical jaws and tears the limb away from the shoulder. The cold metal cannot be expected to feel, to discern, to understand the consequence of its terrible error. But what of a man? How can a man swing an infant by its leg and smash its head against a stone wall? How could Schwammberger and his thousands of similarly employed SS comrades engage in this sort of behavior, day after day, in village after village? Just following orders? The influence of Nazi propaganda? Historical forces?

An ordinary man like Schwammberger tortured Jews in the ghetto by day and then in the evening went home to his wife and child. SS men working with the mobile killing squads in Latvia and Ukraine day after day slaughtered hundreds of Jews beside large pits and then in the evening wrote tender love letters to their sweethearts. The madness seemed so normal.

The fact that there are no complete answers to the riddles of the Holocaust does not mean that the questions should not be asked. But this has been precisely what has happened since Nazi Germany collapsed on May 8, 1945.

Today it seems as if nearly everyone understands at least the most basic history of the Holocaust. At a minimum most people understand that the Holocaust was an attempt to exterminate Europe's Jewish population. But for many years even this elementary concept was widely—and perhaps in some cases even deliberately—obscured.

As one eminent Holocaust historian has noted, even at

Nuremberg, where the Allies indicted nazism at all levels from the SS to the Foreign Ministry to the air force, the prosecutors defined Nazi war crimes on the basis of the nationality of the victims, some of whom just happened to have been Jews. "And so," this historian charged, "even at Nuremberg only the perpetrator was identified, but the identity of the victims was half forgotten."[2]

The Polish government after the war converted the Auschwitz-Birkenau complex into an elaborate museum to honor the millions who perished there. Barracks were converted into exhibition rooms, so that one room became a tribute to the French nationals who died at the camp, another to the Dutch, another to the Romanians, and so on. Hardly any mention was made of the fact that some 1.5 million Jews were killed at the camp.

Indeed, the Poles, after having disowned Polish Jews well before the start of the war, reclaimed and recast Jews as Poles when it came to counting up the victims of the Nazi regime. This rewriting of history, in the words of one Polish historian, amounted to an appropriation of memory. "The three million Polish Jews [killed during the Holocaust] now all became Poles," she has observed, "and when added to the three million Polish victims of the Nazis, made up a total of six million Poles—victims of genocide. The Holocaust was no longer a Jewish property. There was nothing unique in the situation of Jews."[3]

Poland's Jews were not only eliminated physically but erased from the society's collective memory as well. Not until the summer of 1992 did the Polish government finally begin to concede that Jews as Jews had been omitted from the official history of Auschwitz and promise that the mistake would be corrected.

The most extreme perpetrators of the practice of denial have been those who outright reject the Holocaust as a historical reality. There was never any extermination program, these fanatics claim. According to these mythmakers, the Jews fabricated the entire story in order to bankrupt Germany and gain political advantage from a guilt-ridden international community.

The patent absurdity of the claims of these "deniers" ensures that they will remain a fringe element. But in Germany today the ranks of the neo-Nazi movement have swelled as the country staggers under the financial burden of reunification and as refugees from Bosnia and Romania and elsewhere in Eastern Europe stream across the borders. Even though the targets of their hatred are more often Turks and Gypsies than Jews, the disenchanted youths who yell, *"Sieg heil,"* and raise Nazi banners represent a frightening disavowal of the Nazi past just as surely as the handful of actual "deniers."

Hitler and his band of hofbrau hoodlums were not taken seriously until it was far too late. If the neo-Nazis in Germany—or anywhere, for that matter—continue to gain strength, it will be because the majority of people stand by and refuse to condemn their program of hate and violence. If people were half as nervous about the silent conspirators as they were about the loudmouthed ruffians, there would be far less need to worry about the stability of German democracy.

But human beings are a stubborn breed with a short attention span and an even shorter memory. Since the end of the Second World War confrontation with the Nazi legacy and the lasting meaning of the Nazi past has been less than frank, less than wholehearted, less than complete. From the attempts at outright elimination of Jewish memory in Poland to the slack efforts to prosecute Nazi criminals in Germany, more energy has been spent on retiring the Nazi past than on confronting honestly and thoroughly what happened. Perhaps, then, this is another part of the reason why the Holocaust remains a defining historical moment for so many people—German and Jewish—so many years after the fact.

In spite of the efforts to turn away, the Nazi past has continued to influence life in Germany. The past continues to infect the present, it is only fair to mention, despite the efforts of those who have sincerely confronted it, despite the small number of prosecutors who have dedicated themselves to prosecuting Nazi criminals, and despite those monuments that have been raised to honor the memory of victims of the Nazi regime. For all Germans the Nazi period remains a stain on the character and soul of the people. Even after nearly half a century Germany still moves like an elderly veteran, wary and with a pronounced limp.

When the Iraqi dictator Saddam Hussein invaded Kuwait, for example, the Western press referred to him as an Arab Hitler. Western leaders were rallied to the cause by impassioned calls to remember the concessions Europe made to Hitler and the acts of aggression that were tolerated before the Nazi invasion of Poland in 1939 launched World War II. The fact that Hussein was staunchly anti-Israel and counted the PLO among his only supporters seemed to reinforce the allusion to Hitler.

The comparison was a painful reminder for Germany. Making matters far worse were revelations that German businesses had engaged in controversial trade with the Hussein regime. Many Western countries, including the United States, had contributed to the Iraqi's military buildup, right up to the last moment before he turned his armies on tiny Kuwait and poised them for an attack on Saudi Arabia. When Iraq was battling Iran, the Western powers had been happy to support Hussein.

But it was Germany that provided Iraq with materials used in the manufacture of poison gas weapons. And it was a German firm that built Hussein an elaborate multimillion-dollar bunker in Baghdad. The references to Zyklon B and Hitler's underground fortress in Berlin were unmistakable and disturbing.

In recent years reminders of the Nazi past have appeared at seemingly every turn. How could one not share the excitement of the throngs of Berliners clamoring across the Berlin Wall in 1989? How could one not cheer as live television brought pictures to the world of the crowds gathered at the Brandenburg Gate to take part in a joyous celebration of freedom? Yet many felt compelled to temper their excitement with skepticism, not out of a desire to spoil the fun or to punish Germany but out of fear, because they could remember.

When gravestones in a Jewish cemetery in France are toppled by vandals—and such acts do not happen infrequently—the violence is denounced widely. When teenage punks scrawl a swastika on a synagogue in New Jersey, the community is outraged. But the reaction is of a different order when neo-Nazi gangs rampage in Germany, imitating the Hitler salute, brandishing red and black flags.

Germany has inadequately confronted the Nazi past, but that has not made the past go away. The twelve years of the Third Reich cannot simply be deleted from German history, as unfortunate as that is for the Dachauers who remember life before the concentration camp and for other romantic devotees of Goethe, the kaiser, and lederhosen.

Germans will commemorate the fall of the Berlin Wall every November 9, but that date also will always mark a darker day from fifty-one years earlier: *Kristallnacht*. The past will always be a part of the present as long as people remember the past.

Some Germans just cannot bare to be reminded. A young woman from Bremen with long blond hair and broad shoulders spent two years driving a taxi in Berlin around the time of the fall of the wall. She had come to Berlin to escape the memory of an unhappy romance back in her hometown, but after a while she came to see there was more to her desire to run away. The air of celebration around her as Berlin reveled in its restoration as the capital of a reunited Germany did not inspire her. "I'm tired of always living with the past," she said, winding her way along the Spree River in East Berlin. She wondered aloud about Canada, a place she imagined as a vast country with few people. "I must move on from the bad things in my life and find the positive."

Some young Germans express a curiosity about the past, an interest in understanding better the subject about which their parents remained quiet for so long. In the 1990 German film *The Nasty Girl* a young woman confronts a conspiracy of silence when she tries to research her town's involvement in the Second World War for a national essay contest.

In some ways, too, the passing of time, the historical distance, has made it easier to confront the Nazi past. In January 1992 the city of Berlin unveiled a museum at the lakeside villa in the suburb of Wannsee, where Adolf Eichmann and more than a dozen others met to sip brandy and draft the blueprint for the "Final Solution." The museum opened on the fiftieth anniversary of the Wannsee Conference, at which Hitler's deputies coldly plotted the extermination of more than ten million European Jews. Adding to the distinction of the new museum was the fact that it became the first memorial in Germany devoted exclusively to the memory of the Jewish victims of nazism.

Explaining why it took so long to create a lasting memorial to such a vital piece of Nazi history, the museum's founder and curator, Gerhard Schönberner, said, "It is much easier now to deal with the themes of Nazism and the mass murder of Jews than it was 25 years ago. This country is now populated mostly by people who were born after 1945 or who were only small children then. There is the effect of historical distance. People feel an inner freedom and a curiosity that was not there before."[4]

How does one reconcile these two sentiments, the desire to remember and the desire to forget? How does one face

the past, judge it, accept it, and at the same time move on,
progress, live in the present and for the future? This is the
conflict implied in Chancellor Kohl's belligerent defense of
Germany's need to shed the past and live for the future.

Kohl made reconciliation one of the centerpiece themes
of his tenure as German chancellor. According to Kohl (and
a chorus of other German politicians), the Nazi past must
be remembered, yes, and must be studied and commemorated, but Germany cannot always live in the past.

What Kohl really means, however, is that Germany cannot any longer live *with* the past. As the young taxi driver in
Berlin emphasized, the Nazi past has become stifling. In
effect, Germany must live for the future.

In fact, Kohl's message today is little different from the
one German leaders have been trumpeting since the first
days following the Nazi surrender. Then the calls were to
be released from the grips of denazification. When would
the trials end? When would the Allies go home? When
would Germany be allowed back in the family of Western
nations? When would the Allies grant amnesty?

Time has strengthened the call for reconciliation. Kohl's
desire to see Germany released from the burden of the
Nazi past is certainly understandable. But what exactly does
reconciliation mean? What does Kohl want?

Clearly pronouncements go only so far. After all, no one
could have given a more stirring plea for reconciliation than
Ronald Reagan offered at Bitburg in 1985. Six years later,
on the fiftieth anniversary of the Japanese surprise attack on
Pearl Harbor, President George Bush declared, "I have no
rancor in my heart toward Germany or Japan—not at all. . . .
This is no time for recrimination. World War II is over. It
is history."

Just three months after Bush's speech a seventy-one-year-
old German lawmaker resigned from the Brandenburg legislature following the disclosure that he had assisted in killing
six Jews while a German soldier in Ukraine during World

War II. Although the politician, Gustav Just, admitted that he had served on the firing squad, and despite the fact that police files indicated he had volunteered for that assignment, German prosecutors declined to press charges.

Is that what Kohl means by reconciliation? Does he want Germany to stop prosecuting Nazi crimes? Is he still asking for amnesty? Or is he asking for amnesia?

A German supermarket chain in 1991 announced plans to develop land that had once been the site of the Ravensbrück concentration camp just north of Berlin and touched off an international outcry. Does the German chancellor think there should be no protest when the memory of the Holocaust is treated with insensitivity?

In the same year a commercial mining firm announced plans to plumb the shafts of a former SS underground slave labor camp in Germany. Far beneath the ground at the site in central Germany, workers had assembled the V-2 rockets that terrorized Britain late in the war. In the process some twenty thousand Jews and Gypsies were worked and starved to death. Does Chancellor Kohl think that everyone ought simply to forget that the place was used for such purposes?

In March 1992 the German chancellor welcomed outgoing Austrian President Kurt Waldheim, ending a six-year collective cold shoulder by Western leaders against the former United Nations secretary-general. Waldheim had been elected president of Austria in 1986 in spite of allegations—which he denied—that he had participated in Nazi atrocities in the Balkans. Again many groups from around the world protested the gesture. Kohl lashed out at the World Jewish Congress in particular, bellowing, "I don't need any advice."

Germany's desire for forgetting is hardly a uniquely German phenomenon. The tendency to avoid confrontation with the past, to rewrite, romanticize, or outright ignore the past is actually common in history. In the United States, for example, the Watergate crisis was a defining moment in American history, yet the passing of time inspires a rising will to forget. President Nixon's crime, his cover-up, and his betrayal of trust cast a deep stain on the presidency and rocked the country's democratic institutions to their foundations. Now, just twenty years later, Nixon has reemerged as an elder statesman, as an author many times published, as a guest on television talk shows. More and more Nixon is respected; less and less he is reviled.

Another incident is illustrative. During the 1988 presidential race a senior campaign adviser to Vice President George Bush was forced to resign when the press revealed that the official had been involved in dirty politics as a member of the Nixon White House in the early 1970s. The official, Frederic Malek, had run an "errand" for the notoriously paranoid Nixon—namely, to find out how many Jews were employed in the Bureau of Labor Statistics, a federal agency Nixon had decided was out to spoil his efforts to portray the U.S. economy in rosy hues.

In his instructions to Malek, the president expressly directed his deputy to investigate what he termed a "Jewish cabal" in the agency. Malek reported back to the chief executive that thirteen out of thirty-five top officials at the agency were indeed Jewish, at least on the basis of Malek's evaluation of their last names. Two months after Malek's report to Nixon two of those senior officials were reassigned to less visible positions at the Labor Department.

Only three years after his resignation from Vice President Bush's campaign team made front-page news across the country, Malek returned quietly to a senior position in Bush's 1992 reelection drive. In the interim Malek had met with several Jewish groups to smooth over hurt feelings. No one had ever accused Malek of being an anti-Semite or charged that his indiscretion was the worst offense ever committed in American politics. But three years later no one said a word about Malek's return. No one even mentioned the past. It had been forgotten.

How many Americans today actively remember, study, reflect on, or commemorate the many years of black slavery? Every American boy and girl studies slavery in elementary school, but what else is there? What else should there be? How many Americans recall in any meaningful way the Indian wars, the U.S. cavalry campaigns during the 1800s that eliminated tens of thousands of Native Americans and corralled the beaten-down survivors onto reservations? How often do most Americans even think about this shameful chapter in U.S. history?

The point is not to compare the trauma of Watergate in the United States with the devastating impact of the Holocaust on German society or to compare Nixon's crimes or the horrors of slavery or the slaughter of American Indian tribes with the horrors of the Nazi Holocaust. The point is to compare the response to painful moments in history, the powerful human drive to forget.

The trial of Josef Schwammberger and everything the German authorities did to bring the former SS man to trial must be seen in this context. Germany did not bring Schwammberger to trial out of some commitment to justice. Schwammberger for Germany was a matter of political necessity. In taking custody of this elderly Nazi and his half-century-old crimes, Germans hoped that a longtime illness might be healed and that the country might move one step closer to forgetting.

That same hope was behind every other Nazi trial that preceded Schwammberger's, beginning with the trials at Nuremberg. But the Nazi trials did not end, not in the fifties, not in the sixties, not in the seventies, not in the eighties. German leaders starting in the late 1940s called for amnesty and then for reconciliation, but all the while Nazi criminals were brought, however haphazardly and incompletely, to justice.

Josef Schwammberger was indeed brought to justice at

long last. After forty years as a fugitive, he was captured, extradited, tried, and convicted. And so, we say, he was brought to justice. But was he? What was the justice to which Schwammberger was brought?

Typically, in a democratic society, when someone commits a crime, that person is judged according to the system of laws that society has developed. That society, represented by a judge or a jury, finds the accused innocent or guilty. If guilty, the convicted person serves a sentence. Once the person has served the term of the sentence, we consider that person to have paid a debt to society for the crimes committed.

Even in the case of murderers or child molesters or rapists, we accord this right. Unless a person is sentenced to death or to life in prison without parole, we acknowledge that after a period of service a convict becomes an ex-convict. A rapist has not restored the dignity to the woman he assaulted after serving, say, ten years in jail. Even after twenty years he cannot by his confinement in prison remove the pain she must live with all her life. But a society differentiates among crimes, weighs the punishments, and attempts to strike a balance.

What of the Nazi criminals who have been brought to justice? The average sentence over the entire course of Nazi prosecutions has been less than ten years. The average actual time served is about half that number. Does that mean that an SS man who was responsible for dozens, even hundreds of deaths, who participated in the most heinous cruelties, can be said to have paid his debt to society after serving five years in prison? Perhaps after ten years? Twenty? Thirty?

The most serious criminal offenders receive life in prison or even death, in societies that permit capital punishment. Those interested in seeing a defendant punished most seriously, naturally, welcome a life sentence over a shorter, fixed term. The survivors of Przemysl, for example, would have been outraged if Josef Schwammberger had been sentenced to five years in prison instead of life. For what he did, he should receive the maximum sentence allowable, the survivors would readily agree. That Schwammberger did receive the heaviest sentence allowable, we might say, is evidence that justice was done.

But was it? In one sense there really is no practical difference between five years and life, and not only because a man of Schwammberger's age and in his physical condition could easily die in a matter of a couple of years. The reason is that there is no human way that there can be justice in the context of the crimes of the Nazi Holocaust.

In one of the earliest expressions of justice the Jewish Bible refers to "an eye for an eye," a concept often misunderstood as a defense of vengeance. In fact, the statement refers more generally to an idea that has survived through the ages and has become one of the foundations of Western social and legal thought. Simply put, the idea is that the punishment should match the crime. Achieving this balance is necessarily an imperfect science, but the principle informs the efforts in democratic societies to attempt to strike that balance.

A mother might hope for the harshest sentence available to punish the man who gunned down her son in a drive-by shooting on some city corner. No punishment will bring back her son. That fact cannot be changed. But she may believe that there is some justice in the world if her son's assassin is locked up for the rest of his life or—even better—is sent to the electric chair. Even if she is a religious woman, she will surely find it difficult, if not impossible, to forgive, and she will never forget.

What punishment, then, could possibly strike an appropriate balance for the criminals, the murderers of the Holocaust? Even if Germany did still allow capital punishment and if Schwammberger were sentenced to die, what justice would that be? The man who killed so many, who tortured so many, who was for three years a sadistic killer and for nearly fifty years thereafter a terrifying specter in the dreams of those who survived his abuses, would have been killed. Where is the balance?

Simon Wiesenthal tackles a similar question in his 1969 autobiographical essay, *The Sunflower*. In the story, set in wartime Poland, Wiesenthal relates being called away from a work detail at a hospital and brought to the bedside of a dying young SS man. The man, barely able to speak, whispers to Wiesenthal the story of how he participated in a brigade that torched a building filled with Jews and shot at those who tried to escape the burning death trap. The SS man tells Wiesenthal, who has himself already survived terrible hardships, that he regrets his part in the crime. Wiesenthal stands silent through the SS man's stirring confession. Then the man begs Wiesenthal to satisfy a dying man's last wish. The SS man asks for forgiveness.

"Two men who had never known each other had been brought together for a few hours by Fate," Wiesenthal writes. "One asks the other for help. But the other was himself helpless and able to do nothing for him."[5] Without saying a word one way or the other to the dying soldier Wiesenthal leaves the room.

The rest of the story details Wiesenthal's agonizing over whether he should have granted the dying man's wish for forgiveness or whether he was right to decide that it was not his place to forgive on behalf of those whom the SS man had killed, much less on behalf of all Jewry.

The second half of the remarkable book is a symposium, a collection of short essays written by theologians, politicians, journalists, philosophers, and academics commenting on Wiesenthal's story. Some congratulate his decision. Others argue that under the extreme circumstances, his inaction is excusable but that he really ought to have forgiven the man. Others say it is simply unforgivable not to forgive.

But what do the words "I forgive you" really mean? Of course, forgiveness is a concept central to nearly all religious faiths. Forgive others their transgressions, we are taught. But was the Holocaust a transgression? Was the Holocaust a crime? Can any individual personally forgive what happened? Can there be any just punishment?

These questions are complicated. In fact, there may be no absolute answers, just as there may be no absolute answer to the ultimate question of how it was possible for the Holocaust to happen in the first place. But even difficult questions must be asked, no matter how painful or upsetting. The question of forgiveness is better left to the individual, for ultimately forgiveness is a personal matter. Justice, on the other hand, is defined by the shared values of the collective, of the state, of society.

Society has determined that there is no general amnesty for the crimes of the Holocaust. Time and again the German parliament voted to extend the statute of limitations on Nazi crimes of murder. If there is no amnesty, then there can be no forgetting, for as long as there are Nazi criminals, there must be some effort to bring them to justice. And that is, ultimately, the justice that is done.

The actions for which Josef Schwammberger was convicted cannot properly be called crimes. Crimes are acts in violation of the law. Schwammberger's actions shatter the bounds of our understanding of criminal behavior. Someone who kills a dozen men might be considered a mass murderer. Does that make Schwammberger a mass mass murderer?

The laws intended to regulate human behavior did not contemplate, could not have contemplated, killing and torture on the level practiced by the likes of Schwammberger. His actions were Nazi crimes, and by that designation they must be understood as falling within an entirely different quantum of human action. The punishment for the crime of murder cannot simply be multiplied or intensified a thousand times, or three thousand times, to strike the proper balance in finding a just punishment for Schwammberger. No human punishment could possibly compensate for his atrocities.

There must, then, be some other meaning to the idea of "bringing Schwammberger to justice." Because just as one cannot justify turning away from the painful past because it is painful, so one cannot decide not to punish a Josef Schwammberger simply because one believes that no measure of justice as handed down by a man-made system of laws could ever be sufficient.

There must be some other purpose to Schwammberger's trial. Chancellor Kohl and the advocates of reconciliation hoped the "last Nazi trial" would serve that interest. Schwammberger offered a convenient opportunity to make a political statement. If Germany were genuinely serious about prosecuting all unpunished Nazi criminals to the fullest extent of the law, then Schwammberger would not be the "last Nazi."

There still are numerous others, perhaps few with the number of eyewitnesses as were available for Schwammberger's prosecution, but many others nonetheless. No, Schwammberger was for Germany both an act of self-flagellation and an act of defiance. The unspoken message was: See? We have put ourselves through this once again. Now leave us alone.

Argentine President Menem, similarly, did not rush to round up other Nazi fugitives in his country in the wake of Schwammberger's extradition in spite of the fact that Nazi hunters gave him lists of names of known Nazi criminals still living in his country. As far as Menem was concerned, one Nazi was enough. Schwammberger will adequately symbolize Argentina's renunciation of its Nazi-sympathizing past.

These were self-serving attitudes, not ones that reveal a concern for justice. Yet justice was indeed served in the Schwammberger case. Justice resides in the fact that the trial, an act of remembering, occurred at all. While in so many other ways, Germany has sought to repackage the past or turn away from it all together, the trial of Josef Schwammberger, indeed the entire history of the prosecution of the perpetrators of the Nazi Holocaust, has served as a reminder, a recognition of and a confrontation with the Nazi past.

The trials have provided the means to continue asking the difficult questions. Who were these people? What really happened? How could this have happened? The museum exhibits are educational. The memorial stones meaningfully honor the victims. But the trial of Josef Schwammberger and the hundreds of other Nazi trials that came before stand as the truest tribute to both the past and the future.

In bringing Josef Schwammberger to justice, Germany brought him back from oblivion and into memory again, an act of true and lasting significance. The act of judging the transgressors, the criminals, the perpetrators of the Nazi Holocaust—much more so than the judgment itself—stands as the surest, most durable way of confronting the terrible and painful past.

Confronting the past, asking the difficult questions, as can happen only in a democratic society, increases the likelihood that people will work through the past, digest it, understand it, and never repeat it.

CHAPTER 16

THE LAST NAZI/ THE LAST SURVIVOR

Who will remember? We will remember. The
Holocaust survivor.
—Arnold Susskind

And when we will disappear a few years later, I don't
know.
—Sally Susskind

Rose Felner lives today in Przemysl. She has lived in the little town along the San River for more than seventy years, her entire life. For a brief period, after her husband died in 1978, she did try living in New York, but she hated it there. She felt like a stranger. So she moved back home again. She was born in Przemysl, so, she decided, she would die there.[1]

A sweet white-haired woman, Rose Felner now is the last living Jew in Przemysl. There may be a couple of others, she says, but like so many of the estimated five to fifteen thousand Jews in Poland today, they have long ago given up their Jewish identities. Many changed their names during the long years of Soviet domination. Sometimes it was easier if people did not know. Sometimes it was safer.

Roughly half of all Jews killed during the Holocaust were Polish Jews. No country's Jewish community was more devastated. In the country the Nazis chose as the site for their extermination camps, fully 90 percent of the Jewish population was killed. Three million people.

After the war tens of thousands of survivors wandered back from liberated concentration camps elsewhere in Europe or came out of the woods or crawled out from their hiding places. Many, like Arnold and Sally Susskind, returned to Poland only long enough to ascertain whether any other family members had survived. Nearly one hundred thousand Jewish survivors fled Poland in the wake of the Kielce pogrom in 1946. When Israel became the Jewish state in 1948, even more Polish Jews abandoned the place where their forebears had lived for a thousand years.

By 1950 there were still some fifty thousand Polish Jews living in the country that had clearly demonstrated before and since the Nazi occupation that Jews were not really welcome. Some stayed because they hoped that Soviet communism would eliminate anti-Semitism. Some stayed because they were committed to preserving some Jewish presence in Poland, some legacy to the millions who had been lost.

The number of Jews in Poland continued to dwindle steadily over the years. In Przemysl the last rabbi left in 1950, partly because the Soviet-sponsored authorities frowned on all religious institutions but mainly because there was not enough demand for his services. "We couldn't even get a minyan," Felner explains.*

Today the vast majority of those few Jews left in the country are elderly men and women who, like Rose Felner, feel they have nowhere else to go. Their world is haunted by memories of the past, shadows of the dead, but it is the only world they know.

---

*According to Jewish religious practice, there must be at least ten worshipers—a minyan—before any communal prayer service is considered legitimate. Orthodox Jews count only men toward satisfying this requirement.

Rose has a spotless two-room apartment in a soot-encrusted prewar walk-up just a couple of buildings in from one of the city's main thoroughfares. She lives on a modest pension. Her husband was a government economist for many years. She can walk to the market in the center of town. She has a few friends.

"It is a sad life," she admits. "I have my books, the TV, that's all. But I am here with people I know."

Felner has another reason for staying in Przemysl: As the last Jew in a city that was once one-third Jewish she has assumed the role of unofficial caretaker of the Jewish memory. But there is not much one elderly woman can do. Although her own memory is perfectly fine, she cannot hope to stand forever against the forces that are inundating her: the unavoidability of time and the creeping amnesia that is all around her.

Rose Felner is accustomed to speaking softly about the Holocaust. Even before Josef Schwammberger arrived to take command of the ghetto, Rose and her husband, Edmund, were taken in by a married couple who had a hidden attic in their house on the outskirts of town. The couple, a Ukrainian woman and her Jewish husband, also cared for a Jewish infant whose parents had left the child, hoping he would be safer with them. Somehow the Nazis had neglected to search their house, and they made it through to see the Russians liberate the city in 1944.

During the long months in hiding, however, the Felners lived in constant fear. At any moment they knew the Gestapo might burst in and load them onto the next train to Auschwitz or perhaps kill them on the spot. Edmund kept a pistol with them in their attic hideaway. "I remember him saying the bullets were for the Germans and the last one was for himself," Rose relates.

Life in the attic was excruciating. Another family lived directly below the part of the house where the Felners were stashed. This other family could not be trusted not to run to the police if there were any suspicious noises overhead. "So I didn't speak to my husband for two and a half years even though we were in the same room," Rose explains.

Although Rose and her husband escaped with their lives, they suffered tremendous losses. Her two brothers were killed when the Nazis first overran Przemysl in 1939. Her mother and sister were on one of the transports out of the ghetto and to the gas chambers at Auschwitz.

Now that Rose is mostly alone she keeps silent company with the dead and remembers on behalf of those who are no longer there. Occasionally she goes to the Jewish cemetery a half mile from her apartment. She lights candles in small glass containers and places them at the bases of the carved gravestones.

The cemetery itself is a provocative memorial to the lost Jewish community. Through the stone arch and iron gate at the entrance to the cemetery is a small clearing dotted by slate gray and polished black markers. Some stones have been knocked over. Many bear the names of five, a dozen, as many as twenty names, all victims of the Nazi lords, Josef Schwammberger included, who came to drain the city of its Jewish blood. Feuchtbaum, Erlich, Frankel, Ehrenfreund, they all were once part of the longtime diversity of life and culture in the town of Przemysl.

A ring of dense bushes creates the illusion that the cemetery is small, but within the jungle of brambles and high, thick grass are more graves and more toppled headstones. The cleared area just inside the cemetery's front gate, in fact, is only a small part of what was once a much larger memorial park. No one goes into the overgrown part of the cemetery anymore. The dead there have been twice buried.

Rose also makes a point of visiting the commemorative plaque to the ghetto victims that sits in a small courtyard behind a Polish middle school, one specializing in remedial

education. The building formerly housed the Przemysl Judenrat during the days of the ghetto. Hundreds of Jews were
shot against the very wall before which Rose Felner stands
fifty years later. On a dreary, rainy spring afternoon she pulls
another candle from her overcoat pocket, lights it, and places
it next to the burned out candle she left several days earlier.

The key to the courtyard gate is kept in an office in the
school. It is better to keep the memorial locked, Rose says,
even though the result is that the monument is not accessible
to the public. Unless you know exactly where to look, you
would have to stumble onto the courtyard anyway. Besides,
she points out, "We're afraid of vandals."

When Rose Felner is gone, there will be no one to visit
the Jewish cemetery. The grass will cover the rest of the old
gravestones. In time no one will remember that both the
central bus station in Przemysl and the municipal library
were once grand synagogues, thriving centers of worship,
learning, and community. When Rose Felner is gone, no one
will ask for the key to the courtyard to visit the memorial
to the ghetto victims.

Then Josef Schwammberger's work in Przemysl will finally
be done.

Irreconcilable contradictions, it seems, define the story of
Josef Schwammberger. On the one hand, Schwammberger
was a wholly unremarkable individual. He was dull, not
clever; weak, not strong; average, not exceptional. Yet he
had a profound impact on so many lives.

With his lowly rank and medical impediments to higher
calling within the SS, Schwammberger was, in one sense,
but a drop in the bloody sea of the Nazi Holocaust. There
were hundreds of SS men just like him. His cruelty was
commonplace. Yet he was for that very reason, a true Nazi
perpetrator, the real implementer of the Nazi Holocaust, a
major, not minor, Nazi figure. Eichmann had no stomach

for the actual killing that went on in the concentration camps. Schwammberger thrived in that environment.

The survivors who still remember so painfully the look in Schwammberger's eyes when he was about to execute a Jewish prisoner see him today as he was then. For those who lived through the agony, Schwammberger is forever thirty years old and barking commands as if he were the evil king of the world. Those who were not in Przemysl or Rozwadow or Mielec see in the feeble old man called Schwammberger a reminder that the reality of the Holocaust has not changed over time; only we have changed.

In fact, none of the seeming contradictions in Schwammberger's story is irreconcilable. Each observation, in fact, is as true as the other. He was dull and extraordinary. He was both a low-ranking noncom and a major Nazi murderer. His crime and belated punishment suggest both the hopelessness of changing the reality of the past and the hope that such crimes as those Schwammberger committed will never again be allowed to happen.

It is too late for Przemysl. The lives lost there cannot be regained. The centuries of tradition and culture and history cannot be restored from the pits in which they were buried. Jewish life in Przemysl before long will exist only in the memories of some, and then only in books or museums, and perhaps, after a while, not at all. The Nazis lost World War II, but in their war against the Jews they won the battles of tiny Przemysl and hundreds of other villages and towns and cities in Europe.

There are certainly some who saw the trial of the so-called last Nazi as cause for a sigh of relief. No more Nazis means no more trials, which means no more painful recitations of Nazi atrocities to stir up guilt in the hearts of the German people. No more survivors means no more need for stepping delicately around their sensitivities, as a soldier must when he is lost at night in a minefield.

If Josef Schwammberger is the "last Nazi," then that means the effective end of the Nazi past, the end of a fifty-year-long period of hand wringing. Germany can then get on with life after remembering the Holocaust.

But if that is indeed all the Schwammberger story means, if the Schwammberger trial heralds the day Mayor Rommel refers to as the day when nature will have run its course, then perhaps we are doomed after all to repeat the mistakes of our past. If the story of Schwammberger is ultimately a story of forgetting, then perhaps the crackpots who deny the gas chambers ever existed really are a serious threat to our free society. If the story of Schwammberger is really about forgetting, then perhaps the neo-Nazi thugs throwing up the Nazi salute and rampaging against dark-skinned asylum seekers in Germany today are indeed early signs of a return to the grim days when a people was seduced into following a madman.

If, however, the trial and punishment of Josef Schwammberger are acts of remembering, then perhaps he really is the "last Nazi." Choosing to remember means that Schwammberger goes to jail for the rest of his life. More important, the act of confronting the past means that Przemysl, or at least the idea of Przemysl, remains alive in our collective memories.

Refusing to concede to those who want to turn away from the past means remembering the potential dark side of things. It means remembering how a dull man can become a killer, how a gang of street bullies can become a mass movement of hate, how a decision to stand by in the face of wrongdoing can bring a life sentence of shame.

The only irreconcilable difference in the story of Josef Schwammberger is the one between remembering and forgetting.

NOTES

Chapter 1: Memory, Justice, and History

1. Adolf Hitler, *Mein Kampf*, tr. Ralph Manheim (1943; Boston: Houghton Mifflin, 1971), p. 30.
2. Interview with author, January 29, 1992.

Chapter 2: Roots

1. Norman Davies, *God's Playground: A History of Poland* (Oxford: Clarendon, 1981), vol. 1, pp. 79–80.
2. Susskind was interviewed by the author several times, including November 19, 1991, and April 1, 1992.
3. Howard Sachar, *A History of Israel* (New York: Knopf, 1988), pp. 91–92.
4. Ibid., 187.
5. Interview with author, April 27, 1992.

Chapter 3: Uprooting

1. Barbara Jelavich, *Modern Austria: Empire and Republic* (Cambridge, Eng.: Cambridge University Press, 1987), pp. 160, 169.
2. Ibid., pp. 188, 197.
3. Lucy Dawidowicz, *The War against the Jews* (New York: Bantam, 1976), p. 23.
4. Gerald Reitlinger, *The SS: Alibi of a Nation* (New York: Viking, 1957), p. 26
5. Heinz Höhne, *The Order of the Death's Head*, tr. Richard Barry (New York: Coward-McCann, 1970), p. 52.
6. Sarah Gordon, *Hitler, Germans, and the "Jewish Question"* (Princeton: Princeton University Press, 1984), pp. 89–90.
7. Helmut Krausnick et al., *Anatomy of the SS State*, tr. Richard Barry et al. (New York: Walker and Company, 1965), p. 320.
8. Jelavich, p. 198.
9. Celia Heller, *On the Edge of Destruction* (New York: Columbia University Press, 1977), pp. 72, 106.
10. Leni Yahil, *The Holocaust: The Fate of European Jewry* (Oxford, England: Oxford University Press, 1990), p. 190.
11. Martin Gilbert, *The Holocaust* (New York: Holt, 1985), p. 22.
12. Iwona Irwin-Zarecka, *Neutralizing Memory* (New Brunswick, N.J.: Transaction, 1990), p. 41.
13. Ibid., p. 53.

Chapter 4: Endings and Beginnings

1. Gilbert, p. 61.
2. Schwammberger's marriage application and related materials are on file with the U.S.-administered Berlin Documentation Center.
3. Krausnick, p. 356.
4. William Shirer, *The Rise and Fall of the Third Reich* (New York: Ballantine, 1950, 1960), p. 476.
5. All quotations from Hellman are taken, with permission, directly from letters to the author.

6. Gilbert, p. 60.
7. This description comes from Schwammberger's SS biography. See note 2.
8. Shirer, pp. 368–69.
9. Hitler, p. 405.
10. "Mielec," *Encyclopedia Judaica*, 1971 ed.

Chapter 5: Hell

1. Jacob Apenszlak, ed., *The Black Book of Polish Jewry* (New York: Fertig, 1982), p. 12. The eyewitness quoted was Moshe Friedman.

Chapter 6: The Liquidator

1. Interview with author, March 31, 1992.
2. Istvan Deak, "Strategies of Hell," *The New York Review of Books* (October 8, 1992), p. 10.
3. Gilbert, p. 280.
4. Ibid., p. 419.
5. Interview with author, April 2, 1992.
6. Goldenberg gave this description on June 17, 1991, at a deposition held at the German consulate in New York as part of the pretrial proceedings against Schwammberger.
7. Numbers relating to the liquidation of Mielec come from Roman Mogilanski, ed., *The Ghetto Anthology* (Los Angeles: American Congress of Jews from Poland and Survivors of Concentration Camps, 1985).
8. Raul Hilberg, ed., *Documents of Destruction* (Chicago: Quadrangle, 1971), p. 116. Hilberg says the conflict "almost led to shooting between army personnel and police raiders in the town of Przemysl."
9. In the course of gathering testimony for Schwammberger's trial, this incident was mentioned by several Jewish survivors, including Dr. Marcel Tuchman.

Chapter 7: Survivors

1. Viktor E. Frankl, *Man's Search for Meaning* (New York: Touchstone, 1959), p. 82.

2. Chiel was housed at a United Nations relief camp in Austria after the war and gave his statement against Schwammberger to Innsbruck police on August 12, 1946.

3. Balsam, also in a UN refugee camp in Austria, gave his testimony to the Innsbruck police on August 13, 1946.

4. Interview with author, October 11, 1991.

5. Gilbert, p. 819.

Chapter 8: Zero Hour

1. From a speech to the German Bundestag, or parliament, on May 8, 1985, the fortieth anniversary of the German surrender ending World War II in Europe.

2. The description is part of Schwammberger's three-page confession, which he signed on July 31, 1945.

3. The memo is dated July 28, 1948.

4. Frank Buscher, *The U.S. War Crimes Trial Program in Germany, 1946–1955* (New York: Greenwood, 1989), p. 8.

5. Mary Fulbrook, *The Divided Nation* (New York: Oxford, 1992), p. 148.

6. Sabine Reichel, *What Did You Do During the War, Daddy?* (New York: Hill and Wang, 1989), pp. 4–5.

7. Quoted in Ingo Müller, *Hitler's Justice*, trans. Deborah Lucas Schneider (Cambridge, Mass.: Harvard University Press 1991), p. 240.

8. FDR is quoted in Robert Conot, *Judgment at Nuremberg* (New York: Carroll & Graf, 1984), p. 10.

9. For a detailed study of the Rudolph story, as well as an overview of American efforts to protect its Nazi scientists, see Linda Hunt, *Secret Agenda: The Paperclip Conspiracy* (New York: St. Martin's Press, 1991).

10. Henry Friedlander, "The Judiciary and Nazi Crimes in Postwar Germany," *Simon Wiesenthal Center Annual* (Chappaqua: Rossel, 1984), p. 30.

Chapter 9: Into Obscurity

1. Milan Kundera, *The Book of Laughter and Forgetting*, tr. Michael Henry Heim (New York: Penguin, 1986), p. 7.

2. The extradition document dated September 6, 1946, is among the archives of the American war crimes administration, which are held at the National Archives Annex in Suitland, Maryland.

3. Interview with Schwammberger's defense lawyer Achim Bächle, October 21, 1992.

4. For one such account, see "Fugitive Alleged Nazi Charged in WW II Deaths of 3,400," Associated Press, March 1, 1991.

5. Frederick Forsyth, *The Odessa File* (London: Hutchinson, 1972). The novel is based on a true story.

6. Ian Johnson, "Aging Accusers Confront an Elderly Nazi," *Baltimore Sun*, December 16, 1991, p. 1.

7. Memo of January 3, 1948, from the Security Section of the French Control Mission in Innsbruck to the Federal (Austrian) Police Headquarters.

8. The *New York Times* first reported on the State Department memo, written by Vincent La Vista and dated July 14, 1947, nearly forty years after it was prepared. La Vista's report, including sweeping allegations about Vatican aid to Nazis, apparently was not actively checked out by U.S. government officials because La Vista accidentally investigated some individuals who were working undercover for U.S. intelligence. This may say something about La Vista's carelessness or about the nature of postwar American intelligence operations.

9. In recent years the Red Cross and the Catholic Church have come under intense criticism for their involvement in helping scores of Nazi criminals after the war. See, for example, Ralph Blumenthal, "Vatican Is Reported to Have Furnished Aid to Fleeing Nazis," *New York Times*, January 26, 1984, p. A1.

10. Interview with Dr. Miguel Ángel Siri, March 10, 1992. Siri was Schwammberger's defense lawyer in Argentina.

11. Figures are from David Rock, *Argentina 1516–1987* (Berkeley: University of California Press, 1987), pp. 165–66.

12. Haim Avni, *Argentina and the Jews* (Tuscaloosa: University of Alabama Press, 1991), pp. 91–92.

13. Ibid., p. 123.

14. Rock, p. 172.

15. Interview with Raúl Kraiselburd, editor of *El Día*, the main daily newspaper of La Plata, March 4, 1992.

16. Arnaldo Cortesi, "Perón's Henchmen Assault Jews; Argentine Police Arrest Victims," *New York Times*, November 25, 1945, p. A1.

17. "Argentine Police Bar Celebrations," *New York Times*, May 4, 1945, p. A5.

18. One such demonstration occurred on August 17, 1945, when a mob of soldiers and Perón supporters attempted to tear down the offices of a democratic newspaper and attacked civilians celebrating the Allied victory in the war. Just as Hitler would have done, Perón issued a statement blaming the violence, which resulted in two deaths, on Argentine Communists.

19. Frank Kluckhorn, "Portrait of Argentina's 'Strong Man,'" *New York Times Magazine*, December 1, 1946, p. 62.

20. See Hunt, *Secret Agenda*.

21. Avni, pp. 192–93.

22. Günter Grass, *Two States—One Nation?*, tr. Krishna Winston (New York: Harcourt, 1990), p. 6.

23. Ibid., pp. 31–32.

24. Michael Kater, "Political Reeducation in West Germany, 1945–1960," *Simon Wiesenthal Center Annual* (White Plains, N.Y.: Kraus International, 1987), p. 107.

25. Emphasis in the original. Douglas Botting, *From the Ruins of the Reich* (New York: Meridian, 1985), p. 284.

26. Friedlander, pp. 30–31

27. Ibid., p. 31.

28. Müller, p. 243.

29. Buscher, p. 85.

30. Kater, p. 105.

31. Anna J. Merritt and Richard L. Merritt, eds., *Public Opinion in Occupied Germany, the OMGUS Surveys, 1945–1949* (Urbana: University of Illinois Press, 1970).

Chapter 10: Rediscovering The Nazi Past

1. Reuters, August 15, 1992.

2. For a superb discussion about Dachau and memory, see

Timothy W. Ryback, "Report from Dachau," *The New Yorker* (August 3 1992), p. 43.

3. Reinhard Rürup, ed., *Topography of Terror* (Berlin: Verlag, 1989), p. 190.

4. Ibid., p. 7.

5. Interview with author, March 4, 1992.

6. Gideon Hausner, *Justice in Jerusalem* (New York: Harper & Row, 1966), pp. 433–37.

7. Henry Raymont, "Argentine Police Clash with Nazis," *New York Times*, January 29, 1965, p. A1.

8. "Eichmann's Son Released," *New York Times*, August 22, 1965, p. A34.

9. Philip Shabecoff, "At Babi Yar Trial, Only 4 Spectators," *New York Times*, February 14, 1968, p. A11.

10. Flora Lewis, "What German Youth Know about Hitler," *New York Times Magazine*, June 7 1959, p. 72.

11. Ibid., p. 73.

12. Willi Dressen, "The Investigation of Nazi Criminals in Western Germany," Encyclopedia Judaica (Jerusalem: Keter, 1986), p. 134.

13. Arthur J. Olsen, "Germans Pack Courts for War Crime Trials," *New York Times*, November 2, 1958, p. D6.

14. Shabecoff, "At the Babi Yar Trial, Only 4 Spectators."

15. This figure and the related statistics come from the Central Office for the Investigation of National Socialist Crimes in the town of Ludwigsburg and are cumulative through January 1, 1992.

16. Fritz Bauer quoted in Müller, 256.

17. "Nazi's Acquittal Sets Precedent Due to Free Many," *New York Times*, May 22, 1969, p. A6.

18. Philip Shabecoff, "Hostility Abroad Deplored in Bonn," *New York Times*, March 23, 1966, p. A3.

Chapter 11: "What Took You So Long?"

1. Interview with author, June 4, 1992, in Vienna.

2. Police investigative reports on file with the National Archives in Buenos Aires reveal that the Argentine police operated under this mistaken supposition for many years.

3. Wiesenthal's April 26, 1973, note to José Moskovits, then director of the Buenos Aires-based Israelite Association of Survivors of the Nazi Persecution, is quoted in *La Razón*, November 23, 1985.

4. Fulbrook, p. 305.

5. Alvin H. Rosenfeld, "Popularization and Memory," *Lessons and Legacies*, ed. Peter Hayes (Evanston, Ill.: Northwestern, 1991), p. 270.

6. Ted Morgan, *An Uncertain Hour* (New York: Morrow, 1990), p. 16.

7. James M. Markham, "Old Germans and Young: Split Is Deep," *New York Times*, May 8, 1985, p. A1.

8. Hilberg, "Opening Remarks: The Discovery of the Holocaust," *Lessons and Legacies*, p. 17.

9. Details of the investigation are contained in a November 26, 1985, police report on file in the National Archives in Buenos Aires.

10. Ranking wanted Nazi criminals was not a universally popular idea. For example, New York-based Nazi hunter Elliot Welles told the *New York Times* on June 26, 1985, "Jewish blood doesn't go from 1 to 10." Welles was not responding specifically to Wiesenthal.

11. Interview with author, October 24, 1991.

12. Interview with author, March 12, 1992.

Chapter 12: Extradition

1. Interview with author, March 9, 1992.

2. Interview with author, March 12, 1992.

3. Shirley Christian, "Visit By Alfonsín Peacefully Ends Argentine Mutiny," *New York Times*, April 20, 1987, p. A1.

4. Interview with author, March 10, 1992.

5. Interview with author, March 9, 1992.

6. James F. Smith, "Case of Accused Ex-Nazi Strikes a Raw Nerve in Argentina," *Los Angeles Times*, July 17, 1988, p. A12. Secemsky now lives near San Diego.

7. The courtroom exchanges that follow are reconstructed

from official paraphrased transcripts. The Argentine courts do not use verbatim transcripts. As is also the practice in Germany, a court clerk or the judge himself takes notes on the proceeding and then summarizes the testimony afterward.

8. The denaturalization case is captioned "Causa No. 5526 Schwammberger José S/cancelación carta de ciudadanía." The passage quoted appears on page 3 of the opinion.

Chapter 13: The Meaning Of Survival

1. The American Jewish Committee commissioned the opinion study, which was conducted between October 1 and 15, 1990. A U.S. marketing research firm and a German polling company jointly conducted the research.

2. This study, also sponsored by the American Jewish Committee, was conducted by the Gallup Institute of Austria between June 24 and August 21, 1991.

3. See, for example, Dr. Joseph Rebhun, *God and Man in Two Worlds* (Claremont, Calif.: Or, 1985). Also, Max Wolfshaut Dinkes, *Échec et Mat: Récit d'un Survivant de Pchemychl en Galicie* (Paris: L'Associations les Fils et Filles de Déportés Juifs de France, 1983).

4. These books were never meant to be best sellers. They are understandably exceedingly rare. The YIVO Institute archives in New York City has an excellent collection, which includes the memorial book on Przemysl.

5. Michael Marrus, "The Use and Misuse of the Holocaust," *Lessons and Legacies*, p. 113.

Chapter 14: Trying Memories

1. Elie Wiesel, *The Forgotten* (New York: Summit, 1992), p. 12.

2. Interview with senior prosecutor Willi Dressen, August 30, 1991.

3. Ian Johnson, "Aging Accusers Confront an Elderly Nazi," *Baltimore Sun*, December 16, 1991, p. 1.

4. Interview with author, October 21, 1991.

5. Interview with author, October 21, 1991.

6. Schwammberger is quoted in the Frankfurt newspaper *Die Welt*, "He Was Our Executioner, Our God, Our Satan," September 21, 1991, p. 3.

7. Quoted in Telford Taylor, *The Anatomy of the Nuremberg Trials* (New York: Knopf, 1992), p. 45.

8. Stephen Kinzer, "Tale of Nazi Horror Unfurls in Stuttgart Trial," *New York Times*, November 14, 1991, p. A17.

9. Nussbaum re-created his testimony in an interview with the author, April 27, 1992.

10. See Marc Fisher, "Bearing Witness to 'Hell You Can't Imagine,'" *Washington Post*, January 30, 1992, p. A1. Nussbaum, in an interview with the author, provided additional details of the incident.

11. The teacher, Birgit Schindelberger-Barrows, is quoted in the *Los Angeles Times*, "Nazi Hunt: Too Late for Justice?," April 1, 1992, p. 1.

12. Martin Blumenson, "Rommel," *Hitler's Generals*, ed. Correlli Barnett (New York: Grove Weidenfeld, 1989), p. 293.

13. Stephen Kinzer, "A Rommel Defending Foreigners," *New York Times*, November 24, 1991, p. A15.

14. See "'No, That Is Much Too Long Ago,'" *Der Spiegel*, 35 (1991), p. 76. The article, one of the most pro-Schwammberger articles to appear in the mainstream German press, essentially portrays the defendant as an old man who should not be bothered with such ancient accusations.

15. The *Frankfurter Rundschau* editorial is quoted by the *Jewish Telegraphic Agency*, May 3, 1992.

Chapter 15: The Shadow

1. Interview with *Los Angeles Times*, July 28, 1985, during which Kohl responded to criticism over his decision to sell military equipment to moderate Arab countries in the Middle East.

2. Hilberg, "Opening Remarks," p. 11.

3. Irwin-Zarecka, p. 62.

4. Stephen Kinzer, "Germany Marks Place Where Horror Began," *New York Times*, January 20, 1992, p. A1.

5. Simon Wiesenthal, *The Sunflower* (New York: Schocken, 1969), p. 58.

Chapter 16: The Last Nazi/The Last Survivor

1. Interview with author, May 26, 1992.

Selected Bibliography

Apenszlak, Jacob, ed. *The Black Book of Polish Jewry: An Account of the Martyrdom of Polish Jewry under Nazi Occupation.* New York: Fertig, 1982.

Ardagh, John. *Germany and the Germans.* New York: Harper & Row, 1987.

Ashman, Charles, and Robert J. Wagman. *The Nazi Hunters.* New York: Warner Books, 1988.

Avni, Haim. *Argentina and the Jews: A History of Jewish Immigration.* Tuscaloosa: University of Alabama Press, 1991.

Barker, Elisabeth. *Austria 1918–1972.* New York: Macmillan, 1973.

Barnett, Correlli, ed. *Hitler's Generals.* New York: Grove Weidenfeld, 1989.

Bosch, William J. *Judgment on Nuremberg: American Attitudes toward the Major War-Crime Trials.* Chapel Hill: University of North Carolina Press, 1970.

Botting, Douglas. *From the Ruins of the Reich.* New York: Meridian, 1985.

Bower, Tom. *The Paperclip Conspiracy: The Hunt for Nazi Scientists.* Boston: Little, Brown, 1987.

Buscher, Frank M. *The U.S. War Crimes Trial Program in Germany, 1946–1955.* New York: Greenwood Press, 1989.

Conot, Robert E. *Justice at Nuremberg.* New York: Carroll & Graf, 1983.

Davies, Norman. *God's Playground: A History of Poland.* Oxford, England: Clarendon, 1981. 2 vols.

Dawidowicz, Lucy S. *The War against the Jews 1933–1945.* New York: Bantam, 1976.

Dinkes, Max Wolfshaut. *Échec et Mat: Récit d'un Survivant de Pchemychl en Galicie.* Paris: L'Association les Fils et Filles de Déportés Juifs de France, 1983.

Forsyth, Frederick. *The Odessa File.* London: Hutchinson, 1972.

Frankl, Victor E. *Man's Search for Meaning: An Introduction to Logotherapy.* New York: Touchstone, 1984.

Friedlander, Henry. "The Judiciary and Nazi Crimes in Postwar Germany." *Simon Wiesenthal Center Annual,* vol. 1, ed. Alex Grobman. Chappaqua: Rossel, 1984.

Fulbrook, Mary. *The Divided Nation: A History of Germany 1918–1990.* New York: Oxford University Press, 1992.

Gehl, Jurgen. *Austria, Germany, and the Anschluss, 1931–1938.* Westport, Conn.: Greenwood Press, 1979.

Gilbert, Martin. *The Holocaust: A History of the Jews of Europe during the Second World War.* New York: Holt, Rinehart and Winston, 1985.

Gordon, Sarah. *Hitler, Germans, and the "Jewish Question."* Princeton: Princeton University Press, 1984.

Grass, Günter. *Two States—One Nation?,* tr. Krishna Winston and A. S. Wensinger. New York: Harcourt Brace Jovanovich, 1990.

Hausner, Gideon. *Justice in Jerusalem.* New York: Harper & Row, 1966.

Hayes, Peter, ed. *Lessons and Legacies: The Meaning of the Holocaust in a Changing World.* Evanston, Ill.: Northwestern University Press, 1991.

Heinkel, Ernst. *He 1000.* London: Hutchinson & Co., 1956.

Heller, Celia. *On the Edge of Destruction.* New York: Columbia University Press, 1977.

Hilberg, Raul. *Documents of Destruction.* Chicago: Quadrangle, 1971.

Hitler, Adolf. *Mein Kampf*, tr. Ralph Manheim. Boston: Houghton Mifflin, 1971.

Höhne, Heinz. *The Order of the Death's Head*, tr. Richard Barry. New York: Coward-McCann, 1970.

Hunt, Linda. *Secret Agenda: The Paperclip Conspiracy*. New York: St. Martin's Press, 1991.

Irwin-Zarecka, Iwona. *Neutralizing Memory: The Jew in Contemporary Poland*. New Brunswick, N.J.: Transaction, 1990.

Jelavich, Barbara. *Modern Austria: Empire and Republic 1815–1986*. Cambridge, England: Cambridge University Press, 1987.

Kater, Michael H. "Problems of Political Reeducation in West Germany, 1945–1960." *Simon Wiesenthal Center Annual*, vol. 4, ed. Henry Friedlander and Sybil Milton. White Plains, N.Y.: Kraus International, 1987.

Klee, Ernst, Willi Dressen, and Volker Riess, eds. *"The Good Old Days": The Holocaust as Seen by Its Perpetrators and Bystanders*, tr. Deborah Burnstone. New York: Free Press, 1991.

Krausnick, Helmut, et al. *Anatomy of the SS State*, tr. Richard Barry et al. New York: Walker and Company, 1965.

Kundera, Milan. *The Book of Laughter and Forgetting*, tr. Michael Henry Heim. New York: Penguin, 1986.

Levkov, Ilya I., ed. *Bitburg and Beyond: Encounters in American, German and Jewish History*. New York: Shapolsky, 1987.

Lukas, Richard C. *Forgotten Holocaust: The Poles under German Occupation 1939–1944*. Lexington: University Press of Kentucky, 1986.

Menczer, Dr. Arie, ed. *Sefer Przemysl*. Tel Aviv: Irgun Yotzei Przemysl, 1964.

Merritt, Anna J., and Richard L. Merritt. *Public Opinion in Occupied Germany, the OMGUS Surveys, 1945–1949*. Urbana: University of Illinois Press, 1970.

Mogilanski, Roman. *The Ghetto Anthology*. Los Angeles: American Congress of Jews from Poland and Survivors of Concentration Camps, 1985.

Morgan, Ted. *An Uncertain Hour: The French, the Germans, the Jews, the Klaus Barbie Trial, and the City of Lyons, 1940–1945*. New York: Arbor, 1990.

Müller, Ingo. *Hitler's Justice: The Courts of the Third Reich*, tr. Deborah Lucas Schneider. Cambridge, Mass.: Harvard University Press, 1991.

Poland. Ministry of Information. *The Black Book of Poland.* New York: Putnam, 1942.

Rebhun, Dr. Joseph. *God and Man in Two Worlds.* Claremont, Calif.: Or, 1985.

Reichel, Sabine. *What Did You Do in the War, Daddy?: Growing Up German.* New York: Hill and Wang, 1989.

Reitlinger, Gerald. *The SS: Alibi of a Nation 1922–1945.* New York: Viking Press, 1957.

Rock, David. *Argentina 1516–1987: From Spanish Colonization to Alfonsín.* Berkeley: University of California, 1987.

Rothschild, Joseph. *East Central Europe between the Two World Wars,* vol. 9, *A History of East Central Europe.* Seattle: University of Washington Press, 1974.

Ruckerl, Adalbert. *The Investigation of Nazi Crimes 1945–1978.* Hamden, Conn.: Archon, 1980.

Rürup, Reinhard, ed. *Topography of Terror: Gestapo, SS and Reichssicherheitshauptamt on the "Prinz-Albrecht Terrain,"* tr. Werner T. Angress. Berlin: Verlag Willmuth Arenhovel, 1989.

Sachar, Howard M. *A History of Israel: From the Rise of Zionism to Our Time.* New York: Knopf, 1988.

Shirer, William L. *The Rise and Fall of the Third Reich.* New York: Ballantine, 1960.

Stone, I. F. *Underground to Palestine (and Reflections Thirty Years Later).* New York: Pantheon, 1978.

Taylor, Telford. *The Anatomy of the Nuremberg Trials.* New York: Knopf, 1992.

Teicholz, Tom. *The Trial of Ivan the Terrible.* New York: St. Martin's Press, 1990.

Wiesel, Elie. *The Forgotten,* tr. Stephen Becker. New York: Summit, 1992.

Wiesenthal, Simon. *The Murderers among Us,* ed. Joseph Wechsberg. New York: Bantam, 1968.

———. *The Sunflower.* New York: Schocken, 1970.

Yahil, Leni. *The Holocaust: The Fate of European Jewry.* Oxford, England: Oxford University Press, 1990.

Young, James. *Writing and Rewriting the Holocaust.* Bloomington: Indiana University Press, 1988.

INDEX

e